# China's Environmental Policy and Urban Development

# CHINA'S ENVIRONMENTAL POLICY AND URBAN DEVELOPMENT

*Edited by*
Joyce Yanyun Man

*Library of Congress Cataloging-in-Publication Data*

China's environmental policy and urban development / edited by Joyce Yanyun Man.
        pages cm
    Includes bibliographical references and index.
    ISBN 978-1-55844-248-1 (alk. paper)
    1. Urbanization—China.   2. Environmental policy—China.   I. Man, Joyce Y., editor of compilation.
    HT361.C495 2013
        307.760951—dc23                                                        2012048775

*Designed by Westchester Publishing Services*

Composed in 10.5/13 Minion by Westchester Publishing Services in Danbury, Connecticut.
Printed and bound by Puritan Press Inc., in Hollis, New Hampshire.

♻ The paper is Rolland Enviro100, an acid-free, 100 percent PCW recycled sheet.

MANUFACTURED IN THE UNITED STATES OF AMERICA

# Contents

# Illustrations

## FIGURES

# Foreword

For the past 30 years China's economic policies have focused on achieving a high rate of economic growth. These policies have been remarkably successful, and China's constant dollar GDP per capita has grown at approximately 10 percent per year from 1980 to 2010, with little recent slowdown. While this growth is unprecedented in a large country, it has had many costs including the structural transformation of the economy, social adjustment and migration, and environmental degradation. This volume addresses the last of these topics, reporting that environmental costs not included in national income accounts, but associated with economic production, range from 9.7 percent of GDP in 1999 (estimated by the China Council for International Cooperation on Environment and Development) to 3 percent in 2004 (estimated by the Ministry of Environmental Protection).

Economic growth in low-income countries often impacts the environment, and this relationship has been enshrined in the "environmental Kuznets curve" that posits that environmental damage increases with economic growth at low-income levels and then decreases as incomes rise over time. Yet, estimates of the environmental Kuznets curve for China from 1997 to 2007 (reported in this volume) show that environmental outcomes there have improved as incomes have increased, indicating that the country is no longer sacrificing environmental quality for the sake of economic growth. Indeed, a key theme of the chapters in this volume is that both China's environmental policies and performance have begun to embrace the idea of the environment as a priority, and that environmental indicators are responding to such policies and regulations, even while economic growth continues.

Moreover, China has been establishing and strengthening its institutions that are responsible for environmental oversight for some time now. As early as 1979, the Environmental Protection Law was passed for trial implementation. In 1982 the Environmental Protection Agency had a primarily advisory role, and it evolved into a national agency in 1988, became the more independent State Environmental Protection Agency in 1998, and then was elevated to become the Ministry of Environmental Protection in 2008. While the central agency has increased in importance, the responsibility for monitoring and enforcement has been largely (and necessarily) decentralized to environmental bureaus.

The transition of governance has also been accompanied by a change in the style of regulation, with the earlier emphasis on command-and-control regulations (such as emission standards) being replaced to some extent by more economically based instruments, such as taxes on inputs and fees on emissions. The research reported in this volume indicates that the command-and-control regulations are still generally more effective than those using economic incentives.

The performance of managers of municipalities, cities, and provinces is reviewed every year based on a set of criteria that emphasizes economic growth. Yet, many observers believe that additional improvements in environmental outcomes will only occur when these performance criteria give higher priority to improvements in environmental indicators. Evidence for this view is provided by the rapid increase in the control of sulfur dioxide emissions from power plants that followed the inclusion of reduced sulfur emissions in the performance criteria. Providing appropriate incentives for local managers is crucial because of the decentralization of monitoring and enforcement to local environmental bureaus.

While China has much to accomplish in terms of reducing urban air pollution, cleaning up rivers and lakes, and improving energy efficiency, these objectives are becoming more important to its citizens, and the country has been strengthening its environmental governance capacity. More data are available on environmental indicators, and they are contributing to the national dialogue on environmental quality. This volume is intended to contribute to this discussion by reporting on progress, identifying immediate challenges, and assessing new policies and regulatory approaches.

Gregory K. Ingram
President and CEO
Lincoln Institute of Land Policy

# Current Issues in China's
# Environmental Policy

# China's Environmental Policy

*A Critical Survey*

GREGORY C. CHOW

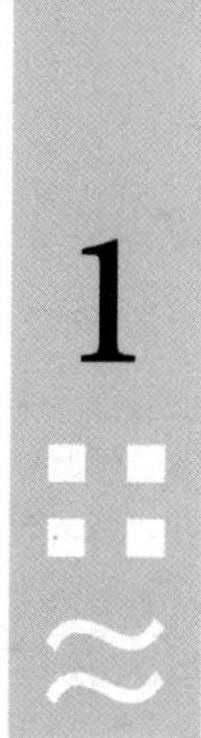

In the past three decades, China has achieved remarkable economic development that is unmatched in human history, but this rapid development has resulted in considerable damage to the natural environment. The environmental problems facing China are serious. In 1998 the World Health Organization (WHO) reported that seven of the ten most polluted cities in the world were in China. Sulfur dioxide ($SO_2$) and soot produced by coal combustion fall as acid rain on approximately 30 percent of China's land area (Flavin 2004). Industrial boilers and furnaces consume almost half of China's coal and are the largest sources of urban air pollution (Tie et al. 2006). In many cities, the burning of coal for cooking and heating accounts for the rest (He, Huo, and Zhang 2002).

Mercury released into the air by coal-fired power plants, captured by raindrops, and transferred to surface water and groundwater has caused serious water pollution. China's water is also polluted by the improper disposal of waste. Supplies of water from the Yellow, Yangtze, and other rivers are running short because of river diversion for agriculture production and electricity generation. In addition, water tables of several important cities, including Beijing and Shanghai, are low, causing a shortage of well water.

The Chinese government has been formulating its environmental policies against this background. Ever since the beginning of economic reform in the late 1970s, the government has paid considerable attention to environmental problems. This chapter surveys the basic laws and policies of the Chinese government on environmental problems, the degree of success in policy implementation, the prospect of solving the environmental problems in the long run, and some recent successes in the development of alternative energy and in controlling pollution. In addition, two proposals will be made for improving the regulation of industrial pollution in China and for controlling carbon emissions in the world.

## Laws and Basic Policies

The 2010 World Exposition in Shanghai provides evidence that the Chinese government views environmental problems as a priority; the green construction of the facilities for the Expo and particularly of the Chinese Pavilion reflects the emphasis the government has placed on protecting and improving the environment. As early as 1979, China passed the Environmental Protection Law for trial implementation. The 1982 Constitution included important provisions to protect the environment. Article 26 of the constitution stipulates that "the state protects and improves the environment in which people live and the ecological environment. It prevents and controls pollution and other public hazards" (National People's Congress 1989). The constitution also asserts that the state has a duty to conserve natural resources and wildlife. Special laws that have been enacted include the Water Pollution Prevention and Control Law of 1984, the Air Pollution Prevention and Control Law of 1987, the Water and Soil Conservation Law of 1991, the Solid Waste Law of 1995, the Energy Conservation Law of 1997, and several important international agreements, such as the Kyoto and Montreal protocols. The Clean Production Promotion Law, enacted in June 2002, established demonstration programs for pollution regulation in 10 major Chinese cities and designated several river valleys as priority areas for the cleanup of pollution.

The State Environmental Protection Administration (SEPA) was established in 1998 to disseminate national environmental policy and regulations, collect data, and provide technological advice to the State Council on both national and international environmental issues. In the spring of 2008, the SEPA was elevated to the Ministry of Environmental Protection to emphasize its importance and to give it more power.

At this point, China is more concerned with air and water pollution than with carbon dioxide ($CO_2$) emissions, which are viewed as a less urgent problem. On 7 June 2007, during the meetings of the Group of 8 (G8) meetings in Germany, President Hu Jintao introduced the principle of "common but differentiated responsibilities" of developing countries in tackling climate change, saying, "We should work together to make sure that the international community upholds the goals and framework established in the United Nations Framework Convention on Climate Change and its Kyoto Protocol [in 1997]," and that developing countries should also carry out "active, practical, and effective cooperation. . . . Considering both historical responsibility and current capability, developed countries should take the lead in reducing carbon emission and help developing countries ease and adapt to climate change. . . . For developing countries, achieving economic growth and improving the lives of our people are top priorities. At the same time, we also need to make every effort to pursue sustainable development in accordance with our national conditions" (Hu 2007). At the UN-sponsored conference on climate change in Copenhagen in January 2009, Premier Wen Jiabao stated that China was determined to do its share in solving the problem of climate change, but would not subject itself to international inspection, a position opposed by the United States (Wen 2009).

From the economic point of view, protection of the environment can be viewed as the government's attempt to correct a major market failure. This failure occurs when natural resources that are freely available in the environment, such as water, are underpriced and overused because users often do not pay the hidden costs of using them. However, the role of the Chinese government is broader than simply correcting this market failure. In the Chinese planning system, which is guided by the National Development and Reform Commission (NDRC), targets are set up to reduce the energy/output ratio and the emissions/energy ratio.

In 2007, for example, Premier Wen Jiabao stated that macrocontrol policy must focus on energy conservation and emissions reduction in order to develop the economy while protecting the environment (Wen 2007). The Chinese government had set a target in the 11th Five-Year Plan of reducing energy consumption per unit of output for every 10,000 yuan (US$1,298) of gross domestic product (GDP) by 20 percent by 2010 (or 4 percent per year), while pollutant discharge (presumably measured by an index of quantities of different pollutants) should drop by 10 percent. The NDRC has also set targets for carbon emissions (National People's Congress 2006).

## Command and Control Versus Economic Incentives

Policies for environmental protection can be divided into two categories. The first is command and control. For example, the U.S. government has specified Corporate Average Fuel Economy (CAFE) standards for automobiles sold in 1978 and 2007. To promote the use of alternative energy technologies, the government can specify that a given share of electricity must be produced from renewable resources. The second category is policies that provide economic incentives to save energy or to reduce pollution. One example is placing a tax on the use of gasoline. Another is requiring emitters to pay for permits according to the amount of their emissions. These permits can be traded among polluters. This is known as a cap-and-trade scheme.

Thus far, the Chinese government has mainly instituted command-and-control laws rather than market-based policies, partly because it has not been able to design a set of market-based policies that estimate the appropriate tax rate. However, it has experimented with such policies. For example, during the Third China-U.S. Strategic Economic Dialogue from 11 to 13 December 2007 in Beijing, China, the two countries agreed to cooperate in introducing emissions permits and other economic incentives to control pollution. A system of emissions trading for sulfur dioxide ($SO_2$) that is similar to that used in the United States is being tested in pilot projects in some Chinese cites and may eventually be applied nationwide (Wang et al. 2003). The Chinese government also plans to reform the pricing of natural gas (Ma 2011),[1] water, and other resources, raise the tax levied on pollutant discharges, establish a "polluter-pays" system, and severely penalize those who violate environmental protection laws (State Council 2011). Future Chinese environmental initiatives may also include formulating a tax structure beneficial to environmental protection and granting preferential loans and subsidies to enterprises that construct

---

[1] In 2011 the NDRC selected Guangdong Province and the Guangxi Zhuang Autonomous Region as experimental units for natural gas pricing reform.

and operate pollution treatment facilities. The government will also provide incentives for companies to use more energy-efficient production facilities and techniques.

On 10 March 2010, the NDRC announced at the National People's Congress and the Chinese People's Political Consultative Conference that it was formulating guidelines for the development of a low-carbon economy, and that small-scale carbon-trading pilot programs would be launched in specific industries and regions. To meet the target of reducing global greenhouse gas emissions by 50 percent by 2050, investment in low-carbon technologies between 2005 and 2050 will total US$1.2 trillion (People's Daily 2010). China has vowed to reduce the intensity of its carbon dioxide emissions per unit of GDP in 2020 by 40 to 45 percent, using 2005 levels that were designated at the Copenhagen conference.

## Enforcement

Even though the laws to protect the environment appear well conceived in general, and the government has set up an administrative structure for environmental protection, the central government has failed to achieve its environmental policy objectives. One reason for this failure is that local governments interested in economic development of their region often allow pollution to occur illegally in order to promote a higher rate of economic growth, and the central government cannot control them. Local government officials benefit from higher levels of output in their region because they receive credits for economic development and sometimes bribes from polluting producers. Given the Chinese system of public land ownership, rent-seeking local bureaucrats who control the use of land tend to approve its use for urban development during their term of office. This has led to overdevelopment of land, which has been an important cause of overheating of the macroeconomy and has created environmental problems.

Premier Wen Jiabao gave the following example of failure to meet targets to protect the environment in April 2007: "The challenge of reducing energy consumption and greenhouse gas emissions has proved arduous as China's economy grew 11.1 percent in the first quarter [of 2007] but power consumption surged 14.9 percent. . . . Energy consumption as a fraction of GDP fell only 1.23 percent in 2006, well short of the annual goal of four percent [as stated in the 11th Five-Year Plan of 2006–2010] (People's Daily 2007)."[2]

The central government has recognized this problem and has updated its policy for evaluating the performance of local government officials to include their record on environmental protection. On 28 October 2007 the National People's Congress enacted the Law on Conserving Energy, which states that work on energy conservation carried out by local government officials should be integrated into the assessment of their political performance along with output growth (National People's Congress 2007). These efforts have yielded positive results, as will be discussed later in this chapter.

---

[2] These quotes from Premier Wen Jiabao were released at the executive meeting of the State Council on 18 April 2007.

In the long run, however, there are three reasons to expect improvement in the implementation of China's environmental policies:

1. The central government is committed to protecting the environment.
2. The central government has the power to enforce environmental laws because the operation of an industrial enterprise requires its approval and sometimes its assistance in the allocation of land or credit. To protect and improve the environment, the government can penalize offenders and can provide economic incentives to act for the economic welfare of society.
3. There is a strong positive correlation between increased income and the demand for a clean environment. As the Chinese economy develops, there will be higher demand for cleaner water, and the Chinese people can afford to pay for these resources. In the long run, although not necessarily in the near future, this favorable income effect should more than offset the unfavorable effects of earlier periods of large-scale output, as the experience of the developed economies has demonstrated. An early increase in pollution followed by a reduction in a later stage of economic development is known as the environmental Kuznets curve. This inverse relationship between pollution and per capita income is expected to take effect eventually in China.

## Recent Successes in Promoting Alternative Energy and Controlling Pollution

Solar energy is still far more expensive to generate than energy from coal, oil, natural gas, or even wind, but the global economic downturn and a decline in European subsidies of purchases of solar panels have lowered its price (Bradsher 2009a). Chinese companies have played a leading role in reducing the price of solar panels by almost half. The production of solar panels has increased because production costs in China are lower than in other countries. Since March 2009 the Chinese central and local governments have given solar panel manufacturers heavy subsidies, including free land and cash for research and development. State-owned banks are flooding the industry with loans at considerably lower interest rates than those available in Europe or the United States. The largest company, Suntech in Wuxi, has become the second-largest manufacturer in the world behind First Solar of the United States. Many firms in China have entered the market. Some are planning to produce in the United States to avoid American protectionist policies against imports from China. Although the production of solar energy is increasing, it is still a very small source, with an expected total capacity in 2020 of 20,000 megawatts, only half the output of coal power plants built in one year (Bradsher 2009a).

The successful development of solar panels indicates that the Chinese government is capable of identifying products that are important to subsidize to promote economic development. Chinese entrepreneurs are ready to take advantage of government subsidies and favorable production and marketing conditions in China to expand production and exports of such products. However, the government's success in promoting the production of clean energy is not limited to solar panels. China doubled its total wind energy capacity in each of the four years from 2006 to

2010 and overtook the United States in 2010 as the world's largest market for installed wind power capacity (Global Wind Energy Council). China is also building considerably more nuclear power plants than the rest of the world combined, and these do not emit carbon dioxide after they are built (Bradsher 2009a).

The control of air pollution by the use of $SO_2$ scrubbers is another success story (Xu 2010). The 10th Five-Year Plan (2001–2005) set a goal of reducing $SO_2$ emissions by 10 percent, but emissions went up by 28 percent during this period. However, in the 11th Five-Year Plan (2006–2010), the trend was reversed. In 2008 China reduced $SO_2$ emissions by 9 percent from the 2005 level, almost reaching the goal of a 10 percent reduction by 2010. The most dramatic change happened at coal-fired power plants: China both installed $SO_2$ scrubbers at newly built coal power plants and retrofitted old plants. At the end of 2008, China had 363 Gigawatts of Electrical output ($GW_e$) of $SO_2$ scrubbers, or 60 percent of the total capacity of coal power generation (601 $GW_e$) (China Electricity Council 2009). By comparison, the ratio at the end of 2005 was only 10 percent.

This achievement resulted from the central government's effort to mobilize both the leaders of local governments and the managers of coal power plants. The 11th Five-Year Plan instituted two measures with regard to local government leaders: (1) promotion or removal of leaders according to their success in the operation of $SO_2$ scrubbers; and (2) use of the power to suspend construction of large projects that might affect the environment (including new coal power plants over 200 $MW_e$) because by law, large construction projects require ratification by the Ministry of Environmental Protection according to its assessment of the environmental impact of the project. To increase the capacity of supervision by site visits, the total personnel at all government levels increased by 39.3 percent, from 37,934 in 2001 to 52,845 in 2006.

In providing incentives to managers of power plants, the most important policy in the 11th Five-Year Plan for the operation of $SO_2$ scrubbers is called the "desulfurized electricity price premium." After installation of $SO_2$ scrubbers, a coal power plant is allowed to sell its electricity to the electric grid at a price 15 Renminbi per Megawatt Hours (RMB/MWh) higher than the original price if the $SO_2$ scrubbers are under normal operation; the plant will be fined 75 RMB/MWh if its $SO_2$ scrubbers are shut down. Although many coal power plants with $SO_2$ scrubbers were receiving the price premium as early as 2004, the penalty and other detailed regulations were not enforced until July 2007.

What are the reasons for the success in controlling $SO_2$ emissions? Can the same strategies help control other forms of air pollution in China? Two factors made $SO_2$ scrubbers successful. First, the source of pollution, coal power plants, is easy to identify and control. Second, the solution, the use of scrubbers, is clear-cut. Hence, it is easy to design policies for local government officials and plant managers to follow. Air pollution created by other industrial producers and by consumers may be more difficult to identify, and the solutions may be less straightforward. However, the success of $SO_2$ scrubbers has demonstrated the central government's resolve and its ability to control air pollution. Because of its resolve, the government can be expected to try to deal with the more difficult cases, even if the effort may be less successful and more time consuming.

## Examples of Successful Government Environmental Policies

The following are some examples of government policies that have been successful in protecting the environment and promoting clean energy. Some of these were suggested by students in a graduate course on the economic analysis of environmental problems at Hong Kong University of Science and Technology in the spring of 2010.

- *Bioenergy:* Under China's National Climate Change Program, China is promoting the development of bioenergy. By 2005, there were more than 17 million household biogas digesters that generated 6,500 million cubic meters of biogas annually. The installed capacity of biomass generation is about 2 gigawatts (GW), of which sugar-cane-fired power capacity is about 1.7GW and landfill-powered capacity is about 0.2GW. In 2006, the reported production capacity of ethanol fuel from crops was 1.02 million tons (National Development and Reform Commission 2007). The Ministry of Agriculture is encouraging the use of marsh gas in rural areas. The government is also promoting the production of alcohol from various plants and the use of alcohol for energy. In the 11th Five-Year Plan, China decided to increase greatly the production of biomass energy—the supply of electricity from the burning of municipal solid waste and agricultural waste—through the construction of power plants to burn these fuels and to expand the production of solid biomass, bioethanol, and biodiesel. The plan included targets to achieve 5 million kilowatts of grid-interconnected wind power and 5.5 million bilowatts of grid-interconnected electricity from biomass combustion.
- *Offsets:* Continued efforts to offset coal consumption include developing natural gas and coal-bed methane infrastructure, increasing the number of combined heat and power plants, adding approximately 3,000 megawatts (MW) of hydropower annually, and developing renewable energy resources, such as wind and photovoltaics, for electricity generation (Chow 2007).
- *Renewable sources of energy:* Renewable sources of energy (including hydroelectricity and excluding nuclear power) accounted for 17.5 percent of China's electricity generation in 2009, second to coal (International Energy Agency 2009). With assistance from the United Nations and the United States, China hopes to embark on a multimillion-dollar renewable energy strategy to combat pollution (Chow 2007). In November 2009 the United States and China established a renewable energy partnership (Council on Foreign Relations 2009). Besides the biofuel, solar, and wind technologies to be developed, the two countries will also focus on modernizing the electrical grid with new transmission lines and smart grid technology.
- *National Working Group:* In 1990 China established a National Working Group for Dealing with Climate Change. In 2007 the group became the National Leading Group for Dealing with Climate Change, directed by the premier. This group has been devoted to fostering the Clean Development Mechanism, which emphasizes the use of renewable energy under an emissions-trading framework.[3]

---

[3] The Clean Development Mechanism is part of the Kyoto Protocol. http://unfcc.int/kyoto_protocol/mechanisms/clean_development_mechanism/items/2718.php

- *Hydropower:* China has made a great effort to develop hydropower. Construction of the Three Gorges Dam began in 1994, and became fully operational in July 2012. It is the world's largest hydroelectric power station. In 2008 China produced 585.2 terawatt hours (TWh) of hydroelectric energy (BP Global 2009).
- *Wind power:* One provision in China's 2005 Renewable Energy Law encourages continued development of wind power. Power grid companies are required to buy all the output of local registered renewable energy producers. The law aims for 70 percent of China's wind turbines to be produced locally. Provincial governments have also incorporated targets for generation capacity of wind power into their five-year plans.
- *Carbon capture:* China is currently developing carbon capture and storage facilities for its coal plants (Bloomberg News 2011).
- *Electric-powered vehicles:* In 2001 the Dongfeng Automobile Company was asked to develop a new type of electric bus for the Beijing 2008 Olympics (Ma et al. 2004). Production was limited because of the speed problem, and only 40 buses were used during the Olympics, but the new technology can be used for family-size vehicles if the costs of production can be reduced.
- *Liquified natural gas:* A number of liquefied natural gas (LNG) stations have been built. The government is also planning to increase imports of natural gas and is building many LNG receiver stations along the coastline. Chinese universities give courses on applications of LNG (Reuters 2010).
- *Prohibition of plastic bags:* In 2008, the Chinese government prohibited the use of plastic bags. China now produces and consumes hundreds of billions fewer plastic bags. Many shoppers carry cloth bags for shopping (New York Times 2008).

## Two Proposals

The Chinese government is considering many useful ideas both to protect China's environment and to control carbon emissions throughout the world. The following are two proposals the government might consider.

## Regulation

1. Industrial polluters would have to pay for pollution permits issued by the local office of China's Ministry of Environmental Protection. Any amount of pollution, however small, would require a permit to pollute or emit that amount. The proceeds from the permits would be returned to local Chinese citizens in some appropriate manner. The number of permits issued (total amount of pollutants discharged) would be determined after consultations with representatives of local citizens who would be affected by the pollution. The citizens and their representatives presumably would balance the harms and benefits of activities that would cause pollution in their area.
2. Because the number of permits issued would be limited, demand would determine the price per permit. The government would first set an initial price for polluters to purchase the permits. If the price was lower than the equilibrium price, the supply of permits would run out, and some polluters would need to

purchase them from others. If the initial price was too high, there would be unsold permits that the government could sell to latecomers at a price lower than the initial price until all permits were sold.

3. Local officials of the state Ministry of Environmental Protection would receive directions from local Chinese citizens through their representatives. Residents in rural areas could be represented by their popularly elected village heads. Urban residents could be represented by their popularly elected representatives of the locality. These representatives would be given responsibility to determine policies to protect the environment and would have incentives and power to enforce them.

This proposal echoes two major policy objectives of the Chinese government in economic development: (1) market reform; and (2) promotion of a democratic government. Under this proposal, market-oriented policies to regulate air and water pollution would be formulated democratically. Citizens would participate in the formulation of environmental policies and would thus help enforce them, rather than simply protesting against the level of pollution, as many have done in recent years.

In the implementation of this policy, it might be difficult to monitor the amount of pollution emitted. This problem could be resolved by requiring polluting factories to report the amount of their emissions, with false reporting subject to a heavy penalty. Government officials might also be reluctant to adopt such a policy. Leaders in the central government would have to demonstrate strong resolve for this policy to be adopted even if they were convinced of its merits.

In response to an inquiry to Premier Wen Jiabao about this proposal, he suggested that this author meet with the vice minister in the Ministry of Environmental Protection in Beijing in July 2008. Several staff members attended the meeting. The meeting was cordial, and the proposal was presented to these officials for their consideration.

## Regulation of Carbon Emissions Through a UN Resolution

1. The total amount of $CO_2$ emissions in the world would be set as the median of amounts submitted as votes by members of the General Assembly of the United Nations. The median rather than the mean would be adopted in order to prevent any member nation from submitting an extreme value to affect the outcome.
2. All countries would be required to have permits for emissions of $CO_2$ and would be forbidden to exceed the amount specified by the permits.
3. Permits would be issued by the UN in proportion to size of a country's population under the principle that each world citizen has an equal right to use the atmosphere, which is a natural resource. Emitting $CO_2$ into the atmosphere is a use of this resource.
4. Emission permits could be traded between any two countries at prices set by mutual agreement.

Developing countries like China with a low level of $CO_2$ emissions per capita would gain financially by selling permits. Developed countries like the United

States that emit a large amount of $CO_2$ per capita would need to buy permits. Buying permits would be an equitable way for the United States to finance the effort of developing countries to limit $CO_2$ emissions, as it has expressed its willingness to do. China might be attracted by this proposal to make clear to the world that it is not emitting an unduly large share of carbon and that it is willing to play its role in the control of total carbon emissions in the world.

## Acknowledgments

I would like to acknowledge financial support from the Gregory C. Chow Econometric Research Program of Princeton University in the preparation of this chapter.

## References

Bloomberg News. 2011. Chinese government drafts plan to develop carbon capture industry. September 22. http://www.bloomberg.com/news/2011-09-22/chinese-government-drafts -plan-to-develop-carbon-capture-storage-industry.html

BP Global. 2009. BP statistical review of world energy. June. www.bp.com/statisticalreview

Bradsher, Keith. 2009a. China outpaces U.S. in cleaner coal-fired plants. *New York Times*, May 10. http://www.nytimes.com/2009/05/11/world/asia/11coal.html

———. 2009b. China racing ahead of US in the drive to go solar. *New York Times*, August 25. http://www.nytimes.com/2009/08/25/business/energy-environment/25solar.html

China Electricity Council. 2009. Quick report of national power generation—2008. Beijing, China.

Chow, Gregory. 2007. China's energy and environmental problems and policies. CEPS Working Paper No. 152. Princeton, NJ: Princeton University. http://www.princeton.edu/ceps/working papers/152chow.pdf

Council on Foreign Relations. 2009. U.S.-China clean energy announcements, November 2009. http://www.cfr.org/china/us-china-clean-energy-announcements-november-2009/p20784

Flavin, Christopher. 2004. Hearing on Asia's environmental challenges: Testimony of Christopher Flavin. Testimony on environmental challenges in Asia at a U.S. House of Representatives Committee on International Relations hearing, Washington, DC. http://www.world watch.org/hearing-asias-environmental-challenges-testimony-christopher-flavin

Global Wind Energy Council. PR China-Total Installed Capacity. http://www.gwec.net/index .php?id=125&L=0%2525252Findex.php%2525253Fid%2525253Dhttp%2525253A%252525

He, Kebin, Hong Huo, and Qiang Zhang. 2002. Urban air pollution in China: Current status, characteristics, and progress. *Annual Review of Energy and Environment* 27:397–431.

Hu, Jintao. 2007. Speech at the collective meeting of leaders of developing countries, a sideline event of the G8 Summit, which groups China, Brazil, India, Mexico, and South Africa, Berlin.

International Energy Agency. 2009. Electricity/Heat in China, People's Republic of in 2009. http://www.iea.org/stats/electricitydata.asp?COUNTRY_CODE=CN

Ma, Wayne. 2011. Beijing lets natural gas prices rise. *Wall Street Journal*, December 27. http:// online.wsj.com/article/SB10001424052970204296804577124371423865252.html

Ma, Chongfang, Yuting Wu, Zhongliang Liu, Xiaoxuan Yu, Shulong Teng, and Xiaoming Liu. 2004. Clean transportation for Beijing 2008 Green Olympics. Paper prepared for Co-OPET Conference on Energy Issues in Transports, Brussels. http://www.bjut.edu.cn/sci/hn/client _c/lunwen/2004_9.pdf

National Development and Reform Commission. 2007. National Climate Change Program. http://www.china.org.cn/english/environment/213624.htm

National People's Congress. 1989. Environmental Protection Law of of the People's Republic of China. Beijing, China.

———. 2006. The Outline of the 11th Five-Year Plan for National Economic and Social Development (2006–2010). Beijing, China.

———. 2007. The Energy Conservation Law of People's Republic of China. Beijing, China.

New York Times. 2008. China bans free plastic shopping bags. http://www.nytimes.com/2008/01/09/world/asia/09iht-plastic.1.9097939.html

People's Daily. 2007. News reports of Hu Jintao. http://english.peopledaily.com.cn/zhuanti/Zhuanti_404.html

———. 2007. China's macro control to focus on energy saving, emission reduction. April 28. http://english.peopledaily.com.cn/200704/28/eng20070428_370564.html

———. 2010. China's top economic planner to launch carbon trading pilot program. March 11. http://english.peopledaily.com.cn/90001/90778/90862/6916176.html

Reuters. 2010. China to build more LNG terminals in Guangdong. March 2. http://news.alibaba.com/article/detail/energy/100255490-1-china-build-more-lng-terminals.html

State Council. 2011. The National Twelfth Five-Year Plan for Environmental Protection. Beijing, China.

Tie, Xuexi, Guy P. Brasseur, Chunsheng Zhao, Claire Granier, Steven Massie, Yu Qin, Pucai Wang, Geli Wang, Peicai Yang, and Andreas Richter. 2006. Chemical charaterization of air pollution in eastern China and the eastern United States. *Atmospheric Environment* 40: 2607–2625. http://login.iup.uni-bremen.de/doas/paper/ae_tie_06.pdf

Wang Jinnan, Yang Jintian, Stephanie Grumet, and Jeremy Schreifels, ed. 2003. SO2 emissions trading program: A feasibility study for China. Beijing: Environmental Science Press. http://www.epa.gov/airmarkets/international/china/feasibility.pdf

Wen, Jiabao. 2007. Speech at the National Teleconference on Energy Conservation and Pollution Reduction, Beijing.

———. 2009. Speech at Copenhagen Climate Conference leaders meeting, Copenhagen.

Xu, Yuan. 2010. China's $SO_2$ emission goal and $SO_2$ scrubbers in the 11th five-year plan. Ph.D. diss., Woodrow Wilson School of Public and International Affairs, Princeton University, Princeton, NJ.

JOYCE YANYUN MAN

# Environmental Policies, Regulations, and Investment in China

The economic reform launched in 1978 has resulted in the rapid growth of China's economy. The growth rate of China's gross domestic product (GDP) has reached double digits for many years, and the rate of urbanization has been growing at an average annual rate of 1 percent. Such remarkable economic growth has taken its toll on the environment. Growing energy consumption, reliance on coal for energy sources, and increasing air and water pollution are threatening China's sustainable future. Environmental pollution and ecological degradation have caused enormous economic losses. According to research by the World Bank (1997), the economic losses caused by environmental problems amounted to 4.43 billion yuan in 1995, about 7.7 percent of GDP. Such losses reached to US$97 billion, about 9.7 percent of GDP, in 1999, according to calculatations by Warford and Li (2002). Chinese government agencies such as the Ministry of Environmental Protection and the National Bureau of Statistics reported economic losses of 511.8 billion yuan and a share of 3.05 percent of GDP in 2004 (State Environmental Protection Administation 2006).

Since the mid-1990s the Chinese government has started initiatives to address environmental problems, and many of its efforts have been very successful. Nevertheless, the debate about economic growth and environmental protection continues. This chapter discusses the evolution of China's regulatory and policy frameworks, the current state of environmental protection, the major economic instruments used to address environmental issues, and the future challenges facing China.

## Environmental Institutional and Regulatory Framework

China did not have a national-level institution responsible for environmental protection and policy design and implementation until 1973, when the Environmental

Protection Steering Office was established under the State Council to advise the State Council on environmental issues. The issuance of "Several Provisions of Environmental Protection and Improvement" by the State Council in 1973 signified the commencement of the development of China's environmental protection regulatory system. In 1978 the Constitution of the People's Republic of China stipulated that the state is responsible for protecting the environment, natural resources, preventing pollution, and other hazards. This was the first time that China had enacted an environmental protection provision into the country's basic national law, adding environmental protection as a responsibility and obligation of the Chinese government. After this significant turning point, the trial enactment of the Environmental Protection Law in 1979 was a legislative landmark. The Environmental Protection Law was later enacted as a part of regular legislation in 1989. It covers a broad spectrum of environmental issues, ranging from the prevention and control of pollution to wildlife protection and establishing a system of environmental management, monitoring, liability, and enforcement (Beyer 2006; Zhang, K. 2007).

Since then, new environmental laws have been enacted, and some old laws have been revised. These include the Marine Environmental Protection Law (1982, amended in 1999), the Forest Law (1984, amended in 1998), the Law on Prevention and Control of Water Pollution (1984, amended in 1996, implemented in 2000), the Grassland Law (1985), the Fisheries Law (1986), the Mineral Resources Law (1986), the Law on Land Administration (1986, amended in 1998), Law on Prevention and Control of Air Pollution (1987), the Water Law (1988, amended in 2002), the Wildlife Protection Law (1988), and the City Planning Law (1989). In the 1990s the Chinese central government undertook new efforts to strengthen its environmental laws and regulations and to promote the principle of sustainable development that was introduced at the 1992 United Nations Conference on Environment and Development. Since 1990 local governments have issued a wide range of local laws and regulations on management, supervision, procedure, and quality standards to implement the national laws (Beyer 2006).

Environmental protection agencies have been raised to a higher level in the Chinese administrative system, and their authority and responsibilites have been increased. In 1973 the first national-level office, the Environmental Protection Leadership Group, was set up under the State Council. In 1983 the Chinese government announced that environmental protection would become a state policy. The Environmental Protection Agency (EPA) was established under the Ministry of Urban and Rural Construction and Environmental Protection in 1982. This was a bureau below a ministry level of a government agency. In 1988 it was promoted to a stand-alone agency under the State Council and was renamed the National Environmental Protection Agency (NEPA). In 1998 its administrative status was further elevated from an agency at subministry level to the ministry level, and it was subsequently renamed the State Environmental Protection Administration (SEPA). In 2008 it was upgraded from an agency under the State Council to an integral component of this chief executive organ in China with a new name, the Ministry of Environmental Protection (MEP). The evolution of the institutional structure from an environmental steering office in 1973 to a cabinet-level ministry in the executive branch of the Chinese government as a part of the State Council signifies the increasing importance of environmental protection in the Chinese government's national policy.

In addition, the administrative structure has become increasingly decentralized since 1992. The central and local governments share responsibilities, functions, and financing in the area of environmental protection. In China, the National People's Congress (NPC), which is the legislative branch, meets once a year and has the authority to enact all basic laws and make amendments to the constitution. Its Standing Committee has the authority to interpret the constitution and the basic laws, as well as to pass laws other than those already prescribed in the constitution. The State Council, China's chief executive branch, is authorized to enact administrative regulations (*xingzheng fagui*), while its ministries, commissions, and departments have authority to issue administrative rules (*xinzheng guizhang*). Because of this restructuring, the MEP is now a major administrative institution of the State Council. It is in charge of national environmental policies, environmental regulations, and national standards and exerts national control and supervision over environmental protection.

The central government's structure has been adopted at the provincial and local levels. Local people's congresses and their standing committees pass local regulations in accordance with national legislation and regulations. From the provincial government to the local governments at levels of cities, counties, and townships, environmental protection bureaus (EPBs) issue and implement local administrative rules in accordance with national laws and regulations, as well as local regulations (Beyer 2006). They are funded by the local government and are the basic units responsible for environmental protection within their jurisdiction. EPBs also supervise compliance with environmental laws and regulations and are often assisted by research institutions and inspection and monitoring centers at higher administrative levels. By 2008 China had established a four-tier environmental compliance system at the central, provincial, prefecture-level cities and county levels and boasted 2,399 environmental inspection institutions with 1,770,000 employees in charge of monitoring, inspection, and supervision of environmental protection nationwide (China government web 2009).

## Environmental Policies

China's environmental policies have also experienced significant changes in the past 30 years. In the late 1970s, three major policies were developed and included in the Environmental Protection Law in 1979 (trial form): environmental impact assessment (EIA); the three synchronizations; and pollution fees on discharges exceeding national or local standards. The EIA aimed at pollution prevention when new and expanding projects with potential adverse effects on the environment were undertaken. This policy, which was reinforced in a new law in 2003, requires that all programs and plans on land use and development projects for natural resources be subject to an environmental impact assessment evaluation (EIA).

The three-synchronizations policy was introduced as the main instrument for pollution prevention and control in 1972. It was incorporated into the 1989

Environmental Protection Law, Article 26, which requires the integration and installation of pollution-prevention and control facilities during all stages of project development, such as design, construction, and operation. It applies to all new factories and major expansions of existing projects (Zhang, S.-q. 2001). The levying of pollution charges was included in the Environmental Protection Laws of 1979 and 1989 on the basis of the polluter-pays principle, which states that polluters are responsible for the elimination and control of pollution and are liable for any damage or loss. In China polluters are required to pay discharge fees and other fees for discharging pollution in excess of national or local standards. The discharge permit system requires that waste sources above a certain size receive a permit before discharging wastes. Limited time treatment was first proposed in 1973 and was included in the Environmental Protection Law in 1989. It imposes deadlines or commitments for heavily polluted towns, industrial sites, rivers, lakes, and ocean bays to improve environmental quality within a limited time (Zhang, S.-q. 2001). Centralized pollution control shifts the focus from individual pollution sources to the entire process. The Law of Clean Production Promotion, enacted in 2002, established a program to promote the sustainable and efficient use of natural resources and to reduce the risks to human health and the environment. Total emission control for major pollutants (TEC) was first proposed in 1995 and was approved by the State Council in 1996. It sets environmental targets for emissions, environmental quality, and waste treatment and focuses on certain heavily polluted regions and rivers (Zhang, S.-q. 2001).

In addition, national and local environmental agencies conduct quantitative assessments of the urban environment to evaluate cities according to a number of indicators of urban environmental construction and management and to identify model cities. Economic instruments, including taxes, incentives, subsidies, fees, and loans, have been used by environmental agencies at national and local levels, as well as within specific industries. These policies promote sound environmental management practices, compliance with the law, and the efficient use of natural resources. The Chinese government has also encouraged public participation by emphasizing education of the public; disseminating information on environmental conditions, statistics, and selected indicators of river and air quality; holding public hearings on environment impact reports; media monitoring; and promoting model cities.

The environmental responsibility system introduced in the 1980s requires that provincial and local government officials be responsible for overall environmental quality in a jurisdiction by signing written contracts or agreements among heads of different levels of government or between government officials and polluting companies (Zhang, S.-q. 2001). Since 2004, green GDP has been used as one of the measures of the performance of provincial and local government officials for credits and promotion.

## Pollution-Levy System and Fee Structures

Most environmental policies in China are command-and-control instruments, which may be effective in environmental protection in the targeted areas and in preventing new pollution from occurring. In addition, China has increasingly been using a range of economic instruments as part of its environmental policies. The pollution-levy system has been fully established and implemented in China. The polluter-pays principle was first proposed in 1978 and later was written into the 1979 Environmental Protection Law (trial), the 1989 Environmental Protection Law, and the laws on air, water, waste and noise. Initially, polluters were required to pay fees and charges for discharges that exceeded pollution concentration standards. In 2003 the State Council issued pollution charges on the concentration exceeding the standard plus the volume of the pollutants, including paying four other kinds of penalty charges commonly referred to as "four small pieces." Currently the pollution charges are levied on sewage (water emissions), exhaust (air emissions), solid waste, hazardous waste, and noise emissions. Chinese governments levied about 113 types of fees and charges by 2008.

Different standards for fees and charges are imposed on each of the five types of emissions, including air, sewage, solid waste, hazardous waste, and noise emissions. The revenue from pollution charges and fees increased from 2002 to 2008. By 2010 total revenue from the pollution-levy system reached 18.8 billion yuan, compared with 6.74 billion in 2002, an increase of 179 percent. During this period, the largest increase in revenues was from exhaust (air) emission fees and charges, up by 1,659 percent, followed by noise emission fees (up by 268.4 percent) and wastewater (up by about 25.1 percent). Hazardous solid waste revenues accounted for less than 1 percent of total emission fees and charges and decreased. Not surprisingly, the fees and charges from exhaust emissions accounted for nearly 78 percent of the total emission revenues in 2010. The shares of revenues from wastewater emission, noise, and hazardous solid waste were 12.58 percent, 7.9 percent, and 0.03 percent of total emission charges and fees, respectively.

The total revenue collected from the pollution-levy system is transferred to the Ministry of Finance at the national level and the Bureaus of Finance at the subnational level. Only about 10 percent of the revenue goes to the central government, and the revenues are earmarked for general purposes of environmental protection, including purchasing monitoring equipment and new technology. The funds are distributed on the basis of proposals provided by the subnational governments (OECD 2007).

In addition to pollution charges, the Chinese government also collects user charges and fees from households and industrial users of environmental services and natural resources. For example, wastewater treatment fees are collected from all customers connected to a centralized water supply system. Municipal solid waste treatment fees are levied on households for garbage collection. Water charges are collected in some cities for the quantity of water used by households and industries. In addition, there are a number of fees for the use of oil and natural gas fields, exploration rights, and mining rights. A mining resource compensation fee has been collected since 1994 on the basis of sales incomes of products from mining operations at a rate of 0.5 percent to 4 percent.

Although pollution-levy systems have been used in China since 1979, these fees are significantly lower than the cost of pollution reduction. Many polluters prefer to pay the charges instead of improving their operations and technology to lower their emissions. Some big enterprises often ignore notices of discharge fees from environmental protection bureaus, and fees are often negotiated rather than being calculated on the basis of a formula or a fixed standard detailed in regulations. Local regulators have too much discretion in enforcing compliance with the rules and regulations and in determining fees, fee reductions, exemptions, and deferrals. User charges and fees are not as widely used as they should be, and the fees in most cases are levied only on costs of operation and rarely reflect fixed costs and investment costs of facilities and project developments (OECD 2007).

## Environmental Investment

Since 1996, we have witnessed a rapid increase in environmental investment expenditure on pollution abatement and control and urban environmental infrastructure. Total environmental investment expenditure increased by 501 percent between 2001 and 2010. In 2010 total investment in the treatment of pollution amounted to 665.4 billion yuan (about US$105.6 billion), an increase of 47 percent from the previous year. It accounted for 1.66 percent of GDP and was largely spent on environmental components for new construction projects that accounted for 30.55 percent of total spending in 2010, urban environmental infrastructure (63.48 percent of the total), and industrial pollution treatment (5.97 percent). Between 2001 and 2010, investment increased among all types of environment investment expenditure, but also grew at the fastest rate during the period from 2001 to 2010. In addition, spending on environmental components for new construction projects increased by 29.4 percent between 2009 and 2010, but expenditures on industrial pollution treatment decreased by 10.3 percent, signifying a policy shift from end-of-pipe treatment to prevention control at the initial stage of development and more emphasis on urban environmental infrastructure investment and pollution-abatement programs.

## Urban Environmental Infrastructure Investment

In 2010 urban environmental infrastructure investment spending reached 422.4 billion yuan, about 64 percent of total environmental investment expenditure. Its share decreased from 53.83 percent in 2001 to 40.11 percent in 2008, a 13.8 percentage drop, but its share went up by 23 percentage points between 2008 and 2010. Total investment on urban environmental infrastructure increased by 135 percent between 2008 and 2010, an indication that there was a big policy shift during the global financial crisis; it amounted to 1.06 percent of GDP in 2010. Investment in gas infrastructure projects accounted for 6.88 percent of total investment in 2010, central heating for 10.26 percent, sewage for about 21.34 percent, gardening and greening projects for 54.38 percent, and city beautification and hygiene projects for 7.14 percent. Investment in sewage and urban gardens and greening projects accounted for nearly 75.72 percent of total investment in urban environmental infrastructure. The share of investment expenditure on gas supply and sewage in total investment decreased by 5.79 and 16.34 percentage points, respectively, between 2001 and 2010, while the share of heating in total urban environmental infrastructure investment decreased by 3.5 percentage points, gardening and greening went up by 27 percentage points, and sanitation went down by 1.35 percentage points. These percentages indicate a policy shift in urban environmental investment to central heating, gardening and greening, and sanitation projects since 2004.

## Industrial Pollution Treatment

Investment expenditure on industrial pollution treatment experienced a rapid increase of 127 percent between 2001 and 2010. It peaked at 55.2 billion yuan in 2007 and then steadily decreased to 39.7 billion yuan in 2010, about 6.0 percent of total environmental investment expenditure in that year. Nevertheless, this share has decreased from 15.77 percent in 2001, about a 10 percentage point drop between the two years. Investment expenditure on wastewater treatment and exhaust (air discharges) treatment accounted for 80.34 percent of total investment in industrial pollution treatment projects in 2010. The investment in wastewater treatment increased from 72.9 billion yuan in 2001 to 130.1 billion yuan in 2010, up by 78 percent, but its share of the total investment in industrial pollution treatment dropped by nearly 9 percentage points during this period, while spending on exhaust (air) emission treatment amounted to 188 billion yuan in 2010, a 187 percent increase over spending in 2001. Exhaust emission treatment's share in total industrial pollution treatment expenditure also went up by nearly 10 percentage points during the 10-year period. In addition, investment in industrial solid waste treatment decreased by 23.7 percent between 2001 and 2010, but expenditure on noise-reduction treatment experienced a rapid increase, up by 136 percent during this period, although it accounted for only 0.38 percent of total investment on industrial pollution treatment in 2010.

## Investment on Pollution Abatement Through Three-Synchronizations Projects

Government expenditure on pollution abatement through environment component for new construction projects grew rapidly from 33.6 billion yuan in 2001 to 203.3 billion yuan in 2010, an amount more than six times greater. Its share in total environmental investment expenditure increased from 30.4 percent in 2001 to 47.81 percent in 2008 and then decreased to 30.6 percent in 2010. Its share in GDP also grew from 0.31 percent in 2001 to 0.51 percent in 2010. It accounted for 4.1 percent of total investment on construction projects and 0.7 percent of the total fixed-assets investment of the entire economy. This result suggests that the Chinese government starts to invest more heavily in pollution control at the development stage of any new or expanding project. It emphasizes new equipment, adaptation, and technical improvement measures and provides assistance at the initial stages of planning, design, and operation.

## Conclusion

The findings of this chapter show that the Chinese government has made great efforts to build an environmental protection system since the mid-1970s and has accomplished a great deal in setting up an institutional structure and compliance system with a full set of laws and regulations and a four-tier enforcement structure with regional environmental supervision bureaus resembling the U.S. Environmental Protection Agency system. The past 30 years have also witnessed the elevation of the administrative status of the environmental administrative structure from a mere environmental protection office to a subministry-level department and then to the cabinet-level Ministry of Environmental Protection in 2008, reflecting the increasing importance of environmental protection in the Chinese government's economic strategic planning and decision-making process.

The passage of environmental protection laws and many other environment-related laws and regulations at both the national and local levels for the objectives of pollution control and treatment and environmental protection demonstrates an increasing reliance on legal and economic instruments to accomplish the ultimate goals of environmental protection. It also reveals that China's environmental policies have experienced a number of transitions. First, China has gone through a shift from a command-and-control policy to more market-oriented economic policies in dealing with pollution control and treatment. Second, it has shifted the focus from just pollution-concentration control to total volume control and concentration standards for more effective policy outcomes. Third, it has changed from end-of-pipe pollution treatment to more comprehensive and integrated prevention measures to promote environmental protection.

The pollution-levy system was established in accordance with the polluter-pays principle and has been protected in a number of laws and regulations. Although the revenue from pollution charges and fees increased by 179 percent from 2002 to 2010, it accounted for only 2.83 percent of total environmental investment expenditure in 2010. This indicates that there is room for improvement in fee rates and structures, enforcement, and collection to make this important economic instrument more effective in changing polluters' behaviors toward more environment-friendly activities through the various stages of production, operation, and consumption. User charges and fees have long been used in China, but the potential of this policy instrument should be further explored to encourage conservation, energy efficiency, and environmental protection. In addition, other economic policy instruments, including cap and trade and direct environmental taxation, should be employed as part of a comprehensive, integrated, and effective set of environmental policies.

The Chinese government has increased its environmental investment expenditure in the past 10 years; the amount reached 665.4 billion yuan in 2010, an increase of 500 percent between 2001 and 2010, and accounted for 1.67 percent of GDP. However, this is still far from the target of 1,400 billion yuan (US$175 billion) announced by the Chinese government for the period from 2006 to 2010.

The policy shifts since 2000s have also been reflected in the spending structure for environment investment. The pollution-abatement and control program has been growing rapidly, and expenditures on it went up by 504 percent from 2001 to 2010, accounting for 30 percent of total environmental treatment investment. However, urban environmental infrastructure investment went up even faster, by 609 percent during this period, and its share in total environmental expenditure increased from 53.8 percent in 2001 to 63.5 percent in 2010. Although emphasis on pollution abatement and control is a sensible policy, the Chinese government should continue to invest in urban environmental infrastructure, which is quite inadequate in many areas, particularly in small towns and less developed regions.

In addition, the Chinese government should encourage partnerships with the private sector in the provision of environmental infrastructure and industrial pollution treatments and should promote public participation and collaboration with nongovernmental and nonprofit organizations among its environmental protection programs. Most important, energy conservation should be pushed to the top of the government's policy agenda in order to realize the objective of a circular economy and sustainable economic growth and development in China.

## References


Beyer, Stefanie. 2006. Environmental law and policy in the People's Republic of China. *Chinese Journal of International Law* 5(1):185–211.

China's Environmental Yearbook Editing Committee. 2002–2011. *China environment yearbook.* Beijing: China Environment Yearbook Editorial Board.

China's Government Web Portal. 2009. Environmental protection achieved striking success. Report Series on China's 60th Anniversary, No. 17. September 28. http://www.gov.cn/gzdt /2009-09/28/content_1428543.htm

Ministry of Environmental Protection of the People's Republic of China. 2003–2011. http://www .mep.gov.cn/

Organisation for Economic Co-operation and Development (OECD). 2007. *OECD environmental performance reviews: China.* Paris: OECD.

State Environmental Protection Administration. 2006. China Green National Accounting-Study Report 2004. Beijing, China. www.cqvip.com/qk/9779x/200606/23185677.html

Warford, Jeremy and Li Yining. 2002. Environmental tax workshop report. China Council for International Cooperation on Environment and Development. Task Force Report Series. Beijing, China. http://www.cciced.net/zlk_1/cbw/procedings/sanjieyici/report/200908/ P020090828563844694683.pdf

World Bank. 1997. "Clear water, blue skies: China's environment in the new century." Washington, DC: World Bank.

Xu, Wen. 2009. Chinese emission fees and charges. Working Paper. Research Institute of Fiscal Sciences, Ministry of Finance of China. Beijing.

Zhang, Kunmin. 2007. Contemporary China's environmental policy: Formation, characteristics and evaluation. *Chinese Population, Resources and the Environment* 17(2):1–6.

Zhang, Shi-qiu. 2001. Environmental regulatory and policy framework in China: An overview. *Journal of Environmental Sciences* 12(1):122–128.

# Government Decentralization, Energy Saving, and Environmental Protection

ZHONGXIANG ZHANG

Confronted with the rising costs and health risks of environmental degradation associated with rapid economic growth, central governments in Asian countries have gradually recognized that the conventional path of encouraging economic growth at the expense of the environment cannot be sustained and must be changed. They are convinced of the need to clean up their countries' development act. Accordingly, they set environmental goals and environmental performance requirements. Environmental ministries or equivalent agencies are empowered to take these responsibilities, but they are often ill equipped for their tasks of enforcing existing regulations and designing, implementing, monitoring, inspecting, and enforcing new effective environmental policies.

The National Environmental Protection Agency of China was for years seen as a powerless entity. Although President Hu Jintao and Prime Minister Wen Jiabao gave the agency a new lease on life and elevated it from a low vice-ministry rank to full ministerial status as the State Environmental Protection Administration (SEPA) and then to its current status as the Ministry of Environmental Protection (MEP) under the State Council (China's cabinet), it still does not have adequate authority. The MEP does not have the ability to block proposed projects that would violate environmental laws and regulations or to remove officials who should be held accountable for noncompliance with environmental regulations. It also lacks the authority to manage local environmental bureaus (Zhang 2007a).

If the MEP decides to impose a penalty on violators of environmental impact assessment (EIA) laws and regulations, as indicated in table 3.1, the maximum fine at its disposal is just 200,000 yuan (about US\$29,500). Even for environmental accidents as serious as the benzene contamination of the Songhuajiang River in northern China in November 2005, an incident that had unprecedented international implications, as well as domestic social, economic, and environmental ramifications, the maximum fine under China's current environmental laws is just 1

"

**TABLE 3.1**

Maximum Fines by Category of Violators of Environmental Laws and Regulations in China

|  | Applicable Laws | Maximum Fines Allowed (10,000 Yuan) |
| --- | --- | --- |
| Exceeding the pollution limit | Atmosphere Pollution Prevention and Control Act | 10 |
| Air pollution accidents | Atmosphere Pollution Prevention and Control Act | 50 |
| EIA violators, imposed only after the grace period | Environmental Impact Assessment (EIA) Law | 20 |
| Extraordinary environmental accidents | Water Pollution Prevention and Control Act | 100 |

SOURCE: Zhang (2008).

million yuan, which was actually imposed one year after that incident. Moreover, the fine can be imposed only once (Zhang 2007a; 2007c; 2007d). As a result, this low, one-time penalty is hardly a deterrent to environmental offenders. To make things worse, even the weak punishments allowed by current environmental laws are still weakly enforced in China because environmental protection agencies at all levels of government are underfunded and inadequately staffed.

Poor compliance and weak enforcement are common in developing Asian countries. Correcting these problems requires a major investment in strengthening the institutions of environmental governance to ensure that they have adequate institutional, financial, and technical capabilities to do their job. This is a necessary step, but it is not enough. The full participation of all stakeholders in protecting the environment is needed.

Over the past three decades, many Asian countries have decentralized allocation and responsibility and have shifted control over resources and decision making to local governments. This devolution of decision making to local levels has placed environmental stewardship in the hands of local officials who are often more concerned with economic growth. Therefore, effective environmental protection must be placed in this context of government decentralization.

In this regard, the cooperation of local governments is crucial to the overall outcome. As often is the case, what the center wants is not necessarily what the center gets. An old Chinese saying goes, "The mountains are high, and the emperor is far away." Central governments need to let go of the notion that they can or even should do it all. Instead, they need to recognize that without local governments' cooperation in policy implementation, it is meaningless to set and defend national environmental goals, no matter how stringent they are.

Taking China as the focus and government decentralization as the context, this chapter first discusses a variety of tactics that the Chinese central government has been using to incentivize local governments. It then examines the objective and subjective factors that lead to the lack of local officials' cooperation on the environment.

Finally, it provides some suggestions for the right incentives for effective environmental protection by local governments.

## Incentives for Local Governments to Be More Environmentally Responsible

Local governments' inability or noncooperation has been a major reason for the failure to meet energy-efficiency and environmental goals set by the national government. The Chinese national government has implemented policies to shut down plants that are inefficient and highly polluting and to keep the frenzied expansion of offending industries under control (Zhang 2010b; 2010d; 2010e). Local officials strongly resist these policies because these companies provide jobs and create tax revenues, as well as personal payoffs. Forcing companies out of business could even trigger local unrest. For example, the National Development and Reform Commission (NDRC), China's top economic planning agency, ordered provincial governments to raise power tariffs for eight energy-guzzling industries, including cement, aluminum, iron and steel, and ferroalloy, from 1 October 2006 onward (see table 3.2). However, it was reported that by mid-April 2007, not only had many local governments failed to implement the differentiated tariffs that charge more for companies classified as "eliminated types" or "restrained types" in these industries, but 14 of them even continued to offer preferential power tariffs for such industries (Zhang 2007a; 2007c; 2007d).

To gain the cooperation of local officials on environmental issues, incentives need to be provided. Under the 2007 evaluation criteria for officials in China, local officials typically have been promoted on the basis of how fast they expand their local economies. That has created an incentive for officials to disregard the environmental costs of economic growth. To correct this distorted view of local officials' accomplishments and to implant environmental consequences in their minds, environmental performance has to be considered as well. If environmental quality does not improve during an official's tenure, that official should not be promoted. This will help local officials realize that they should take their jobs seriously because they have a very real stake in meeting environmental goals.

**TABLE 3.2**

Differentiated Tariffs for Energy-Guzzling Industries in China

| | | Existing Additional Charge (Yuan/kWh) | Additional Charge Since 1 October 2006 (Yuan/kWh) | Additional Charge Since 1 January 2007 (Yuan/kWh) | Additional Charge Since 1 January 2008 (Yuan/kWh) |
|---|---|---|---|---|---|
| Energy-guzzling industries | Eliminated types | 0.05 | 0.10 | 0.15 | 0.20 |
| | Restrained types | 0.02 | 0.03 | 0.04 | 0.05 |

SOURCE: NDRC (2006).

To that end, the central government of China has been using a variety of tactics to incentivize local governments. Since 1997 the SEPA (now the MEP) has run a model environmental city program. Any city that meets about 30 specified environmental indicators for three consecutive years and is among the three best performers of environmental quality in a province is awarded the title. Out of 629 cities in China, 67 had been placed on the honor roll by the end of 2008 (MEP 2009).

To push local governments further on the environmental front, the SEPA unveiled its blacklist of the 10 most polluted cities for the first time in June 2004 to discourage environmentally irresponsible decisions. This shocked local officials who had always worked on the assumption that evil deeds very seldom saw the light of day (Zhang 2007a; 2007b). This public disclosure works effectively because it puts more pressure on local officials to take responsibility for the health of their people and to take action.

Since 2006 the blacklist has expanded to include cities with air quality below the class III standard designed for industrial areas. According to the evaluation of the environmental quality of 595 Chinese cities in 2006, although the number of cities blacklisted was down by 4 from the previous year, there were still 39 cities on the SEPA's blacklist (SEPA 2007). In the 2008 evaluation of 629 cities' environmental quality, released on 21 December 2009, the number of blacklisted cities decreased to seven.[1] Moreover, the category of blacklisted cities has been further expanded to include those cities that are unable to undertake online automatic monitoring, are found not to have undertaken the required urban sewage treatment and to have discharged substandard wastewater, and do not treat urban garbage properly (MEP 2009).

In an attempt to help the general public and officials alike understand how severe the rising environmental degradation associated with China's rapid economic growth is, the SEPA and the National Bureau of Statistics of China (2006) in September 2006 jointly released the first report on the economic costs of pollution, which covered the year 2004. Despite shortcomings in basic data, methodologies, and coverage of items, this report estimates that environmental pollution cost China US$64 billion, or 3.05 percent of gross domestic product (GDP), in 2004. This sends a warning signal that China's rampant environmental pollution problem is undermining its long-term economic growth. The SEPA advocates using green GDP instead of traditional GDP as the economic criterion to evaluate the real performance of local officials.

The SEPA decided in July 2006 to establish six regional environmental protection inspection centers. Unlike local environmental protection agencies budgeted by local governments, these regional centers are directly under the leadership of the

---

[1] China's national air quality standards for residential areas are termed the Chinese "class II standards." The national standards for residential areas are set at the annual average concentrations of total suspended particulate (TSP) matter and particulate matter less than 10 microns in diameter ($PM_{10}$) of 200 and 100 micrograms per cubic meter ($\mu g/m^3$), respectively. In the latest evaluation of Chinese cities' environmental quality in 2008, 76.8 percent of Chinese cities were able to meet or go beyond the class II standard (MEP 2009). That figure was only 37.6 percent in 2006 (SEPA 2007). This suggests that although there has been significant progress in improving urban air quality, about 23 percent of Chinese cities still suffer from air pollution severe enough that they are unable to meet the class II standards, which are much lower than the World Health Organization (WHO) guideline of 90 $\mu g/m^3$ for TSP and 20 $\mu g/m^3$ for $PM_{10}$ (WHO 2000). The WHO abandoned the standards for TSP because time-series epidemiological studies were unable to define a threshold below which no health effects occur.

national environmental regulatory agency. Moreover, they are independent of local governments in their budgets and staffs. Thus, they can resist local governments' short-term interests to better represent national, long-term, and general interests, have an enhanced capability to inspect and resolve serious environmental disputes across provincial borders and river basins, can correct distorted information on local environmental quality, and can rein in the increasing number of local protectionists (Sina Net 2007). This is another way to coerce cooperation between the central government and local governments.

To further enhance the environmental awareness of local officials, the SEPA has tightened approval of construction projects by implementing regional permit restrictions. The so-called regional permit restrictions are based on an ancient Chinese punishment of incriminating relatives and associates related to the main suspect. On 10 January 2007, the SEPA, in an unprecedented move, suspended EIA approval of any new construction projects in four cities (Tangshan in Hebei Province, Luliang in Shanxi Province, Liupanshui in Guizhou Province, and Laiwu in Shandong Province) and of four major national power-generating groups (Datang International, Huaneng Group, China Huadian Corporation, and China Guodian Corporation) until they brought their existing facilities into compliance with environmental regulations. Once their EIA approval rights were suspended, no new construction projects were allowed to be built in these cities and by these power-generating groups until all violators were in compliance with environmental regulations. Given that China's economy is investment driven, local governments are fully aware of the consequences of the suspension of their right to approve new construction projects. Disregarding environmental problems in their regions now can cost them a lot (Zhang 2007a).

This was not the first time the SEPA had imposed administrative measures to punish offenders. Since January 2005, the SEPA has unleashed a series of "environmental protection storms." Its first storm, unleashed on 18 January 2005, blacklisted 30 industrial projects worth 119.7 billion yuan. Many of these projects were considered "national key projects" that had been approved by the powerful NDRC. These industrial projects were not necessarily high polluters, but the SEPA called for a halt to them on the ground that they had not undergone proper EIAs. This first environmental protection storm served as a public education campaign to increase awareness of the EIA law. In the second environmental storm in 2006, the EIA law was further strengthened when it was taken from the project level to the deeper level of planning. In this storm, 163 proposed projects worth 774.6 billion yuan were put on hold on by enforcing the EIA law. But the restriction of regional permits is the strictest administrative measure ever taken by the SEPA in its 30 years of existence (Zhang 2007a; 2007b).

The underlying reason for suspending EIA approval rights is thought to be the desire to promote technology upgrading, industrial restructuring, and sustainable development. Whether it will become an effective punishment will depend on how local governments and companies succeed in changing their attitudes and practices and whether local environmental protection agencies work together with the national agency. Otherwise, suspending approval rights has only temporary effects and does not lead to long-term efficacy.

The new regional permit restrictions seem to be effective. Only one month after the restrictions suspended approval rights for the four cities, one city, Laiwu, quickly responded to the SEPA warnings and recovered its rights. Only two months after the suspension, Huaneng Group and China Guodian Corporation, the two national power-generating groups, came into compliance and recovered their rights (Zhang 2007a).

There have been hardly any reports on environmental protection storms in China's media since the fourth environmental protection storm (July 2007), which targeted river basins in China, but the MEP continues to suspend the rights of those corporations and provinces that approve any new construction projects despite violations of environmental regulations. For example, the Ludila hydropower project by Huadian Power International and the Longkaikou project by Huaneng Power International, both located in Lijiang, Yunnan Province, were found to have blocked the river illegally for the construction effort in January 2010 without reviewing the projects' environmental impact. As a result, in June 2010 the MEP ordered the country's two largest power producers to stop building the dams immediately. Moreover, the MEP suspended approval of hydropower projects along the middle reaches of the Jinsha River and suspended EIA approval of any new construction projects (except for renewable and pollution-abating projects) for the two national power-generating groups. Weifang Steel Group Corporation in Shandong Province started constructing a project that would have produced five million tons of steel. Because this project violated the national industrial policy and the development plan of the steel industry, the MEP suspended EIA approval of any new construction projects in the whole steel sector for the whole province (Sina Net 2009).

China started implementing the bulletin system to release data on energy use per unit of GDP and other indicators by provincial region in 2006 (People's Daily 2005). According to the first bulletin on energy use per unit of GDP and other indicators for 2006, which was released in July 2007, among the 31 Chinese provinces or equivalents, only Beijing met energy-saving and emissions-cutting goals in 2006, cutting its energy use per unit of GDP by 5.25 percent. Tianjin followed close behind, with a 3.98 percent reduction in energy intensity (NBS, NDRC, and Office of the National Energy Leading Group 2007).[2] In 2007, despite concerted efforts to save energy, China cut its energy intensity by only 4.04 percent (NBS, NDRC, and National Energy Administration 2009). There are still big variations in energy-saving performance among the 31 Chinese provinces or equivalents. Beijing still took the lead, cutting its energy intensity by 6 percent, followed by Tianjin at 4.9 percent and Shanghai at 4.66 percent (NBS, NDRC, and National Energy Administration 2008). This was a clear indication of Beijing's commitment to the 2008 Green Olympic Games. In the meantime, there were seven provinces whose energy-saving performances were below the national average. The year 2008 was the first in which China exceeded the annualized target (4.4 percent) for energy saving,

---

[2] In 2006 Beijing became the first provincial region in China to establish the bulletin system to release data on energy use and water use per unit of GDP, releasing these and other indicators quarterly by county. See Zhang (2007b; 2007c; 2007d) for a detailed discussion of why Beijing met the energy-saving goals, but other areas missed them.

cutting its energy intensity by 4.59 percent (NBS, NDRC, and National Energy Administration 2009). This was due partly to the economic crisis that reduced overall demand, particularly for energy-intensive products. Overall, energy intensity was cut by 10.1 percent in the first three years of the 11th Five-Year Plan relative to 2005 levels. At the end of the 11th Five Year Plan, energy intensity was cut by 19 percent.[3] For China's continued success in reducing energy intensity in the 12th Five Year Plan, local governments' cooperation is crucial to the overall outcomes. The MEP could use its power to suspend the right to approve new construction projects in those provinces if they fail to comply with the energy-saving and environmental goals (Zhang 2007a).

Shifting control over resources and decision making to local governments as the result of economic reforms in China over the past three decades has led to insufficient investment in energy saving. Its share in total investment in the energy industry in China declined from about 13.4 percent in 1983 to about 3 percent in 2005 (Zhang 2007c; 2007d; 2010d). China needs to increase investment in energy conservation and energy-efficiency improvements. Faced with the prospect of failure to meet the ambitious energy-intensity target, the central government provided an additional 10 billion yuan in mid-2007, following the 11.3 billion yuan already allocated early in that year (a total of 21.3 billion yuan, about US$3.2 billion, or 4.5 percent of the total investment in the energy sector in 2005) specifically for energy saving, of which 9 billion yuan went to support the Ten Key Energy-Saving Programs, 13 times the funding support in 2006 (0.68 billion yuan). This is a helpful step in promoting energy conservation, but the amount of funds allocated for energy saving needs to increase still more. To encourage local governments to eliminate outdated production capacities, payment transfers should be made both from the central government to provincial governments in the less developed regions and from the provincial governments to those cities and counties in which a large amount of outdated production capacity has been closed down. Moreover, the transfer amount needs to be indexed to the real energy saving as the result of closing down outdated production capacity (Zhang 2007c; 2007d; 2010d). The Chinese government has gradually recognized the importance of transfer payments in getting local government to cooperate. This is reflected in the central government's decision in November 2007 to transfer 2 billion yuan to provincial governments. This is a very positive development, but this amount falls far short of what is needed and must increase further, in particular because the central government accounts for less than 25 percent of the country's total government expenditure but receives over 50 percent of the total government revenue in China (see table 3.3). The good news is that the Chinese central government has recognized these needs; it increased the amount of funding allocated for energy saving to 41.8 billion yuan in 2008 (including the 4 billion yuan allocated for urban sewage treatment in 2007) from 23.5 billion yuan in 2007 (State Council 2008). The year 2010 was the final year of China's energy-efficiency drive of the 11th Five-Year Plan. With energy intensity

---

[3] The reliability of both energy-use and GDP data matters in meeting this energy-intensity target. See Zhang (2010a; 2010c) for discussions of the reliability and revisions of China's statistical data on energy and GDP and of their implications for meeting China's existing energy-saving goal in 2010 and its proposed carbon-intensity target in 2020.

**TABLE 3.3**

Shares of Central and Local Governments in Government Revenue and Expenditure in China, 1993–2008

| | Government Revenue | | Government Expenditure | |
|---|---|---|---|---|
| | Central Government (%) | Local Governments (%) | Central Government (%) | Local Governments (%) |
| 1993 | 22.0 | 78.0 | 28.3 | 71.7 |
| 1994 | 55.7 | 44.3 | 30.3 | 69.7 |
| 1995 | 52.2 | 47.8 | 29.2 | 70.8 |
| 1996 | 49.4 | 50.6 | 27.1 | 72.9 |
| 1997 | 48.9 | 51.1 | 27.4 | 72.6 |
| 1998 | 49.5 | 50.5 | 28.9 | 71.1 |
| 1999 | 51.1 | 48.9 | 31.5 | 68.5 |
| 2000 | 52.2 | 47.8 | 34.7 | 65.3 |
| 2001 | 52.4 | 47.6 | 30.5 | 69.5 |
| 2002 | 55.0 | 45.0 | 30.7 | 69.3 |
| 2003 | 54.6 | 45.4 | 30.1 | 69.9 |
| 2004 | 54.9 | 45.1 | 27.7 | 72.3 |
| 2005 | 52.3 | 47.7 | 25.9 | 74.1 |
| 2006 | 52.8 | 47.2 | 24.7 | 75.3 |
| 2007 | 54.1 | 45.9 | 23.0 | 77.0 |
| 2008 | 53.3 | 46.7 | 21.3 | 78.7 |

SOURCE: National Bureau of Statistics (2009).

cut by 14.38 percent in the first four years (2006 to 2009) of the 11th Five-Year Plan relative to its 2005 levels (Xinhua Net 2010), meeting the national energy-intensity target required an energy-intensity reduction of 5.62 percent in 2010. This required energy-saving rate is even higher than the annual saving rate of 5.25 percent during the period 1980 to 2000, in which China achieved a quadrupling of its GDP while cutting its energy intensity by about three-quarters (Zhang 2003). Recognizing how challenging it would be to achieve that goal, the Chinese central government doubled the amount of its allocated fund for energy saving relative to its level in 2008, earmarking 83.3 billion yuan in 2010 (Xinhua Net 2010).

## Objective and Subjective Factors in Local Governments' Noncooperation

Because of China's vast size and diversity, it is impossible for the central government in Beijing to operate single-handedly in pursuing nationwide energy-saving and environmental outcomes. The ability of, and incentives for, lower-level governments to implement energy-saving and pollution-cutting policies effectively are therefore critical, particularly because the past three decades of economic reforms have seen a shift in control over resources and decision making to local governments.

This devolution of decision making to local governments has placed environmental stewardship in the hands of local officials. These officials often are more concerned with economic growth than with environmental damage because, as noted earlier, local officials typically have been promoted on the basis of how fast they expand their local economies. Moreover, objectively speaking, the current fiscal system in China plays a part in driving local governments to seek higher GDP growth because it makes it hard to reconcile the interests of the central and local governments (Zhang 2007c; 2007d; 2010d). Since the tax-sharing system was adopted in China in 1994, taxes have been grouped into taxes collected by the central government, taxes collected by local governments, and taxes shared between the central and local governments. All those taxes that have steady sources and broad bases and are easily collected, such as the consumption tax, tariffs, and the vehicle purchase tax, are assigned to the central government. The value-added tax (VAT) and the income tax are split between the central and local governments, with 75 percent of the VAT and 60 percent of the income tax going to the central government. As a result, the central government's revenue increased by 200 percent in 1994 relative to its 1993 level, and the share of the central government in total government revenue reached 55.7 percent in 1994, compared with 22.0 percent in the previous year (see table 3.3). In the meantime, the share of the central government in total government expenditure rose by just 2 percent. By 2008 local governments accounted for only 46.7 percent of total government revenue, but their expenditures accounted for 78.7 percent of total government expenditures in China. To afford their expenditures on culture and education, supporting agricultural production, subsidizing social security, and other programs, local governments have little choice but to focus on local development and GDP. Doing so will enable them to enlarge their tax revenues by collecting an urban maintenance and development tax, a contract tax, an arable land occupation tax, an urban land use tax, and other development-related taxes.

Another example of the inequitable tax-sharing scheme in China is related to the tariffs on energy-guzzling industries mentioned earlier in this chapter, which many local governments failed to implement. This is not the only time China's provinces and regions have violated this nationwide policy. Some provinces and regions have been offering preferential power tariffs to struggling local energy-intensive industries (Stanway 2009). Partly to strengthen China's long-standing efforts to restructure its inefficient heavy industries, and partly faced with the prospect of the failure to meet the ambitious energy-intensity target set for 2010, the NDRC and five other ministries and agencies jointly ordered utilities to stop offering preferential power tariffs to energy-intensive industries by 10 June 2010. Such industries will be charged punitive differentiated tariffs. Those utilities that fail to implement the differentiated tariffs will have to pay a fine that is five times that of the differentiated tariffs multiplied by the volume of sold electricity (Zhu 2010). The reason for the repeated violation of the nationwide policy is the lack of incentive for local governments to implement it because all the revenue collected from these additional charges goes to the central government. These revenues should be collected by local governments for unrestricted use, but the central government requires local governments to use the revenue specifically for industrial upgrading, energy saving, and emissions cutting (Zhang 2007c; 2007d, 2010d).

The evidence presented here suggests the need to carefully examine those objective and subjective factors that lead to the lack of local officials' cooperation on the environment, and to provide the right incentives to get their cooperation. One way to ensure that local officials realize that they should take their environmental responsibilities seriously is to develop criteria that incorporate energy conservation and environmental performance into the overall evaluation of local officials' performances, which will affect their promotions. To ensure that the energy-saving goal under the so-called Top 1000 Enterprises Energy Conservation Action Program is met (Zhang 2010d), achieving energy-efficiency improvements has become a criterion for job-performance evaluations of the heads of these enterprises. This will help them realize that they have a very real stake in meeting energy-saving goals. This criterion should be strengthened and extended to hold local officials accountable for saving energy and reducing pollution. Evaluation of local officials should abandon the unique importance of GDP. Instead, evaluation needs to look not only at economic growth of a region, but even more at the model and quality of its development. This has spurred several provinces, such as Jiangsu, to set higher standards for officials' energy-saving and environmental performance. They stipulate that if the energy-conservation target is not met and environmental quality does not improve during an official's tenure, that official cannot be promoted.

Alleviating the financial burden of local governments is another incentive for them not to focus on economic growth alone. Enlarging their tax revenues is the key to helping them cover a substantial amount of the aforementioned government expenditures. The central government must cultivate a steady and sizable source of revenue for local governments. Enacting property taxes or real estate taxes for local governments is urgently needed. In the tax-sharing system adopted in 1994, onshore resource taxes are assigned to local governments, while the central government collects revenues from offshore resource taxes. Currently, resource taxes in China are levied on the basis of extracted volume of resources. Since 1984 resource taxes have been levied at rates of 2 to 5 yuan per ton of raw coal and 8 yuan per ton of coking coal, with a weighted average of 3.5 yuan per ton of coal. For crude oil, the corresponding tax is 8 to 30 yuan per ton. The prices of coal and oil have increased significantly since 1984, but their resource taxes have remained unchanged over the past 25 years. As a result, the resource taxes raised amounted to only 30 billion yuan in 2008, accounting for about 0.56 percent of China's total tax revenues and about 21 percent of the national government expenditure of 145 billion yuan for environmental protection (National Bureau of Statistics 2009). Therefore, to avoid wasteful extraction and use of resources while alleviating the financial burden of local governments, the current system of levying taxes on resources in China should be changed. Such taxes should be levied on the basis of revenues. In addition, current resource taxes are levied on only seven types of resources, including coal, oil, and natural gas. This coverage is too narrow and falls far short of the purposes of both preserving resources and protecting the environment. Thus, overhauling resource taxes should also include broadening their coverage so that more resources will be subject to resource taxation.

Clearly, broadening current coverage and significantly increasing the level of resource taxation would also help increase local governments' revenues while conserving resources and preserving the environment. The good news is that the Chinese central government has started a pilot reform of resource taxes in Xinjiang, an area of abundant resources and numerous opportunities for growth and expansion on China's northwestern border. Since 1 June 2010, crude oil and natural gas have been taxed on the basis of revenues rather than volume in Xinjiang. Although this new resource tax was enacted as part of a massive support package to help Xinjiang achieve leapfrog-like development, which is considered a strategic choice to deepen the country's Western Development Strategy and tap new sources of economic growth for China, it will help increase revenues significantly for Xinjiang. It is estimated that the new resource tax at a rate of 5 percent will generate additional annual revenues of at least 3.2 billion yuan for Xinjiang (Liu and Zhang 2010). This is a significant increase in comparison with the total resource tax revenues of 1.1 billion yuan in 2008, including those from other resources than crude oil and natural gas (National Bureau of Statistics 2009). This will contribute about 15 percent of the total tax revenues for Xinjiang, in comparison with the current contribution level of about 3.8 percent.

## Conclusion

Strengthening the MEP and other environmental agencies and providing proper incentives to local officials to secure the cooperation are essential if China is to achieve its goals of protecting the environment. China also needs to take serious efforts to plan and design nationwide functional zoning, which was sketched out in the 11th Five-Year Plan. The underlying basis is that a region can be classified as an optimized development zone, a prioritized development zone, a restrained development zone, or a prohibited development zone, depending on its population, resource endowments, and environmental assimilating capacity. Each functional zone is given differing development objectives. These objectives are in turn aligned with different evaluation criteria for officials. In a region that needs to develop its industries, evaluation of local officials will be based on how fast they expand their local economies; in a region that needs to develop its service sector, evaluation will target the contribution of high-tech value added. By contrast, in a region whose ecology services need to be preserved, evaluation will focus on green GDP. Planning and designing nationwide functional zoning may go beyond current administrative regions. Clearly, this is easier said than done, but put in place and implemented effectively, a functional zoning policy not only will help correct the current distorted incentive system, but, more importantly, will put China on a more sustainable development path. There has been much progress since the policy's enactment.

It should be emphasized that enacting the aforementioned policies and measures targeted toward saving energy and cutting pollution displays the goodwill and determination of China's leaders. To actually achieve the desired outcomes, however, requires strict implementation and coordination of these policies and measures. It is expected that leaders of local governments are to be held accountable for energy saving and pollution cutting in their jurisdiction, and that achieving the goals of energy-efficiency improvements and pollution reduction has become a key component of their job-performance evaluations. But no senior officials have ever been reported to take responsibility for failing to meet the energy-saving and pollution-cutting targets to date, let alone to step down from their positions on these grounds, with the exception of the mayor of Beijing Municipality and the governor of Shanxi Province, who stepped down because of mismanagement of the severe acute respiratory syndrome epidemic and coal-mining accidents. Clearly, implementation is the key. This will be a decisive factor in determining the prospects for sustainable development in China. There is no doubt that dealing with unprecedented environmental pollution and health risks poses a significant challenge for China. The whole world is waiting to see whether China can turn this challenge into a win-win outcome for both China and the global environment.

## References


Liu, Shucheng, and Binshang Zhang. 2010. Xinjiang starts levying the resource tax based on revenues, additional revenues of yuan 1.6 billion expected in the second half of 2010. *Sina News.* June 8. http://news.sina.com.cn/c/2010-06-08/110120434200.shtml

Ministry of Environmental Protection of China (MEP). 2009. A circular on the 2008 evaluation on cities' environmental quality. Beijing. http://www.mep.gov.cn/gkml/hbb/bgth/200912/t20091229_183597.html

National Bureau of Statistics. 2009. *China statistical yearbook.* Beijing: China Statistics Press.

National Bureau of Statistics, National Development and Reform Commission, and National Energy Administration. 2008. Bulletin on energy use per unit of GDP and other indicators by region: Beijing. http://www.stats.gov.cn/tjgb/qttjgb/qgqttjgb/t20080714_402491870.htm

———. 2009. Bulletin on energy use per unit of GDP and other indicators by region: Beijing. http://www.stats.gov.cn/tjgb/qttjgb/qgqttjgb/t20090630_402568721.htm

National Bureau of Statistics, National Development and Reform Commission, and Office of the National Energy Leading Group. 2007. Bulletin on energy use per unit of GDP and other indicators by region: Beijing. http://hzs.ndrc.gov.cn/newjn/t20070809_152873.htm

National Development and Reform Commission (NDRC). 2006. Suggestions for improving the policy on differentiated tariffs: Beijing. http://www.gov.cn/zwgk/2006-09/22/content_396258.htm

People's Daily. 2005. China is going to start implementing the bulletin system to release data on energy use per unit of GDP. http://news.sina.com.cn/c/2005-12-17/05457728754s.shtml

Sina Net. 2007. Regional environmental protection inspection system: Today and future. July 20. http://finance.sina.com.cn/economist/jingjiguancha/20070720/17203806186.shtml

———. 2009. Ministry of Environmental Protection suspended approval of hydropower projects along the middle reaches of Jinsha River. June 11. http://news.sina.com.cn/c/2009-06-11/112517997932.shtml

Stanway, David. 2009. China blocks regional power price cuts. March 17. http://uk.reuters.com/article/oilRpt/idUKPEK31823420090317

State Council. 2008. Work plan for energy saving and pollution cutting. Beijing. (July). http://www.ccchina.gov.cn/cn/NewsInfo.asp?NewsId=14127

State Environmental Protection Administration of China (SEPA). 2007. SEPA released the latest evaluation on cities' environmental quality: Beijing. http://www.sepa.gov.cn/xcjy/zwhb/200706/t20070611_104908.htm

State Environmental Protection Administration of China (SEPA) and National Bureau of Statistics (NBS). 2006. China Green National Accounting study report 2004. Public Version. Beijing (September).

World Health Organization (WHO). 2000. *World Health Organization guidelines for air quality.* Geneva: WHO.

Xinhua Net. 2010. NDRC: The 11th five-year pollution-cutting goals met ahead of the schedule. March 10. http://news.sina.com.cn/c/2010-03-10/152019834186.shtml

Zhang, Zhongxiang. 2003. Why did the energy intensity fall in China's industrial sector in the 1990s? The relative importance of structural change and intensity change. *Energy Economics* 25(6):625–638.

———. 2007a. China's reds embrace green. *Far Eastern Economic Review* 170(5):33–37.

———. 2007b. China is moving away from the pattern of "develop first and then treat the pollution." *Energy Policy* 35:3547–3549.

———. 2007c. Energy and environmental policy in mainland China. Keynote address at the Cross-Straits Conference on Energy Economics and Policy, Chinese Association for Energy Economics, Taipei (November 7–8).

———. 2007d. Greening China: Can Hu and Wen turn a test of their leadership into a legacy? Paper presented at the plenary session on sustainable development at the first Harvard College China-India Development and Relations Symposium, New York City (March 30).

———. 2008. Asian energy and environmental policy: Promoting growth while preserving the environment. *Energy Policy* 36:3905–3924.

———. 2009. Multilateral trade measures in a post-2012 climate change regime: What can be taken from the Montreal Protocol and the WTO? *Energy Policy* 37:5105–5112.

———. 2010a. Assessing China's energy conservation and carbon intensity: How will the future differ from the past? In *China: The next twenty years of reform and development*, ed. Ross Garnaut, Jane Golley, and Ligang Song, 99–125. Canberra: Australian National University E-Press and Brookings Institution Press.

———. 2010b. China in the transition to a low-carbon economy. *Energy Policy* 38:6638–6653.

———. 2010c. Copenhagen and beyond: Reflections on China's stance and responses. In *Climate change policies: Global challenges and future prospects*, ed. Emilio Cerdá and Xavier Labandeira, 239–253. Cheltenham, U.K.: Edward Elgar.

———. 2010d. Is it fair to treat China as a Christmas tree to hang everybody's complaints? Putting its own energy-saving into perspective. *Energy Economics* 32:S47–S56.

———. 2010e. The U.S. proposed carbon tariffs, WTO scrutiny and China's responses. *International Economics and Economic Policy* 7:203–225.

Zhu, Jianhong. 2010. Six ministries and agencies claim those utilities that failed to implement the differentiated tariffs will face a penalty equaling to five times that of supposed revenues. *People Net*, May 22. http://finance.sina.com.cn/chanjing/cyxw/20100522/07037984663.shtml

# Urban Development
# and the Environment

# Decentralization and the Environment
## Industrial Air Pollution in Chinese Cities

CANFEI HE AND FENGHUA PAN

Economic reform in China is a dual decentralization process in which power has been shifted from the central government to the locales and decision making has been transferred from local governments to firms and households (Qian and Weingast 1997). The devolution of political and administrative power to lower-level governments has led to improved economic efficiency and has augmented economic growth in China (Lin and Liu 2000; Shi and Zhou 2007). Marketization allows firms and households to make the best decisions about the use of resources and has promoted industrial and regional growth in China (Anderson and Ge 2004; Chen and Feng 2000; Demurger et al. 2002; Liu and Li 2001).

Economic reform, however, has posed serious problems for environmental protection efforts in China (Jahiel 1997). There are daily media reports of rivers and lakes poisoned by pollution, farmlands tainted by industrial pollution, and cities choking on smog in China (Dean and Lovely 2008). The high-growth, resource-intensive, and export-oriented development strategy that China has pursued, coupled with the norms and institutional relationships designed to support this development strategy, has played a critical role in the deterioration of China's urban environment (Chan and Yao 2008; Jahiel 1997; 1998). As Naughton (2007, 503) notes, "The challenges of water availability, resilience of the natural environment and atmospheric degradation and climate change are among the most serious that China confronts."

Institutionally, market and power decentralization may be responsible for these problems. Marketization has gradually introduced market forces and has allowed multiple ownerships in the Chinese economy. Theoretically, state-owned enterprises

This study was partially supported by the Natural Science Foundation of China (No. 40830747) and the Ministry of Science and Technology (2008ZX07102-001).

(SOEs) have more bargaining power than privately owned enterprises and strong connections with local governments and have less incentive to reduce their air pollution. In reality, SOEs may pay more attention to social impacts in their decision-making processes, and their environmental performance could theoretically be better than that of private-sector enterprises. Non-SOEs are profit oriented and have less incentive to internalize environmental costs in the context of decentralization. More market decentralization could be associated with more pollution. But non-SOEs are at a disadvantage in bargaining with local government agencies and may encounter stricter enforcement of environmental regulations and punishments for environmental pollution. If this is the case, they are likely to have better environmental performance.

As a consequence, market decentralization may generate mixed environmental results because of different environmental behaviors of various types of industrial enterprises. Power decentralization has given local officials the means and the incentive to develop their local economies. The pervasive emphasis on development, consumerism, and profit in government proclamations has further motivated local governments to intervene against regulations, such as those on environmental protection, that are deemed unfavorable to growth (Oi 1995). Fiscal decentralization could trigger a race to the bottom, in which cities lower their environmental standards to compete for capital and attract pollution-intensive industries. Power decentralization may thereby lead to environmental degradation in Chinese cities.

Using data on sulfur dioxide ($SO_2$) emissions and industrial dust at the prefecture cities in China during 2003–2008, this chapter tests the environmental impacts of market and power decentralization in China. The results suggest that SOEs have damaged China's environment. Moreover, market decentralization has been harmful to urban environments, especially in the central and western regions and in small and medium-sized cities. Power decentralization has also contributed to environmental degradation, which is more noticeable in the coastal and central regions and in medium-sized and small cities. Evidently, market decentralization, coupled with administrative decentralization, has led to a trade-off between economic growth and environmental degradation in China.

This chapter first discusses the environmental impacts of market decentralization and power decentralization in China. It then reports the structural and spatial pattern of industrial pollution. Finally, it investigates the determinants of industrial pollution intensity and concludes with a summary of major findings.

## Decentralization and the Environment in China

China's economic reform has been a two-pronged process, market decentralization and power decentralization. Market decentralization returns decision-making power to households and enterprises, while power decentralization shifts power from the central government to local governments. Power and fiscal decentralization has induced local governments to implement lax environmental regulations that reduce the incentives of industrial enterprises to internalize environmental costs. The dual decentralization process may result in poor environmental performance (figure 4.1).

**FIGURE 4.1**

Theoretical Framework: Decentralization and Regional Environmental Performance in China

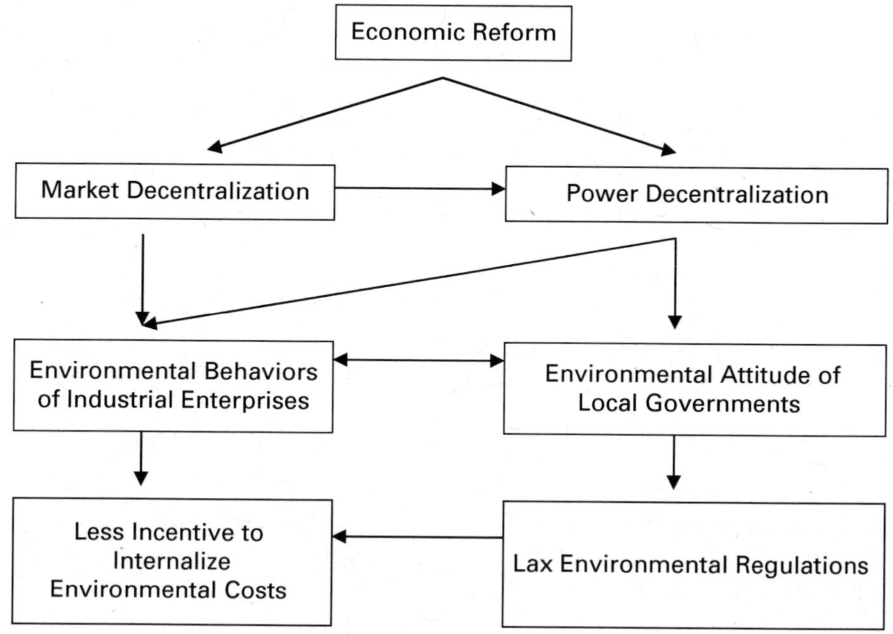


## Market Decentralization and Environmental Behavior of Industrial Enterprises

The goal of economic reform is to transform the Chinese economic system into a market-oriented economy. In the command economy, firms were executors of state orders. As the economic transition proceeds, markets play an increasingly important role in resource allocation. Firms gain more decision-making power to manage their operations. Market decentralization has encouraged the development of many types of non-state-owned enterprises, including collectively owned, privately owned, or cooperative enterprises; jointly owned, limited-liability enterprises; shared-holding enterprises; and foreign-owned enterprises. In China different types of industrial enterprises may differ in their environmental behaviors for economic and political reasons.

On the one hand, SOEs may have incentives to internalize the environmental costs resulting from their pollution discharges in order to achieve higher national or local social welfare. SOEs are also more likely to be equipped with advanced technology to deal with air pollution. As a consequence, the dominance of SOEs may provide opportunities to reduce air pollution in Chinese cities. On the other hand, SOEs have stronger bargaining power with central and local governments regarding environmental regulations than privately owned enterprises (Wang et al. 2001). Furthermore, SOEs have strong connections with governments, and some managers of SOEs hold higher political status than the local environmental authorities. As a result, SOEs may be able to elicit a lower pollution payment or punishment and may have less incentive to decrease their pollution. Existing studies provide evidence to support the argument that the dominance of SOEs in a city may degrade its environmental quality. For instance, using plant-level data, Wang and Wheeler (2000) found that SOEs are more likely to pollute than private enterprises in China. Wang and Jin (2002) reported that foreign-owned enterprises and collectively owned enterprises have better environmental performance in water pollution discharge intensity, while SOEs and privately owned enterprises in China are the worst performers.

Privately owned enterprises (POEs) are able to use resources more efficiently and to generate less air pollution with the same resources. They may have lower bargaining power with local environmental authorities with respect to the enforcement of pollution charges and regulations (Wang et al. 2001). Better environmental quality could be achieved with a greater presence of non-state-owned enterprises. For instance, using annual data for 44 developing countries from 1987 to 1995, Talukdar and Meisner (2001) showed a significantly negative relationship between the share of private-sector investment in total domestic investment or its share of output value in the national GDP and carbon dioxide ($CO_2$) emission levels, suggesting that an increased role of the private sector in an economy is more likely to help the environment of the economy. However, although non-SOEs may have higher efficiency in resource use, they are more profit oriented, may not seek to internalize environmental externalities, and may compromise the environment to avoid the potential cost of environmental investments (Eiser, Reicher, and Podpadec 1996).

Under fiscal decentralization, local governments eagerly seek revenues. In the meantime, local environmental protection agencies start to be in charge of implementing environmental regulations. China's non-state-owned sector has been growing very rapidly, which implies that it will become increasingly difficult to enforce policy as institutional channels of state control over industry become weaker (Jahiel 1997). As a result, it is likely that market decentralization results in more pollution.

Foreign enterprises have played a critical role in diversifying China's industrial structures. The environmental behavior of foreign enterprises is debatable. If regions are identical except for exogenous differences in pollution policy, the pollution-haven hypothesis proposes that it is cheaper to produce dirty goods in a region with weaker environmental regulation. Investments induced by environmental regulation differences create a pollution haven in poor regions. Pollution-intensive industries migrate to regions with weaker environmental regulations, mostly to save production costs. Foreign enterprises therefore may be harmful to the environment of developing countries whose environmental regulations are relatively weak.

However, foreign enterprises are likely to help the environment in developing regions through technology effects. Foreign investment may bring advanced technological and managerial innovations that both improve the environment and promote economic progress, facilitating an international ratcheting up of environmental standards. Investment liberalization can provide favorable conditions for the diffusion of global environmental norms and standards by creating opportunities and necessities for environmental institution building and policy processes in host economies (Shin 2004). Foreign direct investment (FDI) may induce policy changes in developing countries to cope with possible environmental damage. Wang and Jin

(2002) found that foreign-owned firms have better environmental performance than state-owned and privately owned firms. They suggest that foreign firms pollute less because they use superior technology in production and are more energy efficient. Shin (2004) examined the effects of trade and investment liberalization on the environment in two Chinese cities, Shenyang and Dalian, and found that economic openness positively affected domestic environmental policy by providing the necessity and opportunities for strengthening environmental institutions. Jie He (2006; 2009), however, provided convincing evidence to support the pollution-haven hypothesis and found that more FDI in a province was associated with more air pollution.

There are other types of industrial enterprises, including collectively owned enterprises (COEs), cooperative enterprises (CEs), jointly owned enterprises (JOEs), limited-liability enterprises (LLEs), and shared-holding enterprises (SHEs). Those enterprises are owned by multiple owners, some of which are local governmental agencies. The environmental behaviors of multiowner enterprises depend on the nature of the owners. If local governmental agencies are partially involved, the industrial enterprises are likely to act like SOEs. If private owners dominate, their environmental behaviors will be similar to those of privately owned enterprises.

## Power Decentralization and Environmental Attitudes of Local Governments

Economic reform in China has resulted in considerable decentralization of power from the central government to more regional loci. As a result, local governments have the primary responsibility for economic development in their jurisdictions and great autonomy in pursuing it. Since the late 1980s, the Chinese central government has also given much autonomy and responsibility in environmental policy to local authorities, so that provincial and municipal governments have to compete with one another in environmental as well as economic performance (Jahiel 1997; 1998). Environmental protection agencies now report to higher levels of the national environmental protection administrative apparatus and to the local governments where they reside. Environmental decentralization has removed central government guarantees of financial resources for floundering localities and has deprived localities of the financial security they once had. Local governments provide environmental agencies with their annual budgetary funds, evaluate the work of the environmental agencies, and determine increases in personnel and even the allocation of such resources as cars and office buildings.

This budgetary constraint has created increasing difficulties for local environment protection agencies. As a consequence, China's environmental protection apparatus has suffered from insufficient authority and lack of coordination among institutional actors (Jahiel 1998). The fragmented authority structure undermines the effective enforcement of environmental policies in China. Van Rooij and Lo (2010) found considerable regional variations in the enforcement of environmental pollution violations, with coastal areas in China having more and higher punishments than those inland. Such factors as central government support, community pressure, local government commitment, enforcement capacity, characteristics of regulated firms, and general economic conditions are responsible for the variations. The root of enforcement problems of environmental policies lies with the institutional arrangement, in which the local governments fund and directly manage China's main local environmental enforcement authorities (Jahiel 1998; Van Rooij and Lo 2010).

Fiscal decentralization has enhanced the importance of local revenues (Young 2000; Zhao and Zhang 1999). Under the central planning system, local governments had no authority over the structure of local expenditure and no particular incentive to collect revenues. In 1980 China introduced a revenue-sharing system called the fiscal contracting system because the central and provincial governments started to tap different revenue bases rather than receiving funding from one big pot. The Chinese government initiated a new tax-sharing system that introduced a clear distinction between national and local taxes in 1994. The new system proposed a value-added tax (VAT) as the major indirect tax to be collected by the central government and shared by local governments at a fixed ratio of 75:25. Fiscal decentralization inherently and explicitly emphasized autarchic development because the localities had to self-finance their budgets and their development (Zhao and Zhang 1999).

The effect of environmental and fiscal decentralization has been that many local officials have become entrepreneurial, trying to promote growth in their particular locality. This entrepreneurship by local leaders has translated into an economic boom for many localities, but its effect on environmental regulations has been far less beneficial. With the transformation from administrators to entrepreneurs, local governments are shifting from regulation to advocacy of their local enterprises (Oi 1995). Meanwhile, fiscal decentralization has induced fierce interregional competition, which may trigger a race to the bottom in which regions lower environmental standards to compete for investments and firms. Decentralization of economic decision making to local governments and factory managers, combined with calls for rapid economic growth and production for profit, has created further incentives for local governments and managers to pursue economic growth and profitability at the expense of environmental degradation (Jahiel 1997). Local governments have a strong motive to circumvent those policies that might constrain local growth, such as environmental regulations (Lieberthal 1995). Reform incentives thus "have actually distorted the role of local governments as agents of the central state," making local authorities more lax in enforcement of environmental regulations (Jahiel 1997, 85).

Destructive regulatory competition in the form of a race to the bottom would lower environmental quality when power is decentralized. Using the UN's Global Environment Monitoring System Water data in 47 countries, Sigman (2009) found higher regional levels of pollutants of biochemical oxygen demand and fecal coliform with more environmental and fiscal decentralization. Existing studies have reported that China's local governments have consistently undermined pollution enforcement in order to protect local economic interests (Jahiel 1997; 1998; Ma and Ortolano 2000; Sinkule and Ortolano 1995; Swanson, Kuhn, and Xu 2001; Tang et al. 1997; Tang, Lo, and Fryxell 2003; Van Rooij 2006). With fiscal and environmental decentralization, pollution-intensive industries gain opportunities to grow in regions facing hard budgets with limited local revenues.

Overall, market decentralization has significantly stimulated economic growth and has changed the ownership structure of the Chinese economy through the growing share of non-state-owned enterprises and the decreasing status of SOEs. Power and fiscal decentralization has stimulated industrial growth and has triggered a race to the bottom with regard to environmental regulations. Although market decentralization may generate mixed environmental performance, power and administrative decentralization should lead to environmental degradation in China. There may be a trade-off between decentralization and environmental degradation in China. The following section tests these theoretical propositions.

## Empirical Analysis of Industrial Air Pollution

### Variables and Models

To test the environmental impacts of decentralization, a systematic investigation of determinants of industrial air pollution is conducted by applying a panel data regression model. The explanatory variables include proxies for marketization and fiscal decentralization, controlling for industrial composition. The model is as follows:

$$
\begin{aligned}
\mathrm{Ln}TSO_{2it}\,(\text{or }\mathrm{Ln}TDUST_{it}) = {}& \beta_1 \mathrm{Ln}PGDP_{it} + \beta_2 (\mathrm{Ln}PGDP_{it})^2 + \beta_3 \mathrm{Ln}SOES_{it} \\
& + \beta_4 \mathrm{Ln}COES_{it} + \beta_5 \mathrm{Ln}COOP_{it} + \beta_6 \mathrm{Ln}JOIN_{it} \\
& + \beta_7 \mathrm{Ln}LIMD_{it} + \beta_8 \mathrm{Ln}SHARE_{it} + \beta_9 \mathrm{Ln}PRIV_{it} \\
& + \beta_{10} \mathrm{Ln}HTM_{it} + \beta_{11} \mathrm{Ln}FDI_{it} + \beta_{12} \mathrm{Ln}LEXRE_{it} \\
& + \beta_3 \mathrm{Ln}VTAX_{it} + \sum_{k=1}^{9} \alpha_k \mathrm{Ln}INDU_{itk} \\
& + \lambda_t + \nu_{it},\ i = 1,\,\ldots,N,\ t = 1,2,3,4
\end{aligned}
$$

That is, the pollution intensity ($TSO_2$ or $TDUST$) in city $i$ in year $t$ is a function of theoretically discussed variables. The variables $i$ and $t$ denote city and time, $\lambda_t$ the unobservable time effect, and $\nu_{it}$ the remainder stochastic disturbance term. Note that $\lambda_t$ is city invariant and accounts for any time-specific effect that is not included in the regression. Per capita gross domestic product (GDP) and its square are included to test the existence of the environmental Kuznets curve (EKC) at the city level. The use of per capita GDP and squared per capita GDP to capture scale and technique effects is consistent with the literature on the environmental Kuznets curve, within which the inverted-U-shaped relationship between per capita GDP and pollution is explained largely in terms of the dominance of scale effects at low levels of income and the dominance of technique effects at high income levels.

The particular interest of this analysis is the environmental effects of decentralization. Market decentralization has played a significant role in changing the intensity of industrial pollution in Chinese cities, but the net effect is unclear. Market decentralization has diversified the ownership structure of the Chinese city, with growing shares of non-SOEs. The analysis includes the percentages of different types of enterprises in gross industrial output to test the environmental impacts of market decentralization, including state-owned enterprises (*SOES*), collectively owned enterprises (*COES*), cooperative enterprises (*COOP*), jointly owned enterprises

(*JOIN*), limited-liability corporations (*LIMD*), shared-holding enterprises (*SHARE*), privately owned enterprises (*PRIV*), industrial enterprises from Hong Kong, Taiwan, and Macao (*HTM*), and foreign enterprises (*FDI*). Power decentralization is difficult to quantify. The race to the bottom in environmental regulations, however, is associated with decentralization, which has created incentives for local governments to attract or develop pollution-intensive industries. This analysis employs two variables to serve as proxies for the effect of fiscal decentralization: the percentage of local expenditure in local revenue (*LEXRE*) and the percentage of the value-added tax in local revenue (*VTAX*). Both variables are expected to have positive coefficients.

Finally, this analysis intends to control for industrial composition in Chinese cities by including the percentages of gross industrial output of pollution-intensive industries (*INDU*). These industries include mining, papermaking and paper products, petroleum refining and coking, chemical materials and products, chemical fibers, nonmetal mineral products, ferrous metal smelting and pressing, nonferrous metal smelting and pressing, and power, natural gas, and water production. All variables are summarized in table 4.1.

## Empirical Results

Because of the significant declining trend of industrial air-pollution intensity during 2004–2007, the time-fixed-effect model was applied to estimate the coefficients of explanatory variables. The panel data regression results for both industrial $SO_2$

**TABLE 4.1**

Definitions of Dependent and Independent Variables

| Variable | Definition |
| --- | --- |
| $TSO_2$ | Total industrial $SO_2$ emissions/gross industrial output |
| TDUST | Total industrial dust/gross industrial output |
| PGDP | GDP per capita |
| SOES | Share of state-owned or controlled enterprises in gross industrial output |
| COES | Share of collectively owned enterprises in gross industrial output |
| COOP | Share of cooperative enterprises in gross industrial output |
| JOIN | Share of jointly owned enterprises in gross industrial output |
| LIMD | Share of limited-liability corporations in gross industrial output |
| SHARE | Share of shared-holding enterprises in gross industrial output |
| PRIV | Share of privately owned enterprises in gross industrial output |
| HTM | Share of enterprises from Hong Kong, Taiwan, and Macao in gross industrial output |
| FDI | Share of foreign enterprises in gross industrial output |
| LEXRE | Local expenditure/local revenue |
| VTAX | Share of value-added tax in local revenue |
| INDU | Share of individual pollution-intensive industries in gross industrial output, including mining ($INDU_1$), papermaking and paper products ($INDU_2$), petroleum refining and coking ($INDU_3$), chemical materials and products ($INDU_4$), chemical fibers ($INDU_5$), nonmetal mineral products ($INDU_6$), ferrous metal smelting and pressing ($INDU_7$), nonferrous metal smelting and pressing ($INDU_8$), and power, natural gas, and water production ($INDU_9$) |

and industrial dust intensities are presented in table 4.2. The Breusch-Pagan tests indicate the existence of heteroscedasticity, and all estimates are corrected for heteroscedasticity.

The statistical results provide strong evidence to support the EKC effect in Chinese cities. There is a statistically significant inverted-U-shaped relationship between Ln$PGDP$ and Ln$TSO_2$ (or Ln$TDUST$) when industrial structure is controlled for. Air-pollution intensity is lower in underdeveloped cities. As cities grow economically, their economies become increasingly pollution intensive. When per capita GDP reaches a certain level, air-pollution intensity gradually decreases because of technique effects. This result could largely explain the spatial pattern of pollution intensity, with smaller intensities in the coastal cities but high intensities in the central cities. The finding indicates the dominance of scale effects at low levels of income, but the dominance of technique effects at high income levels. There is

## TABLE 4.2

Regression Results for Industrial Dust and SO$_2$ Intensity

| | Ln$TSO_2$ | | | Ln$TDUST$ | | |
|---|---|---|---|---|---|---|
| | Model 1 | Model 2 | Model 3 | Model 1 | Model 2 | Model 3 |
| Ln$PGDP$ | 1.7097** | 3.1147*** | 1.7481** | 2.1621** | 4.7135*** | 3.0353*** |
| Ln$PGDP$*Ln$PGDP$ | −0.1114*** | −0.1867*** | −0.1109** | −0.1501*** | −0.2777*** | −0.1832*** |
| Ln$SOES$ | 0.1197*** | | 0.1327*** | 0.1618*** | | 0.1892*** |
| Ln$COES$ | −0.0036 | | 0.0009 | 0.0166 | | 0.0300 |
| Ln$COOP$ | −0.0411 | | −0.0333 | −0.0827 | | −0.0707 |
| Ln$JOIN$ | −0.0772 | | −0.0793 | −0.0547 | | −0.0508 |
| Ln$LIMD$ | 0.4488*** | | 0.4548*** | 0.4307*** | | 0.4507*** |
| Ln$SHARE$ | 0.0212 | | 0.0359 | 0.1031*** | | 0.1156*** |
| Ln$PRIV$ | −0.0146 | | 0.0057 | 0.1306** | | 0.1454*** |
| Ln$HTM$ | −0.0411 | | −0.0367 | −0.1200*** | | −0.0888* |
| Ln$FDI$ | −0.0185 | | −0.0045 | −0.0228 | | −0.0027 |
| Ln$LEXRE$ | | 0.1661* | 0.1116 | | 0.5125*** | 0.4353*** |
| Ln$VTAX$ | | 0.2476*** | 0.2472*** | | 0.1202* | 0.1625** |
| Ln$INDU_1$ | 0.1969*** | 0.2290*** | 0.1823*** | 0.2298*** | 0.2823*** | 0.2198*** |
| Ln$INDU_2$ | −0.1095** | −0.1510*** | −0.1004** | −0.1253** | −0.1678*** | −0.1115** |
| Ln$INDU_3$ | −0.0202 | −0.0284 | −0.0183 | 0.0134 | 0.0098 | 0.0173 |
| Ln$INDU_4$ | 0.1081*** | 0.1193*** | 0.1096*** | 0.0551 | 0.0915** | 0.0647 |
| Ln$INDU_5$ | −0.1048** | −0.1324*** | −0.1060** | −0.0504 | −0.0755 | −0.0481 |
| Ln$INDU_6$ | −0.0515 | −0.1021* | −0.0356 | 0.0456 | −0.1364 | 0.0447 |
| Ln$INDU_7$ | 0.0661*** | 0.0865*** | 0.0683*** | 0.0897** | 0.0823*** | 0.0630** |
| Ln$INDU_8$ | 0.0760*** | 0.1057*** | 0.0751*** | 0.0145 | 0.0524* | 0.0258 |
| Ln$INDU_9$ | 0.0685* | 0.0992** | 0.0607 | 0.0080 | 0.0086 | 0.0189 |
| Time dummy | Included | Included | Included | Included | Included | Included |
| Observations | 1,144 | 1,144 | 1,144 | 1,144 | 1,144 | 1,144 |
| Adjusted $R^2$ | 0.4511 | 0.3935 | 0.4584 | 0.5232 | 0.4747 | 0.5319 |
| $F$-value | 41.85 | 47.36 | 39.69 | 55.54 | 65.55 | 52.96 |
| Breusch-Pagan $\chi^2$ | 207.84 | 120.22 | 227.94 | 207.84 | 95.81 | 95.62 |

NOTE: Results are corrected for heteroscedasticity.

* $p<0.10$; ** $p<0.05$; *** $p<0.01$.

certainly a structural effect. Resource-based industries, including mining, chemical materials and products, ferrous and nonferrous metal smelting and rolling, and power, natural gas, and water production significantly increase pollution intensity in Chinese cities. Interestingly, papermaking and paper products and chemical fibers are negatively associated with air-pollution intensities. The EKC effect suggests that economic development and economic restructuring would improve environmental quality in Chinese cities.

There is evidence to show that market decentralization has degraded China's environment if one controls for industrial structural effects and the EKC effect. On the one hand, Ln$SOES$ is highly and positively associated with industrial pollution intensity in Chinese cities when industrial structures are controlled for. The dominance of SOEs in Chinese cities would lead to higher $SO_2$ emissions and dust per industrial output and degrade the environment. This is consistent with the finding of Wang and Wheeler (2000) that SOEs are more likely to pollute than privately owned enterprises. It is indeed true that SOEs, especially those under the administration of upper levels of governments, have stronger bargaining power than POEs with local governments regarding environmental regulations, are able to elicit lower pollution payments or punishments, and have less incentive to decrease their air pollution (Wang et al. 2001). Meanwhile, power decentralization has granted local governments incentives to protect SOEs under their administration, which are the base of political power, as well as sources of private benefits and fiscal revenues (Bai et al. 2004; He, C., Wei, and Xie 2008). Local protectionism in turn has created incentives for SOEs to perform poorly in environmental protection. The poor environmental performance of SOEs is the result of fiscal and environmental decentralization.

On the other hand, some market-driven industrial enterprises are significantly positively related to air-pollution intensity in Chinese cities. The coefficient of Ln$LIMD$ is positive and significant in both $SO_2$ and dust models, while the coefficients of Ln$PRIV$ and Ln$SHARE$ are positive and significant in the dust models. More output by limited-liability corporations is associated with higher $SO_2$ intensity in Chinese cities, and more industrial output by privately owned and shared-holding enterprises is associated with higher dust intensities. The results indicate that limited-liability corporations, privately owned enterprises, and shared-holding enterprises may emit more $SO_2$ or industrial dust and contribute to environmental degradation in Chinese cities. Wang and Jin (2002) found that SOEs and privately owned enterprises in China are the worst performers in water-pollution discharge. Profit-driven enterprises have less incentive to internalize environmental costs when they face lax environmental regulations. Foreign-funded enterprises seem to improve air quality in Chinese cities. Both Ln$HTM$ and Ln$FDI$ have negative coefficients in the $SO_2$ and dust models, and Ln$HTM$ is significant in the dust models. The net environmental effect of foreign enterprises is positive, which is consistent with the finding of Shin (2004) that economic openness positively affected domestic environmental policy by providing the necessity and opportunities for strengthening environmental institutions in Shenyang and Dalian. This result also agrees with the finding of Wang and Jin (2002) that foreign enterprises have better environmental performance than SOEs and POEs. The findings fundamentally reject the notion of pollution havens in developing economies.

As expected, fiscal decentralization has played a significant role in degrading China's environment. Both Ln*LEXRE* and Ln*VTAX* are positively associated with air-pollution intensity when pollution-intensive industries are controlled for. *LEXRE* is applied to quantify the difficulties of local budgets. *VTAX* measures the dependence of local revenues on industrial development. The results suggest that both straitened local budgets and more dependence on the value-added tax mean more air pollution. Fiscal decentralization and designated local tax structures create strong pressure and incentives to develop pollution-intensive industries and to enhance local revenues. Cities suffering from tight budgets are also more lax in the enforcement of environmental regulations and thus create opportunities for pollution-intensive industries to develop. Meanwhile, local governments also protect high-value-added, pollution-intensive industries.

Overall, the statistical results from the full sample provide evidence to support the hypothesis that decentralization has contributed to the deterioration of environmental quality in Chinese cities. Market decentralization, together with power decentralization, has reduced the incentives for market-driven enterprises to internalize environmental costs, leading to an economic system that is less effective in controlling pollution. Fiscal and power decentralization grants authority and responsibilities to local governments, which have developed a passive attitude toward environmental protection that has led to a development model that is unfriendly to the environment.

## Environmental Impact of Decentralization in Different Regions

There are remarkable regional differences in economic development, geographical location, industrial structure, technology, institutional environment, and government policies in China. There may be significant regional differences in environmental performance in the coastal, central, and western regions. To see the regional differences in the environmental effects of decentralization, this analysis divides Chinese cities into three groups: cities located in the coastal, central, and western provinces. The statistical results are reported in table 4.3. All models are highly significant. The models perform best in the coastal cities and most poorly in the western cities. The results show significant regional differences in the environmental behaviors of industrial enterprises and the environmental attitudes of local governments.

There is a U-shaped rather than an inverted-U-shaped relationship between Ln*PGDP* and Ln*TSO$_2$* and Ln*TDUST* in the coastal cities. The EKC effects are likely to occur in the central cities. When the effects of decentralization and industrial composition are controlled for, no significant relationship between Ln*PGDP* and pollution intensity can be found in the western cities. The inverted EKC effect is possibly related to the heavy industrialization in some coastal cities in the past ten years by developing petroleum refining and coking, ferrous metal smelting and processing, chemical materials and products, and machinery and equipment. This

**TABLE 4.3**

Regression Results for Pollution Intensity in Coastal, Central, and Western Cities

| | Coastal Region | | Central Region | | Western Region | |
| --- | --- | --- | --- | --- | --- | --- |
| | $LnTSO_2$ | $LnTDUST$ | $LnTSO_2$ | $LnTDUST$ | $LnTSO_2$ | $LnTDUST$ |
| $LnPGDP$ | −5.9364*** | −5.3650*** | 3.1919* | 3.5652* | 0.0470 | −1.4757 |
| $LnPGDP*$ | 0.2617*** | 0.2216*** | −0.1634* | −0.1844* | −0.0252 | 0.0586 |
| $LnSOES$ | 0.1503*** | 0.2596*** | 0.1869*** | 0.0352 | −0.0864 | −0.0723 |
| $LnCOES$ | 0.2212*** | 0.1369 | −0.2031*** | −0.1139** | −0.0347 | −0.1545 |
| $LnCOOP$ | −0.0448 | −0.1525 | −0.0321 | −0.0995 | 0.0435 | 0.3636*** |
| $LnJOIN$ | −0.0882 | 0.0535 | 0.0350 | −0.0812 | 0.3950** | 0.3882** |
| $LnLIMD$ | 0.2616*** | 0.2803*** | 0.4418*** | 0.3375*** | 0.5445*** | 0.3093*** |
| $LnSHARE$ | 0.0970* | 0.1621** | 0.0457 | 0.0139 | −0.1152** | −0.0957 |
| $LnPRIV$ | 0.0028 | 0.2350** | 0.1780** | 0.2333*** | −0.1627 | −0.0698 |
| $LnHTM$ | −0.1244** | −0.0994 | 0.0677 | 0.0216 | 0.0822 | −0.0570 |
| $LnFDI$ | 0.0961 | 0.0878 | −0.0767* | −0.0369 | 0.0318 | 0.1022 |
| $LnLEXRE$ | 0.1680 | 0.3925* | 0.2910*** | 0.5954*** | −0.2870 | 0.1075 |
| $LnVTAX$ | 0.3292** | 0.0478 | 0.2885*** | 0.1381 | 0.2070 | 0.2388 |
| $LnINDU_1$ | 0.1526*** | 0.1534*** | 0.2207*** | 0.2573*** | 0.0099 | 0.0475 |
| $LnINDU_2$ | 0.0362 | −0.1257 | −0.0183 | 0.1009 | −0.2091* | −0.0930 |
| $LnINDU_3$ | −0.0580* | 0.0088 | −0.0311 | 0.0539* | 0.0587 | 0.0555 |
| $LnINDU_4$ | 0.1679*** | 0.1584** | 0.017 | −0.0278 | 0.0859 | 0.0896 |
| $LnINDU_5$ | −0.0412 | 0.0198 | −0.0401 | 0.0603 | 0.2059* | −0.0666 |
| $LnINDU_6$ | −0.2138*** | −0.0831 | 0.0200 | −0.0452 | 0.1878* | 0.1806 |
| $LnINDU_7$ | 0.1245*** | 0.1536*** | 0.0608*** | 0.0716*** | 0.0404 | 0.0811 |
| $LnINDU_8$ | 0.0823* | 0.0832 | 0.0859*** | −0.0043 | −0.0445 | −0.0335 |
| $LnINDU_9$ | −0.0497 | −0.2052*** | 0.1367** | 0.0991* | 0.1536** | 0.1785 |
| Time dummy | Included | Included | Included | Included | Included | Included |
| Observations | 460 | 460 | 440 | 440 | 244 | 244 |
| Adjusted $R^2$ | 0.4903 | 0.5730 | 0.4440 | 0.4576 | 0.3186 | 0.3570 |
| $F$-value | 18.66 | 25.63 | 15.02 | 15.82 | 5.55 | 6.40 |
| Breusch-Pagan $\chi^2$ | 239.87 | 139.66 | 70.50 | 103.32 | 44.29 | 35.03 |

NOTE: Results are corrected for heteroscedasticity.

* $p<0.10$; ** $p<0.05$; *** $p<0.01$.

heavy industrialization is justifiable economically. First, facing rising costs of labor and land, coastal cities have been pursuing a strategy of industrial upgrading, promoting the development of heavy industries; second, the coastal cities are well prepared to develop heavy industries because of capital accumulation from labor- and resource-intensive industries in the 1980s and 1990s; third, international industrial relocation is moving heavy industries to China for markets; finally, heavy industries have huge market potential as China continues to grow. There has been a heated debate in the last couple of years about whether China's coastal region needs heavy industrialization, which has imposed a serious environmental challenge there that could last a long time. The western region does not observe a significant relationship between economic development and air-pollution intensity when industrial structure is controlled for. Its underdevelopment may have discouraged the disastrous effect of economic development on the environment in the western region.

Significant differences in the environmental behaviors of industrial enterprises in the different regions can be observed. First, the results indicate that SOEs hurt the environment in the coastal and central regions but are likely to clean the air in the western region. In the coastal and central cities, SOEs are largely in heavy industries, such as chemical materials and chemical products, ferrous metal mineral smelting and processing, and equipment and machinery, which are more likely to pollute than labor-intensive industries. More important, industrial enterprises in those heavy industries are major contributors to local economies and local revenues, so SOEs have more bargaining power to elicit lower pollution punishments. Second, coefficients of Ln*COES* are positive in the coastal models and but significant only in the $SO_2$ model, implying that collectively owned enterprises in the coastal cities are environmentally harmful. Some collectively owned enterprises in the coastal cities are former township enterprises, relatively small and poorly equipped compared with SOEs and foreign enterprises. They are not environmentally effective. Coefficients of Ln*COES* are negative and significant in both $SO_2$ and dust models in the central cities, but are insignificant in the western cities. In the less developed central cities, the state still controls the heavy and high-value-added, pollution-intensive industries. Collectively owned enterprises are largely in the market-driven light industries and thereby are more environmentally effective.

Third, cooperative enterprises and jointly owned enterprises have no significant environmental impacts in the coastal and central cities but are unfriendly to the environment in the western cities. Limited-liability corporations have significantly contributed to environmental degradation in all three regions. Shared-holding enterprises and privately owned enterprises are environmentally harmful in the coastal and central regions, but are likely to help the environment in the western region. Comparatively, the inland region is weak in community pressure, local government commitment, enforcement capacity, and general economic conditions and may be lax in the enforcement of environmental regulations and environmental pollution violations (Van Rooij and Lo 2010). Market-driven enterprises in the inland regions lack sufficient incentives to internalize environmental costs and thus produce more air pollution. Surprisingly, limited-liability corporations, shared-holding enterprises, and privately owned enterprises are also harmful to the urban environment in the coastal region, which in general has more and higher punishments than those in inland China (Jahiel 1998; Van Rooij and Lo 2010). In the economically liberalized coastal region, those market-oriented enterprises are also major contributors to local revenues and local economic growth. With fiscal decentralization, local governments have incentives to accommodate them and to implement lax environmental regulations. In addition, HTM enterprises and foreign enterprises are associated with lower $SO_2$ emissions intensity in the coastal region and the central region, respectively. The poor environmental performance of market-driven enterprises provides convincing evidence to support the proposition that market decentralization is responsible for China's environmental degradation.

There are regional differences in the environmental attitudes of local governments. Both Ln*LEXRE* and Ln*VTAX* are insignificant in the western region but are expectedly significant in the central region. There is only weak evidence on the environmental impact of fiscal decentralization in the coastal region. Incentives for economic development and pressure on local revenues would be expected to induce the development of pollution-intensive industries in the central cities. In the past couple of years, the central region has gained favorable policy support from the central government and has thereby realized rapid economic growth. The central cities have competed to attract industries from the coastal region, which are often forced to relocate because of environmental pollution. Although the western region faces budgetary challenges, it has consistently received a significant amount of financial transfers from the central government, which have reduced the fiscal pressure on local governments. In addition, the central government has made enormous investments by implementing the strategy of "Develop the West." The western region is extremely environmentally vulnerable, and the central government has imposed more pressure on local governments to protect the local environment.

## Environmental Impact of Decentralization in Cities of Different Sizes

Cities differ in size and technology. The environmental impacts of decentralization may differ across city groups. This analysis divides Chinese cities into three groups based on their population in 2004: large cities (population greater than 5 million), medium cities (population of 2 to 5 million), and small cities (population smaller than 2 million). The panel regression results are presented in table 4.4. All models are highly significant, with $R^2$ larger than 0.50.

First, no significant evidence for the EKC is observed in the small cities, but industrial dusts quickly drop as per capita GDP increases in the large and medium cities, which are able to adopt more advanced technology in their industrial production. As a result, the technique effects in large and medium cities are expected to be more significant. Both scale and technique effects have not played roles in influencing the environment in the small cities, which may have less capacity to utilize advanced technologies.

Second, decentralization is mainly good for environment quality in large cities, while medium and small cities largely suffer from decentralization. As usual, Ln$SOES$ has a positive coefficient in all model specifications, but the coefficients are significant in both $SO_2$ and dust models only in the medium cities. SOEs are significantly and positively associated with industrial dust intensity in the large cities. The good news is that market-driven enterprises are negatively associated with air-pollution intensity in the large cities. Large cities have incentives to improve their natural environment to attract high-tech industries and professional services to upgrade their industrial structures. As a consequence, large cities may enforce stricter environmental regulations on market-driven enterprises, which typically have lower bargaining power with local environmental authorities about the enforcement of pollution charges and regulations (Wang et al. 2001). Foreign enterprises are also likely to contribute to environment improvement, contrary to the pollution-haven hypothesis. Foreign enterprises, which are able to enter large cities, are likely to be major multinational corporations that belong to capital- and technology-intensive industries. They may bring environment-friendly advanced technologies and management and implement higher environmental standards. For instance,

**TABLE 4.4**

Regression Results for Pollution Intensity in Large, Medium, and Small Cities

| | Large Cities | | Medium Cities | | Small Cities | |
|---|---|---|---|---|---|---|
| | $LnTSO_2$ | $LnTDUST$ | $LnTSO_2$ | $LnTDUST$ | $LnTSO_2$ | $LnTDUST$ |
| $LnPGDP$ | 0.9002 | 2.5934 | −0.3914 | 1.6059 | 1.6188 | −1.1164 |
| $LnPGDP^*$ | −0.0832 | −0.1892** | −0.0109 | −0.1153* | −0.1013 | 0.0148 |
| $LnSOES$ | 0.0101 | 0.1755** | 0.3690*** | 0.4089*** | 0.0283 | 0.0818 |
| $LnCOES$ | −0.2121*** | −0.0991 | 0.1296*** | 0.1550*** | 0.0751 | 0.0957 |
| $LnCOOP$ | −0.2176*** | −0.2862*** | −0.1686** | −0.1422* | 0.4649*** | 0.3344*** |
| $LnJOIN$ | 0.0597 | 0.0613 | −0.3164* | 0.0646 | −0.1266 | −0.3208* |
| $LnLIMD$ | 0.2664*** | −0.0287 | 0.6271*** | 0.7149*** | 0.3312*** | 0.4260*** |
| $LnSHARE$ | 0.0580 | −0.1232* | 0.2134*** | 0.2935*** | −0.0915 | 0.0446 |
| $LnPRIV$ | −0.0481 | −0.0551 | 0.1356** | 0.2592*** | 0.0509 | 0.2800** |
| $LnHTM$ | −0.0616 | −0.1975*** | 0.0658 | 0.0559 | −0.2355** | −0.2790** |
| $LnFDI$ | −0.1343** | −0.0730 | 0.1866*** | 0.1758*** | 0.1256 | 0.0951 |
| $LnLEXRE$ | −0.2270 | −0.0448 | −0.0282 | 0.4121*** | 0.1471 | 0.2232 |
| $LnVTAX$ | 0.1021 | −0.2040 | −0.0688 | −0.1216 | 0.8029*** | 0.8140*** |
| $LnINDU_1$ | 0.1471*** | 0.1396*** | 0.1616*** | 0.2238*** | 0.1127* | 0.1075* |
| $LnINDU_2$ | 0.1140 | 0.1724* | 0.0228 | −0.0595 | −0.2840*** | −0.2147** |
| $LnINDU_3$ | 0.0222 | 0.0401 | 0.0037 | 0.0404 | 0.0269 | 0.0689 |
| $LnINDU_4$ | −0.1655*** | −0.3047*** | 0.1179** | 0.1358** | 0.2252** | 0.1631* |
| $LnINDU_5$ | −0.0731 | 0.0123 | −0.0690 | −0.0100 | −0.2670 | −0.1861 |
| $LnINDU_6$ | 0.0209 | 0.1431 | −0.1167* | −0.0692 | −0.0191 | −0.1037 |
| $LnINDU_7$ | 0.1446*** | 0.2278*** | 0.1011*** | 0.0462 | 0.0606 | 0.0848* |
| $LnINDU_8$ | 0.0981** | 0.0541 | −0.0133 | 0.0013 | 0.1123* | 0.0015 |
| $LnINDU_9$ | −0.1422** | 0.2296*** | 0.1019** | −0.1084** | 0.0786 | 0.0860 |
| Time dummy | Included | Included | Included | Included | Included | Included |
| Observations | 340 | 340 | 576 | 576 | 228 | 228 |
| Adjusted $R^2$ | 0.5866 | 0.6154 | 0.5022 | 0.5366 | 0.5143 | 0.6227 |
| $F$-Value | 20.24 | 22.70 | 24.21 | 27.64 | 10.61 | 15.98 |
| Breusch-Pagan $\chi^2$ | 72.82 | 85.45 | 217.69 | 98.99 | 116.67 | 30.24 |

NOTE: Large cities are those with population greater than 5 million; medium cities, with population between 2 million and 5 million; and small cities, with population smaller than 2 million. Results are corrected for heteroscedasticity.

$^* p < 0.10$; $^{**} p < 0.05$; $^{***} p < 0.01$.

foreign investments dominate in the electric and electronics industries in Beijing, Shanghai, Tianjin, and Shenzhen and reduce air-pollution intensity.

$LnCOES$, $LnLIMD$, $LnSHARE$, $LnPRIV$, and $LnFDI$ all have significant and positive coefficients in the medium cities. Only cooperative enterprises and jointly owned enterprises are negatively associated with air pollution in the medium cities. $LnCOOP$, $LnLIMD$, and $LnPRIV$ are positively associated with air-pollution intensity in the small cities. The results suggest that market-driven enterprises may result in more air pollution in medium and small cities, which face higher pressure to achieve economic growth and are in the process of fast industrialization and urbanization. $LnVTAX$ is positively significant in small cities. $LnLEXRE$ is positive and significant in the dust model of medium cities. With power and fiscal decentralization, local governments in the medium and small cities are more likely to engage in a race to the bottom by implementing lax environmental regulations.

Market-driven enterprises have less incentive to internalize environmental negative externalities and are able to elicit lower pollution payments or punishments in medium and small cities. It is worthwhile to point out that HTM enterprises are able to improve environmental quality in small cities. HTM enterprises in small cities are largely in traditional labor-intensive industries, such as food manufacturing, garments, shoe and hat making, toy making, leather, and fur and down products. Compared with domestic enterprises in the small cities, HTM enterprises may have better equipment and advanced technologies and thus contribute to environmental improvement. Overall, large cities are likely to benefit environmentally from market and power decentralization, while medium and small cities may suffer from decentralization.

## Conclusion

China's industrial production has been cleaner, with decreasing pollution intensity, during the past decade. Pollution-intensive industries particularly have made significant achievements in reducing pollution intensity. Industrial pollution is clustered in some Chinese cities. The Yangtze River Delta, the Shandong Peninsula, the Capital region, central and northern China, northeastern China, the Sichuan basin, and the Pearl River Delta are the hot spots. The coastal region is much less pollution intensive than the inland region.

Statistical results confirm the EKC effect in Chinese cities and imply that economic development can mitigate industrial pollution through technique effects. SOEs have contributed to environmental degradation in Chinese cities. Market-driven enterprises are positively associated with air-pollution intensity, indicating that market decentralization may be harmful to urban environments, especially in the central and western regions and in the small and medium cities. Power and fiscal decentralization has induced a race to the bottom by lowering environmental regulations to attract taxable and high-value-added, pollution-intensive industries, especially in the coastal and central regions and in the medium and small cities. The environmental impacts of decentralization in China are highly influenced by the environmental behaviors of different types of industrial enterprises and different environmental attitudes of local governments.

To a certain degree, China's economic achievement has occurred at the expense of environmental quality. Previous studies examined the effects of scale, technology and structure on environmental pollution. The analysis in this chapter has highlighted the importance of regional decentralization. On the one hand, decentralization is a critical part of economic reform and has constituted a significant institutional advantage for China's economic development since the late 1970s. On the other hand, decentralization has been shown to result in environmental degradation not only in the coastal region, but also in the western region. Meanwhile, SOEs clearly are harmful to urban environments. The environmental effects of SOEs and decentralization are associated with lower environmental standards and lax environmental enforcement and implementation. Evidently, there is a trade-off between economic growth and environmental degradation associated with decentralization. It is critical to increase the incentives for industrial enterprises to internalize environmental costs by strengthening the enforcement of environmental regulations, which depends on the environmental attitudes of local governments. As a consequence, the fundamental solution to China's environmental degradation depends on the efforts of local governments. Achieving cooperation of local governments will require a set of reforms, including changing local revenue structures and performance evaluations of local officials and improving the status of environmental enforcement agencies.

## References


Anderson, Gordon, and Ying Ge. 2004. Do economic reforms accelerate urban growth? The case of China. *Urban Studies* 41(11):2197–2210.

Bai, Chong-En, Yingjuan Du, Zhigang Tao, and Sarah Y. Tong. 2004. Local protectionism and regional specialization: Evidence from China's industries. *Journal of International Economics* 63:397–417.

Chan, Chak K., and Xiaohong Yao. 2008. Air pollution in mega cities in China. *Atmospheric Environment* 42:1–42.

Chen, Baizhu, and Yi Feng. 2000. Determinants of economic growth in China: Private enterprise, education and openness. *China Economic Review* 11:1–15.

Dean, Judith M., and Mary E. Lovely. 2008. *Trade growth, production fragmentation, and China's environment.* NBER Working Paper 13860. Cambridge: National Bureau of Economic Research.

Demurger, Sylvie, Jeffrey D. Sachs, Wing Thye Woo, Shuming Bao, and Gene Chang. 2002. The relative contributions of location and preferential policies in China's regional development: Being in the right place and having the right incentives. *China Economic Review* 13:444–465.

Eiser, J. Richard, Steven D. Reicher, and Tessa J. Podpadec. 1996. Attitudes to privatization of U.K. public utilities: Anticipating industrial practice and environmental effects. *Journal of Consumer Policy* 19(2):193–208.

He, Canfei, Yehua Wei, and Xiuzhen Xie. 2008. Globalization, institutional change and industrial location: Economic transition and industrial concentration in China. *Regional Studies* 42(7):923–945.

He, Jie. 2006. Pollution haven hypothesis and environmental impacts of foreign direct investment: The case of industrial emission of sulfur dioxide ($SO_2$) in Chinese provinces. *Ecological Economics* 60:228–245.

———. 2009. China's industrial $SO_2$ emissions and its economic determinants: EKC's reduced vs. structural model and the role of international trade. *Environment and Development Economics* 14:227–262.

Jahiel, Abigail R. 1997. The contradictory impact of reform on environmental protection in China. *China Quarterly* 149:81–103.

———. 1998. The organization of environmental protection in China. *China Quarterly* 156:757–787.

Lieberthal, Kenneth. 1995. *Governing China: From revolution through reform.* New York: W. W. Norton.

Lin, Justin Yifu, and Zhiqiang Liu. 2000. Fiscal decentralization and economic growth in China. *Economic Development and Cultural Change* 49(1):1–21.

Liu, Tung, and Kui-wai Li. 2001. Impact of liberalization of financial resources in China's economic growth: Evidence from provinces. *Journal of Asian Economics* 12:245–262.

Ma, Xiaoying, and Leonard Ortolano. 2000. *Environmental regulation in China.* Lanham, MD: Rowman and Littlefield.

Naughton, Barry. 2007. *The Chinese economy: Transitions and growth.* Cambridge, MA: MIT Press.

Oi, Jean C. 1995. The role of the local state in China's transitional economy. *China Quarterly* 144:1132–1149.

Qian, Yingyi, and Barry R. Weingast. 1997. Federalism as a commitment to preserving market incentives. *Journal of Economic Perspectives* 11:83–92.

Shi, Yunpeng, and Li'an Zhou. 2007. Regional decentralization and economic efficiency: Evidence from separate planning cities in China. [In Chinese.] *Economic Research* 1:17–28.

Shin, Sangbum. 2004. Economic globalization and the environment in China: A comparative case study of Shenyang and Dalian. *Journal of Environment and Development* 13:263–294.

Sigman, Hilary. 2009. Decentralization and environmental quality: An international analysis of water pollution. Berkeley: University of California at Berkeley, Berkeley Program in Law and Economics. http://www.escholarship.org/uc/item/9qj772pj

Sinkule, Barbara J., and Leonard Ortolano. 1995. *Implementing environmental policy in China.* Westport, CT: Praeger.

Swanson, Kate E., Richard G. Kuhn, and Wei Xu. 2001. Environmental policy implementation in rural China: A case study of Yuhang, Zhejiang. *Environmental Management* 27:481–491.

Talukdar, Dababrata, and M. Craig Meisner. 2001. Does the private sector help or hurt the environment? Evidence from carbon dioxide pollution in developing countries. *World Development* 29:827–840.

Tang, Shui-yan, Carlos Wing-Hung Lo, Kai-Chee Cheung, and Jack Man-keung Lo. 1997. Institutional constraints on environmental management in urban China: Environmental impact assessment in Guangzhou and Shanghai. *China Quarterly* 152:863–874.

Tang, Shui-yan, Carlos Wing-Hung Lo, and Gerald E. Fryxell. 2003. Enforcement styles, organizational commitment, and enforcement effectiveness: An empirical study of local environmental protection officials in urban China. *Environment and Planning* 35:75–94.

Van Rooij, B. 2006. *Regulating land and pollution in China: Lawmaking, compliance, and enforcement; Theory and cases.* Leiden, The Netherlands: Leiden University Press.

Van Rooij, Benjamin, and Carlos Wing-Hung Lo. 2010. Fragile convergence: Understanding variation in the enforcement of China's industrial pollution law. *Law and Policy* 32:14–37.

Wang, Hua, and Yanhong Jin. 2002. Industrial ownership and environmental performance: Evidence from China. Policy Research Working Paper 2936. Washington, DC: World Bank.

Wang, Hua, Nlandu Mamingi, Benoit Laplante, and Susmita Dasgupta. 2001. Incomplete enforcement of pollution regulation: Bargaining power of Chinese factories. Policy Research Working Paper 2756. Washington, DC: World Bank.

Wang, Hua, and David Wheeler. 2000. Endogenous enforcement and effectiveness of China's pollution levy system. Policy Research Working Paper 2336. Washington, DC: World Bank.

Young, Alwyn. 2000. The razor's edge: Distortions and incremental reform in the People's Republic of China. NBER Working Paper 7828. Cambridge: National Bureau of Economic Research (NBER).

Zhao, Xiao Bin, and Li Zhang. 1999. Decentralization reforms and regionalism in China: A review. *International Regional Science Review* 22:251–281.

# Income Growth, Urbanization, Changing Lifestyles, and CO$_2$ Emissions in China

MINJUN SHI AND YAN WANG

In the decade from 1995 to 2004, income growth and urbanization have caused significant changes in household consumption and lifestyles in China. The most remarkable changes in lifestyle are the growth of private vehicle usage and of expenditures on housing. Studies have shown that lifestyle changes and household consumption have become driving forces in increasing energy use and CO$_2$ emissions (Lenzen 1998; Peet, Carter, and Baines 1985; Weber and Fahl 1993; Wier et al. 2001). The direct and indirect energy requirements induced by changing lifestyle and household consumption have attracted attention (Reinders, Vringer, and Blok 2003). In the United States more than 80 percent of total energy use and CO$_2$ emissions are a consequence of consumer demands and the economic activities to support these demands (Bin and Dowlatabadi 2005). In the Netherlands, Korea, and Brazil the share of indirect energy requirements in total energy use that is caused by consumption demands varies from 50 to 60 percent (Cohena, Lenzen, and Schaeffer 2005; Park and Heo 2007; Vringer and Blok 1995). Even in India it is estimated that 47 percent of total energy use was indirect energy use in 1993 and 1994 (Pachauri and Spreng 2002).

Wei and colleagues estimated that approximately 26 percent of total energy consumption and 30 percent of CO$_2$ emissions are a consequence of residents' consumption demands in China (Wei et al. 2007). However, they did not examine how changing lifestyles drove the increase of energy use and CO$_2$ emissions with income growth and urbanization. Moreover, it is expected that changes in household consumption and lifestyle driven by income growth and urbanization will cause further growth of CO$_2$ emissions. This chapter estimates the effects of these changes and then projects the impacts of improvement in patterns of household consumption on mitigating CO$_2$ emissions by 2020 on the basis of input-output analysis and a scenario-simulation approach.

## Method

### Input-Output Analysis

The general method used for estimating embodied $CO_2$ emissions caused by household consumption is outlined in Lenzen (1998) and Bin and Dowlatabadi (2005). Input-output analysis and the consumer lifestyle approach are the main methods in their works. The functions are as follows:

$$E = E^{dir} + E^{ind} = E^{dir} + Q^{emb}\,Y; \tag{1}$$

$$Q^{emb} = Q^{dir}\,(I-A)^{-1}; \tag{2}$$

$$C = C^{dir} + C^{ind}; \tag{3}$$

$$C^{dir} = CO_2 coefficient_m \times E^{dir}; \tag{4}$$

$$C^{ind} = C^{emb}Y; \tag{5}$$

$$C^{emb} = CO_2 coefficient_m \times Q^{dir}\,(I-A)^{-1}. \tag{6}$$

$E$:     energy use caused by consumption of urban residents.
$E^{dir}$:     direct energy use of urban residents.
$E^{ind}$:     indirect energy use of urban residents.
$(I-A)^{-1}$:     Leontief inverse matrix.
$Q^{dir}$:     direct energy intensity of sectors.
$Q^{emb}$:     indirect energy intensity of sectors.
$Y$:     matrix of consumption of urban residents.
$C$:     $CO_2$ emissions caused by consumption of urban residents.
$C^{dir}$:     direct $CO_2$ emissions of urban residents.
$C^{ind}$:     indirect $CO_2$ emissions of urban residents.
$C^{emb}$:     indirect $CO_2$ emissions intensity from consumption of urban residents.
$CO_2\,coefficient_m$:     carbon coefficient of fuel $m$.

### Structure Decomposition Analysis of $CO_2$ Emissions

In order to analyze the influence of technology changes on the amount of $CO_2$ emissions caused by consumption, structure decomposition analysis is used to decompose the amount of $CO_2$ emissions caused by consumption per capita. The functions are as follows:

$$C^{ind} = C^{emb}Y.$$

Therefore,

$$\Delta C^{ind} = C_2^{emb}Y_2 - C_1^{emb}Y_1 = (C_2^{emb}Y_2 - C_1^{emb}Y_2) + (C_1^{emb}Y_2 - C_1^{emb}Y_1)$$
$$= \Delta C^{emb}Y_2 + C_1^{emb}\Delta Y \tag{7}$$

$\Delta C^{ind}$:    change of indirect $CO_2$ emissions from consumption of urban residents.

$C_1^{emb}$:    matrix of indirect $CO_2$ emission intensity from consumption of urban residents in 1995.

$C_2^{emb}$:    matrix of indirect $CO_2$ emission intensity from consumption of urban residents in 2004.

$Y_1$:    matrix of consumption of urban residents in 1995.

$Y_2$:    matrix of consumption of urban residents in 2004.

$\Delta Y$:    change of consumption of urban residents from 1995 to 2004.

$\Delta C^{emb}$:    change of indirect $CO_2$ emission intensity.

## Scenario Simulation

### Scenario Design

The scenario-simulation approach is used to estimate per capita $CO_2$ emissions induced by consumption of urban residents in 2015 and 2020. The main driving factors affecting $CO_2$ emission are examined, including income growth, technological progress, urbanization, and adjustments of lifestyle. Changes in household consumption driven by income growth, urbanization, and energy technological progress are taken into account in the baseline scenarios. In order to examine the effect of lifestyle adjustments on $CO_2$ emissions reduction, changes in transport behavior and improvements in home energy use efficiency are taken into account in the low-carbon scenario. Table 5.1 outlines the scenarios.

### Simulation Model

$$C^{fk} = \sum_{j=1}^{m} CO_2 efficient_j^f \times Y_j^{fk} \qquad (j=1,2,\ldots,n); \qquad (8)$$

$$CO_2 efficient_j^f = CO_2 efficient^{*\,fk}_{\ j}(I - A^f)^{-1} \qquad (j=1,2,\ldots,n); \qquad (9)$$

$$Y_i^f = \sum_{j=1}^{n} Y_j^{fk} = \left(1 + \varepsilon_i \times \frac{L_i^f - L_i^c}{L_i^c}\right) \times Y_j^c \qquad (i=1,2,\ldots,7). \qquad (10)$$

$C^{fk}$ is per capita $CO_2$ emissions in scenario $k$ for the year $f$; $Y_j^{fk}$ denotes the expenditure for goods and service of sector $j$ in scenario $k$ between the different income group $i$ for the year $f$; $Y_j^f$ is the expenditure of residents of income group $i$ for the

**TABLE 5.1**

Scenarios

| | |
|---|---|
| Baseline scenario | Income growth |
| | Technological progress |
| Urbanization | Low-carbon scenario |
| | Lifestyle change |

terminal year $f$; $L_i^c$ is the income of residents of income group $i$ for the terminal year $f$; $L_i^c$ is the income of residents of income group $i$ for the beginning year $c$; $\varepsilon_i$ is the income elasticity of income group $i$; $CO_2 efficient_{ij}^{f}$ is the carbon coefficient of sector $j$ for the terminal year $f$; and $CO_2 efficient^{*}{}_{ij}^{fk}$ is the direct carbon coefficient of sector $j$ for the terminal year $f$.

*Parameters*

The per capita income of each income group in 2015 and 2020 is estimated according to the appropriate growth rate. The per capita consumption expenditure of each income group in 2015 and 2020 is estimated on the basis of a regression function. The $CO_2$ emission intensities of all sectors in 2015 and 2020 come from the report of the ERI Low Carbon Economy Research Team. Data on population and urbanization rates in 2015 and 2020 are derived from relevant sources (International Eurasian Academy of Sciences 2010). The parameters of living and transport behavior refer mainly to the report commissioned by the National Development and Reform Commission entitled *The path of low-carbon development towards 2050 in China*.

## Data Sources

Data on home energy use and final energy use come from the *China Energy Statistical Yearbook* (National Bureau of Statistics 1997–2006). Data on consumption expenditures of urban residents come from the *China Statistical Yearbook* (National Bureau of Statistics 1996–2005b) and the *Chinese Price and Urban Household Survey Yearbook* (National Bureau of Statistics 1996–2005a). Other data sources include 40 sector input-output tables of China in 1997 and 60 sector input-output tables in 2002 (National Bureau of Statistics 1997 and 2002).

To avoid double calculation, only fossil-fuel energy sources, including coal, petroleum, and natural gas, are considered. Hydropower, nuclear power, and renewable energy are not taken into account.

## Lifestyle Changes with Income Growth and Urbanization

In China the per capita disposable income of urban residents increased from 4,283 yuan in 1995 to 9,422 yuan in 2004. The per capita net income of rural residents increased from 1,578 yuan in 1995 to 2,936 yuan in 2004. Meanwhile, the urbanization rate rose from 29 percent in 1995 to 42 percent in 2004 (National Bureau of Statistics 1996–2005b). At least 13 percent of the total population was transformed from rural residents to urban residents during this period.

Income growth and urbanization have caused significant changes in household consumption and lifestyle. With income growth, the per capita consumption expenditure of urban residents increased from 3,538 yuan in 1995 to 7,182 yuan in 2004, and the per capita consumption expenditure of rural residents increased from 1,310 yuan in 1995 to 2,185 yuan in 2004 (National Bureau of Statistics 1996–2005b). The correlation coefficient between per capita income and per capita expenditure of urban residents is 0.92, which shows a significant relationship between income and consumption expenditure (figure 5.1).

**FIGURE 5.1**

Correlation Between Per Capita Income and Expenditure

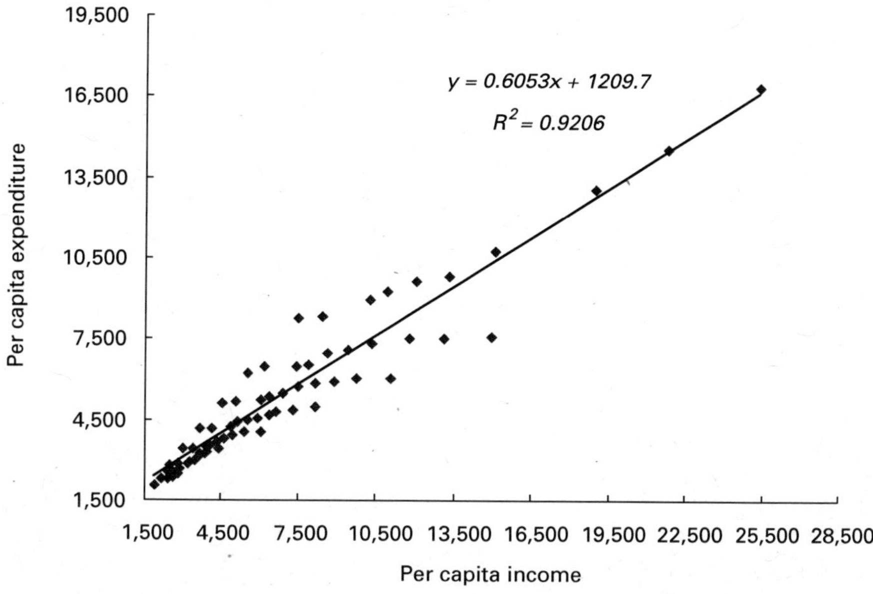


SOURCE: National Bureau of Statistics (1996–2005).

With income growth, transport behavior and expenditures on housing have experienced significant changes. Private car and motorcycle ownership by urban residents has increased by 11.5 times and 3.9 times from 1995 to 2004. Motorcycle ownership by rural residents has increased by 7.4 times. Average house floor space has increased by 153 percent for urban residents and 133 percent for rural residents in the past decade. Average residential expenditure has increased by 293 percent for urban residents and 178 percent for rural residents (National Bureau of Statistics 1996–2005b). Income growth has been the driving force of the increase in household consumption and especially of changes in transport behavior and housing expenditures.

## Changing Lifestyles and Consumption-Induced CO$_2$ Emissions in the Past Decade

### Impact of Changing Lifestyle on Consumption-Induced CO$_2$ Emissions

Increases in household consumption and changes in lifestyle that are driven by income growth and urbanization have caused a remarkable increase in CO$_2$ emissions. With the growth of household income and consumption expenditure, overall per capita CO$_2$ emissions of urban residents increased from 1,853 kg of CO$_2$ in 1995 to 2,498 kg of CO$_2$ in 2004. Per capita CO$_2$ emissions of rural residents increased from 616 kg of CO$_2$ in 1995 to 900 kg of CO$_2$ in 2004. Indirect consumption-induced CO$_2$ emissions of urban residents increased from 1,093 kg of CO$_2$ in 1995 to 1,971 kg of CO$_2$ in 2004, and per capita indirect consumption-induced CO$_2$

Change in Per Capita $CO_2$ Emissions with Income Growth

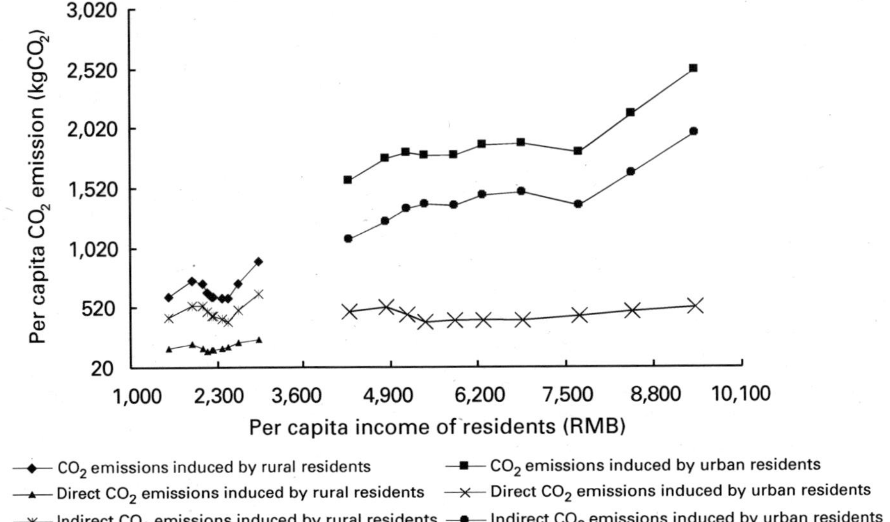


SOURCES: National Bureau of Statistics (1997; 2002); National Bureau of Statistics (1996–2005).

emissions of rural residents has increased from 435 kg of $CO_2$ in 1995 to 641 kg of $CO_2$ in 2004 (National Bureau of Statistics 1996–2005a) (figure 5.2).

Increasing consumption-induced $CO_2$ emissions with changes in transport behavior and housing expenditures have been a conspicuous feature in the data period. Per capita $CO_2$ emissions caused by transport behaviors of urban residents increased from 52 kg of $CO_2$ in 1995 to 249 kg of $CO_2$ in 2004. Per capita $CO_2$ emissions induced by housing expenditures of urban residents increased from 630 kg of $CO_2$ in 1995 to 783 kg of $CO_2$ in 2004. Increasing private vehicle and fuel expenditures have led to a significant growth in $CO_2$ emissions. Per capita $CO_2$ emissions induced by private vehicle and fuel expenditures increased by 538 percent, from 34 kg of $CO_2$ in 1995 to 183 kg of $CO_2$ in 2004 (National Bureau of Statistics 1996–2005a). Within the growth in housing expenditures, $CO_2$ emissions caused by building activities increased, while $CO_2$ emissions caused by direct home energy use decreased.

## Differences Across Income Groups

There are significant differences in lifestyle and consumption-induced $CO_2$ emissions among different income groups of urban households. Higher-income groups have higher $CO_2$ emissions caused by their higher consumption expenditures. Moreover, higher-income groups have a much larger increase in $CO_2$ emissions with income growth than low-income groups (figure 5.3).

The differences in $CO_2$ emissions across income groups can be explained to a great extent by the different housing expenditures and transport behaviors of these groups. The higher-income groups have much higher housing and transport expenditures that have induced more $CO_2$ emissions (figures 5.4 and 5.5). The corre-

## Change in Per Capita Consumption-Induced $CO_2$ Emissions Across Income Groups

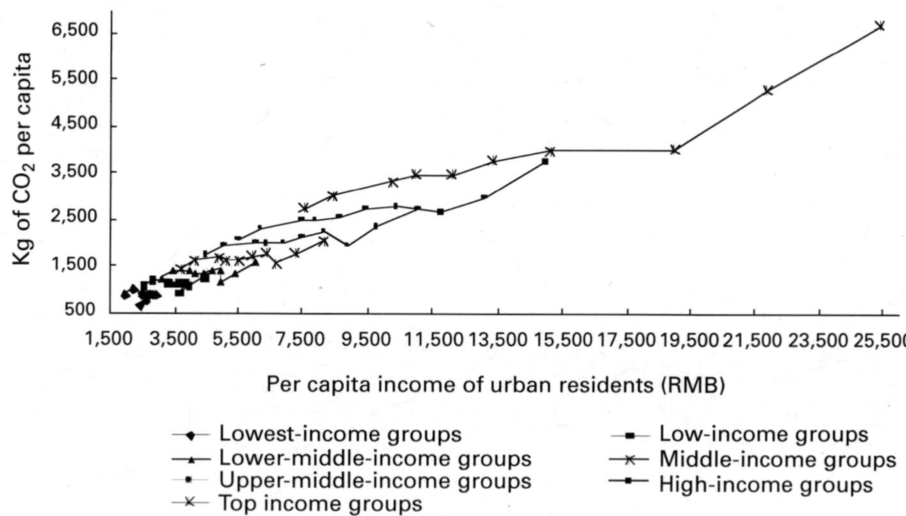


SOURCES: National Bureau of Statistics (1997; 2002); National Bureau of Statistics (1996–2005a).



## Change in Per Capita $CO_2$ Emissions Induced by Housing Expenditures

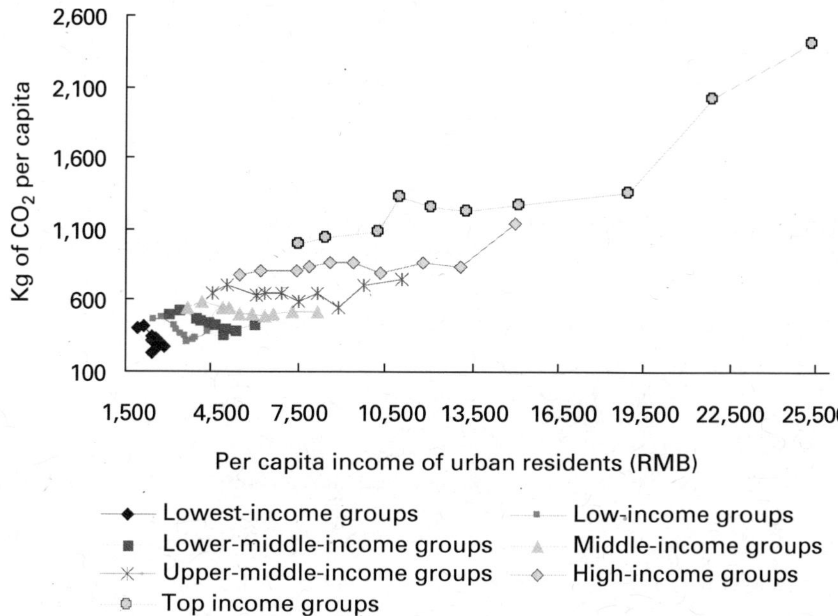


SOURCES: National Bureau of Statistics (1997; 2002); National Bureau of Statistics (1996–2005a).

Change in Per Capita CO$_2$ Emissions Induced by Transport Expenditures

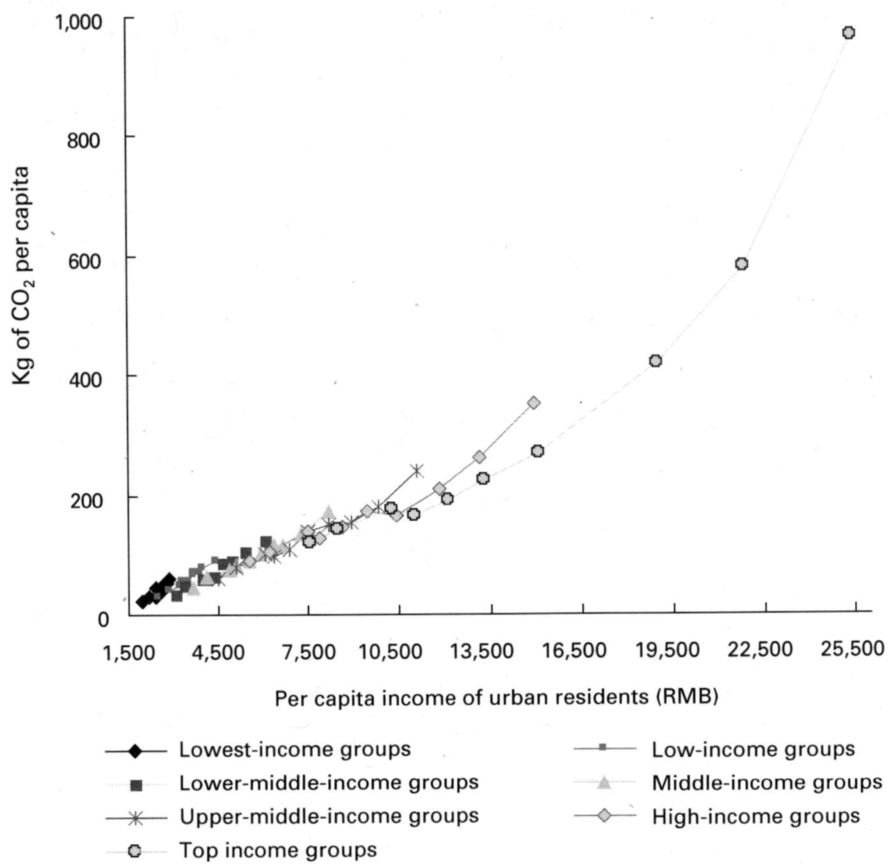


SOURCES: National Bureau of Statistics (1997; 2002); National Bureau of Statistics (1996–2005a).

lation coefficient between per capita income and consumption-induced CO$_2$ emissions of urban residents is 0.935. This indicates that income growth has been a driving force in the increase of CO$_2$ emissions because of associated changes in consumption patterns and lifestyles.

## Impacts of Urbanization

The urbanization rate in China increased from 29 percent in 1995 to 42 percent in 2004. Because of the differences in consumption patterns and lifestyles between rural residents and urban residents, urbanization may directly drive changes in consumption patterns and lifestyles of residents, especially changes in transport behavior and housing expenditures, which have led to an increase of 0.264 billion tons of CO$_2$ emissions. That accounts for 25.46 percent of the total increase of CO$_2$ emissions during this period (National Bureau of Statistics 1996–2005a) (figure 5.6).

**FIGURE 5.6**

Change in $CO_2$ Emissions of Housing and Transport with Urbanization

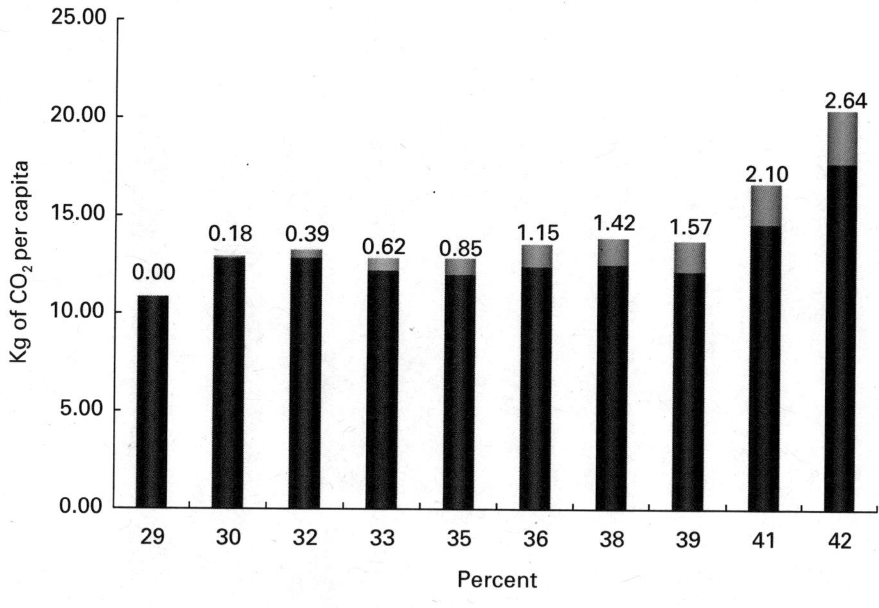


SOURCES: National Bureau of Statistics (1997; 2002); National Bureau of Statistics (1996–2005a).

## Factor Decomposition of $CO_2$ Emissions Caused by Consumption

Two factors determine changes in consumption-induced per capita $CO_2$ emissions: increases in consumption expenditures and technological improvements in energy use. Factor decomposition analysis may help separate the effects of these factors. The results of factor decomposition show that technological improvements in energy use have somewhat offset the effects of increased consumption expenditures on the growth of $CO_2$ emissions. The results show that increased consumption expenditures induced an increase in per capita $CO_2$ emissions of 1,670 kg from 1995 to 2004. However, technological improvements led to a decrease in consumption-induced per capita $CO_2$ emissions of 755 kg (National Bureau of Statistics 1996–2005a). The net increase in consumption-induced per capita $CO_2$ emissions was 915 kg (figure 5.7). The effect of technological improvement on $CO_2$ emissions varies across different income groups. Technological improvement led to a much greater decrease of $CO_2$ emissions for higher-income groups; there was a decrease of 3,688 kg of $CO_2$ for the highest-income group, but of only 281 kg for the lowest-income group (National Bureau of Statistics 1996–2005a).

**FIGURE 5.7**

Impact of Consumption and Technological Improvements on Increases of $CO_2$ Emissions in Different Income Groups, 1995–2004

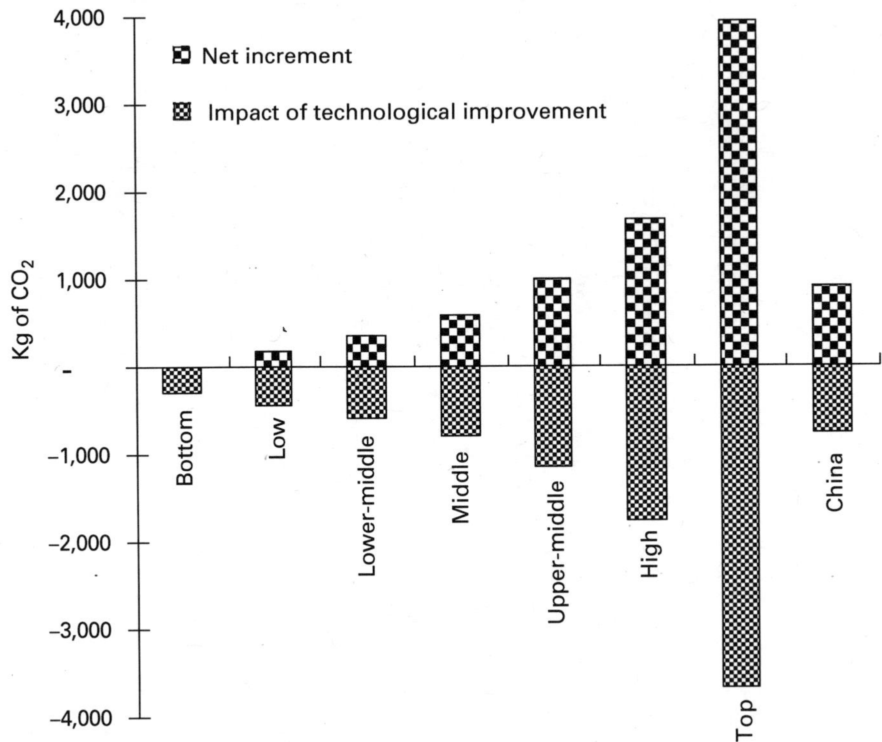


SOURCES: National Bureau of Statistics (1997; 2002); National Bureau of Statistics (1996–2005a).

## Prospect for Consumption-Induced $CO_2$ Emissions by 2020

### Estimated $CO_2$ Emissions with Increasing Income, Consumption, and Urbanization

Growth in household consumption driven by income growth and urbanization may cause further increases in $CO_2$ emissions in the future. A scenario simulation based on projections of future income growth and consumption of urban residents indicates that if technology remains at its present level, per capita $CO_2$ emissions of urban residents might reach 5,542 kg in 2015 and 7,993 kg in 2020, 3.1 times and 4.4 times higher, respectively, than in 2002. If progress in energy use technologies is considered, per capita $CO_2$ emissions of urban residents under the baseline scenario might reach 3,459 kg in 2015 and 4,582 kg in 2020, a decrease of 38 percent of per capita $CO_2$ emission in 2015 and 43 percent in 2020. However, under the baseline scenario, with both income growth and technological progress, per capita $CO_2$ emissions of urban residents will still be 1.9 times the 2002 level in 2015 and 2.5 times the 2002 level in 2020 (table 5.2).

It is expected that the urbanization rate will rise from 42 percent in 2004 to 55 percent in 2015 and 60 percent in 2020 (Zhang and Wang 2010). According to the

**TABLE 5.2**

Consumption-Induced $CO_2$ Emissions by Income Groups, 2015 and 2020

| Year | Income Groups | Scenarios | | |
| | | Income Growth (kg of $CO_2$ Per Capita) | Technological Progress (kg of $CO_2$ Per Capita) | Low-Carbon Lifestyle (kg of $CO_2$ Per Capita) |
|---|---|---|---|---|
| 2012 | Average | 5,226 | 2,968 | 2,702 |
| | Bottom | 1,967 | 1,290 | 1,246 |
| | Low | 2,914 | 1,800 | 1,713 |
| | Lower-middle | 3,418 | 2,262 | 2,187 |
| | Middle | 5,019 | 3,085 | 2,930 |
| | Upper-middle | 6,082 | 3,794 | 3,616 |
| | High | 7,567 | 4,765 | 4,550 |
| | Top | 11,783 | 7,377 | 7,027 |
| 2020 | Average | 7,993 | 4,582 | 4,165 |
| | Bottom | 3,367 | 1,860 | 1,680 |
| | Low | 4,423 | 2,482 | 2,250 |
| | Lower-middle | 5,226 | 2,968 | 2,702 |
| | Middle | 6,911 | 3,964 | 3,615 |
| | Upper-middle | 8,327 | 4,789 | 4,357 |
| | High | 10,042 | 5,804 | 5,270 |
| | Top | 14,936 | 8,628 | 7,800 |

SOURCES: National Bureau of Statistics (1997, 2002); National Bureau of Statistics (1996–2005a).

authors' estimation, the increase of $CO_2$ emissions caused by the growth in the number of urban residents will reach 0.78 billion tons in 2015 and 1.40 billion tons in 2020.

It is estimated that the Chinese population will reach 1.39 billion in 2015 and 1.42 billion in 2020 according to the historical data of the population in China. If $CO_2$ emissions of rural residents are kept at their present level and the urbanization rate rises to 55 percent in 2015 and 60 percent in 2020, the national $CO_2$ emissions induced by consumer demands and the economic activities to support these demands will reach 3.02 billion tons in 2015 and 4.24 billion tons in 2020. China's mitigation target is 8.8 to 9.5 billion tons of $CO_2$ emissions in 2020. That means that about 45 to 48 percent of total $CO_2$ emissions will be a consequence of residents' lifestyles and the economic activities to support consumption demands. These estimation results imply that China needs to make a great effort to develop a green low-carbon lifestyle.

## Effects of Adjusting Consumption Pattern Toward a Green Low-Carbon Lifestyle

In order to estimate the effects of adjusting consumption patterns on $CO_2$ emissions, the shift to a green low-carbon lifestyle is considered to depend primarily on two factors: (1) adjustment of transport behavior to increase the use of public

Impact of Future Urbanization on Consumption-Induced $CO_2$ Emissions

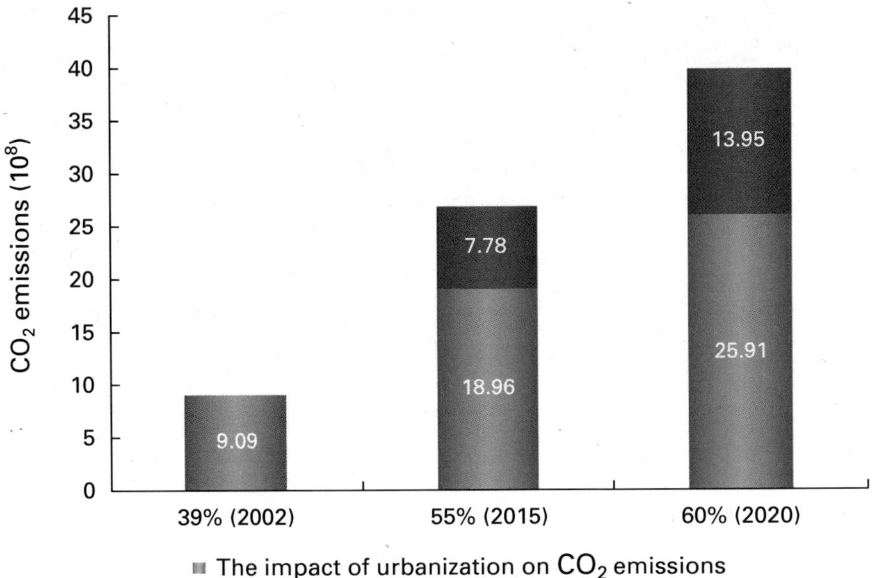


SOURCES: National Bureau of Statistics (1997; 2002); National Bureau of Statistics (1996–2005a).

transportation and to reduce the use of private vehicles; and (2) improvement of home energy use efficiency to reduce $CO_2$ emissions caused by housing expenditures.

The results of scenario simulation indicate that developing a green low-carbon lifestyle may considerably reduce per capita consumption-induced $CO_2$ emissions. Per capita $CO_2$ emissions of urban residents may decline to 3,297 kg in 2015 and 4,165 kg in 2020.

Under the low-carbon scenario, if $CO_2$ emissions of rural residents are kept at the present level and the urbanization rate rises to 55 percent in 2015 and 60 percent in 2020, national $CO_2$ emissions induced by consumer demands and the economic activities to support these demands will reach 2.89 billion tons in 2015 and 3.89 billion tons in 2020, a reduction of 0.13 billion tons in 2015 and 0.35 billion tons in 2020 from the amounts in the baseline scenario (figure 5.8).

## Findings and Policy Implications

The findings of the preceding analysis can be summarized as follows:

1. Income growth and urbanization have been the driving forces of increases in household consumption and changes in lifestyle, especially changes in transport behavior and housing expenditures. These increases in household consumption and lifestyle changes, especially the growing use of private vehicles, have caused a great increase in $CO_2$ emissions.

2. Energy technological improvements have somewhat offset the effects of increased consumption expenditure on the growth of $CO_2$ emission. It is estimated that technological improvements in energy use led to a 45 percent decrease in $CO_2$ emissions induced by increased consumption expenditures from 1995 to 2004. Furthermore, technological improvement led to a much greater decrease in $CO_2$ emissions for higher-income groups.

3. Growth in household consumption driven by income growth and urbanization may lead to further increases in $CO_2$ emissions in the future.

4. It is estimated that about 45 to 48 percent of total $CO_2$ emissions in 2020 will be a consequence of residents' lifestyles and the economic activities to support consumption demands in China. That implies that China needs to make a great effort to develop a green low-carbon lifestyle in order to realize its mitigation target in 2020.

5. Developing a green low-carbon lifestyle may contribute to a considerable reduction in consumption-induced $CO_2$ emissions.

## References


Bin, Shui, and Hadi Dowlatabadi. 2005. Consumer lifestyle approach to US energy use and the related $CO_2$ emissions. *Energy Policy* 33:197–208.

Cohena, Claude, Manfred Lenzen, and Roberto Schaeffer. 2005. Energy requirements of households in Brazil. *Energy Policy* 33:555–562.

Fan, Ying, Qiao-Mei Liang, Yi-Ming Wei, and Norio Okada. 2007. Multi-regional input-output model for regional energy requirements and $CO_2$ emissions in China. *Energy Policy* 35:247–257.

International Eurasian Academy of Sciences. 2010. *China urban development report 2009.* [In Chinese.] Beijing: China City Press.

Lenzen, Manfred. 1998. Primary energy and greenhouse gases embodied in Australian final consumption: An input-output analysis. *Energy Policy* 26:495–506.

National Bureau of Statistics. 1996–2005a. *Chinese price and urban household survey yearbook.* Beijing: China Statistics Press.

———. 1996–2005b. *China statistical yearbook.* Beijing: China Statistics Press.

———. Department of Industry and Transport Statistics and National Development and Reform Commission. 1997–2006. *China energy statistical yearbook.* Beijing: China Statistics Press.

———. 1997, 2002. *National input-output table of China.* Beijing: China Statistics Press.

Pachauri, Shonali, and Daniel Spreng. 2002. Direct and indirect energy requirements of households in India. *Energy Policy* 30:511–523.

Park, Hi-Chun, and Eun-Nyeong Heo. 2007. The direct and indirect household energy requirements in the Republic of Korea from 1980 to 2000: An input-output analysis. *Energy Policy* 35:2839–2851.

Peet, N. J., J. Carter, and J. T. Baines. 1985. Energy in the New Zealand household, 1974–1980. *Energy* 10(11):1197–1208.

Reinders, Angelia Hubertina Mechtildus Elisabeth, Kees Vringer, and Kornelis Blok. 2003. The direct and indirect energy requirements of households in the European Union. *Energy Policy* 31:139–153.

Vringer, Kees, and Kornelis Blok. 1995. The direct and indirect energy requirements of households in the Netherlands. *Energy Policy* 23:893–910.

Weber, Christoph, and U. Fahl. 1993. Energy consumption and satisfying their needs: An analysis with the help of the input-output calculation. (Energieverbrauch und Bedürfnisbefriedigung: Eine Analyse mit Hilfe der energetischen Input-Output-Rechnung.) *Energiewirtschaftliche Tagesfragen* 43(9):605–612.

Wei, Yi-Ming, Lan-Cui Liu, Ying Fan, and Gang Wu. 2007. The impact of lifestyle on energy use and $CO_2$ emissions: An empirical analysis of China's residents. *Energy Policy* 35:247–257.
Wier, Mette, Manfred Lenzen, Jesper Munksgaard, and Sinne Smed. 2001. Effects of household consumption patterns on CO2 requirements. *Economic Systems Research* 13(3):259–274.
Zhang, Ping, and Hong-Miao Wang. 2010. Transition of development pattern. http://www.cass .net.cn/file/20101019286008.html

# Passenger Transportation Systems in Large Chinese Cities and Life-Cycle Greenhouse Gas Emissions

**6**

RUI WANG

Chinese cities are facing serious consequences of rapid motorization, including congestion, air pollution, energy price hikes, and greenhouse gas emissions. Peak-hour speeds often drop below 15 or even 10 kilometers per hour in large cities. Numerous cities are on the list of the World Health Organization's most polluted cities. Many people attribute the oil price surge since 2007 to China's exploding appetite for energy. The fact that China is now the world's largest carbon dioxide emitter urges policy makers and researchers to scrutinize possible solutions in every sector to lower the global impacts of China's growth.

China is likely experiencing the grandest urbanization process in human history. The urbanization rate increased from 29 percent in 1995 to 45 percent in 2008, and more than 10 million new urban dwellers were added annually (NBS). This vast agglomeration process has been accompanied by dramatic changes in urban transportation activities. Residents in Chinese cities are not only traveling longer distances, but also are taking more trips and increasingly relying on modes of transportation that use fossil-fuel energy. As people in China, primarily urban residents, become wealthier, the auto ownership rate accelerates rapidly. According to the China Association of Automobile Manufactures, China became the largest market in the world for automobiles and trucks in late 2008, and more than a million autos and trucks have been sold each month since March 2009 (CAAM).

A more fearful fact is that room for future growth in mobility seems enormous. China's overall auto ownership rate was just 18 cars per 1,000 people in 2008, compared with 104 in Brazil and 213 in Russia (Haddock and Jullens 2009). Together with India, another rapidly motorizing country, which registered 11 cars per 1,000 people in 2008, China will probably produce an unprecedented global wave of motorization if its economy continues to grow. This trend is further affirmed by the infrastructure-led economic development of China. The national expressway system started to operate only in 1988, but by the end of 2001, China's national expressway system became the second-longest in the world (China Transport Statistics). By the end of 2008, total route length in operation exceeded 60,000 km, surpassing the goal in the original plan for 2010 (Ministry of Transport of the People's Republic of China 2004). The construction of highways is speeding up thanks to the government's economic stimulus plan, which started in 2009. There seems to be little doubt that the Chinese national expressway system will outgrow the U.S. interstate highway system, currently the world's largest, very soon. China's in-service urban rail transit lines reached a total of 933 km at the end of 2009. By 2015 the government plans to invest 700 billion yuan (US$102.5 billion) in urban rail construction (China Daily 2010). Presently there are 11 Chinese cities with subways, but 20 more are in the process of constructing them.

The urban transportation problems caused by rapid motorization in China and other similar emerging economies pose major challenges. If poorly constructed policies are designed and implemented, the gain in life quality for people who own cars will be compromised by the time and energy lost in congestion, and by the huge risks of global climate change. Policy makers have already been trying various solutions, such as green/intelligent transportation technologies, smart growth which tackles problems related to urban sprawl, and even demand management. However, given the uncertainty of technological progress, the high density of most Chinese cities, and the expectation that travel demand will keep expanding, one must also emphasize smart infrastructure investment. Infrastructure investment decisions are often large scale and indivisble in rapidly growing cities, especially with the Chinese government's economic stimulus focus on infrastructure. However, because of China's status as a developing country, greenhouse gas (GHG) emissions are not likely to be considered when making economic decisions in the foreseeable future as GHG is not priced. Without an economy-wide carbon price, the full picture of carbon externalities resulting from policy decisions can be revealed only through integrating climate-change effects into transportation planning decisions. Furthermore, if one believes that climate-change mitigation is critical, then infrastructure investment should be seriously scrutinized because a significant portion of life-cycle GHGs will be emitted even before the infrastructure becomes operational.

This chapter provides initial evidence for decision makers and researchers on the significance of life-cycle GHG emissions in urban transportation. In particular, it examines how big the difference is likely to be if evaluation of urban transportation systems in China shifts from consideration of operational GHG emissions to consideration of life-cycle GHG emissions.

## Two Literatures Come Together: Intermodal Comparison and Transportation Life-Cycle Analysis

The literature on intermodal comparison for urban transportation planning begins with the seminal work of Meyer, Kain, and Wohl (1965). Their research compared the capital and operating costs of rail, buses, and automobiles for commuters in typical U.S. urban corridors. They found that the relative costs of these modes depended on traffic volumes in corridors, with automobiles being the least costly in corridors with low volume, buses the least costly in intermediate- or higher-volume corridors, and rail sometimes the least costly in high-volume corridors. Their work was followed by a number of other studies. For example, Boyd, Wetzler, and Asher (1973; 1978) added traveler time cost to the comparison between rail and buses, while Keeler and Small (1975) conducted a full-cost comparison of rail, bus, and auto transportation with optimized modal investments and operations. Studies of intermodal comparison (e.g., Kain 1997; Pickrell 1990; U.S. GAO 2001) focus more on actual versus forecast system performance than on systematic but abstract comparison of aggregated costs. Generally, previous studies agree that socially optimal modal planning depends on corridor volume, but the exact volume thresholds between autos, buses, and rail remain controversial.

Life-cycle analysis attempts to provide a systematic approach to measure resource consumption and environmental releases in air, water, and soil that are associated with products, processes, and services. It takes into consideration that all product life-cycle stages (extracting and processing raw materials, manufacturing, transportation and distribution, use and reuse, and recycling and waste management) have environmental and economic impacts. Life-cycle analysis is particularly suitable for GHG emissions not only because they are largely unregulated and are not priced, but also because GHGs, unlike conventional air pollutants, have the same climate effects regardless of where they are emitted.

Transportation policies and evaluation tools, such as the Corporate Average Fuel Economy (CAFE) standards and MOBILE6, an estimation tool for mobile emissions developed by the U.S. government, have long been primarily concerned with tailpipe emissions. With the growing interest in alternative fuels and vehicle technologies, research integrating the full fuel cycle in evaluating alternative fuels or fuel-vehicle technology systems (e.g., Delucchi 2003; Hackney and de Neufville 2001; Ogden, Williams, and Larson 2004) emerged. Important evaluation/simulation tools, such as the Greenhouse Gases, Regulated Emissions, and Energy Use in Transportation model, have been developed.[1] However, most of these studies and tools focus only on automobiles rather than comparing alternative systems of passenger travel. The very few transportation life-cycle analyses of alternative modes (e.g., Cherry, Weinert, and Yang 2009) generally ignore emissions originating from infrastructure. However, if only fuel or fuel-engine life cycles are included in analyses, comparisons may favor infrastructure-intensive modes, such as rail systems.

A notable exception is Chester's dissertation (2008), which establishes a life-cycle energy/GHG inventory of major passenger modes in the United States. Not surprisingly, Chester's work finds that significant contributors to life-cycle energy consumption and GHG emissions from modes such as automobiles, buses, and rail include not only petroleum refining and vehicle manufacturing, but also infrastructure construction. It is worthwhile to summarize his results to show how emissions from other life-cycle components compare with those from the use phase, and to compare the noninfrastructure portion of Chester's results with other available estimates.

---

[1] For more information on detailed process-based evaluation tools, visit the EPA's Transportation and Climate: Tools, Analysis and Publications website: http://www.epa.gov/OTAQ/climate/publications.htm.

**TABLE 6.1**

Comparison of Operational GHG emissions in the United States and China (gCO$_2$/VMT)

|  | China | United States |
|---|---|---|
| Car | 317 | 370 |
| Bus | 2,017 | 2,480 |
| Rail | 8,211 | 1,524[a] |

SOURCES: Chester (2008); Wang (2008a).

NOTES: 1 VMT = 1.609 VKT, with vehicle defined as motor vehicle or train car.

[a]Based on a bottom-up calculation using the BART parameters.

Table 6.1 compares Chester's average operational emissions from urban passenger vehicles with typical values in China. Although on average, cars and buses emit 15 to 20 percent less GHG per vehicle mile traveled (VMT) in China than in the United States, the operation of urban rail emits more than five times as much GHG per VMT, primarily because of the dramatic difference in CO$_2$ emission factors from electricity between the San Francisco Bay Area (Chester's results are based on Bay Area Rapid Transit [BART]) and China.

Tables 6.2.a, 6.2b, and 6.2c summarize the relative energy consumption and GHG emissions of different life-cycle components of passenger cars, buses, and rail in Chester (2008) and other comparable studies in the United States and China. For passenger cars, the major nonuse life-cycle energy/GHG components are infrastructure construction, fuel production and distribution, and vehicle manufacturing. The importance of these components relative to the use phase is similar between measures of energy consumption and GHG emissions. Overall, total life-cycle energy consumption is 54.1 percent higher than that from the use phase. The corresponding difference in GHG emissions is 60.1 percent. A similar pattern is found for diesel buses, except that infrastructure construction is far less important. Total bus life-cycle energy consumption is 37 percent higher than that from the use phase, and GHG emissions are 33 percent higher. The result for rail is somewhat different. Total rail life-cycle energy consumption is 60 percent higher than that from the use phase, and GHG emissions are 57 percent higher. The major components of life-cycle energy consumption besides the use phase are infrastructure construction and fuel production and distribution. However, the fuel-cycle component is much less important in life-cycle GHG emissions. This may be due to the fact that the energy (electricity) used to operate BART is considered much less carbon intensive than the energy used to produce the system's infrastructure.

A small number of other studies (Delucchi 2003; 2005; Karman 2006) provide partial comparisons with Chester's results for passenger cars and buses. Given the complexity of life-cycle analysis, it is not surprising to see some differences in their findings; the other studies all report higher fuel and vehicle upstream emissions relative to operational emissions. The results of Delucchi and Karman are similar

**TABLE 6.2A**

Relative Importance of Life-Cycle Components in GHG Emissions and Energy Consumption for Passenger Cars

| Country and year | Chester (2008) U.S. 2005 | | Delucchi (2003) U.S. 2015 (%) | Delucchi (2005) U.S. 2010 (%) | Delucchi (2005) China 2010 (%) |
|---|---|---|---|---|---|
| | $gCO_2e$ (%) | MJ (%) | | | |
| Vehicle manufacturing | 12.2 | 11.5 | 17.4 | 19.6 | 20.2 |
| Fuel production and distribution | 16.5 | 14.2 | 27 | 22.9 | 22 |
| Vehicle operation | 100 | 100.0 | 100 | 100 | 100 |
| Vehicle parts and maintenance | 3.8 | 6.4 | | 2.8 | 2.7 |
| Infrastructure construction | 19.7 | 18.1 | | | |
| Infrastructure operation and maintenance | 2.2 | 0.9 | | | |
| Parking construction | 4.3 | 2.5 | | | |
| Parking operation and maintenance | 1.4 | 0.5 | | | |
| TOTAL | 160.1 | 154.1 | | | |

SOURCES: Chester (2008); Delucchi (2003, 2005).

NOTES: MJ = Megajoule; $gCO_2$ = grams of $CO_2$ equivalent.

**TABLE 6.2B**

Relative Importance of Life-Cycle Components in GHG Emissions and Energy Consumption for Buses

| Country and year | Chester (2008) U.S. 2005 | | Delucchi (2003) U.S. 2015 (%) | Karman (2006) Beijing 2003 (%) |
|---|---|---|---|---|
| | $gCO_2e$ (%) | MJ (%) | | |
| Vehicle manufacturing | 12.9 | 12.4 | 5.5 | 3.5 |
| Fuel production and distribution | 15.3 | 12.7 | 19 | 22 |
| Vehicle operation | 100 | 100.0 | 100 | 100 |
| Vehicle parts and maintenance | 1.8 | 1.8 | | |
| Infrastructure construction | 2.7 | 2.4 | | |
| Infrastructure operation and maintenance | 4.2 | 3.7 | | |
| TOTAL | 137 | 133 | | |

SOURCES: Chester (2008); Delucchi (2003, 2005).

NOTES: MJ = Megajoule; $gCO_2$ = grams of $CO_2$ equivalent.

primarily because they use the same life-cycle data inventory. Interestingly, Delucchi's results on the relative importance of vehicle manufacturing and fuel production and distribution compared with vehicle operation for passenger cars are very similar for the United States and China. Overall, because none of the results consider infrastructure, it is impossible to compare alternative results about full life-cycle emissions with Chester's work.

**TABLE 6.2C**

Relative Importance of Life-Cycle Components in GHG
Emissions and Energy Consumption for Rail

|  | Chester (2008) U.S. 2005 | |
|---|---|---|
|  | gCO$_2$e/VMT (%) | MJ/VMT (%) |
| Vehicle manufacturing | 2.7 | 2.7 |
| Fuel production and distribution | 3.5 | 20.4 |
| Vehicle operation | 76.1 | 82.0 |
| Vehicle parts and maintenance | 2.4 | 2.7 |
| Infrastructure construction | 44.3 | 27.3 |
| Infrastructure operation and maintenance | 18.6 | 12.1 |
| Parking construction | 9.8 | 7.0 |
| Parking operation and maintenance | 3.0 | 3.2 |
| Total operational | 100 | 100 |
| Total upstream | 60 | 57.3 |
| TOTAL | 160 | 157.3 |

SOURCES: Chester (2008).

NOTES: MJ = Megajoule; gCO$_2$ = grams of CO$_2$ equivalent.

## A Typical Large Chinese City and Its Passenger Transportation Systems

Chester's (2008) inventory study compares different technologies from a technological rather than a travel-system perspective. It is important to put such a comparison in the context of urban transportation infrastructure planning, in which transit trips are generally intermodal and should therefore be compared as part of alternative urban passenger travel systems. This study positions the infrastructure planning question in the context of China's cities by specifying the critical size of cities and typical passenger transportation systems defined by common urban land use patterns in China.

Large cities with a population between 1.5 million and 3 million (there were 26 of them in China by the end of 2007) are of particular interest for two reasons. First, 12 of the 14 cities with a population larger than 3 million have already been operating and/or constructing rail transit systems, while none of the cities with populations smaller than 1.5 million have a rail transit system plan that is close to being approved by the state for cost and ridership reasons. Second, such cities, which are generally provincial or subprovincial economic centers, are among the fastest-growing cities in population and motorization. China's rapid growth is forcing regional-center cities to invest heavily and hastily in transportation systems, often without appropriate assessment of a very diverse range of competing options. This becomes increasingly important as skyrocketing housing costs in megacities spur the growth of previously less attractive provincial capitals and prefecture-level cities. More cities are expected to enter this critical size category in the near future.

Assumptions about corridors and travel demand patterns in corridors follow the characterization of a typical large Chinese city. Besides high population density (see the international comparison in Bertaud and Malpezzi 2003), Chinese cities share certain characteristics different from many industrialized cities in market economies because of historic and institutional backgrounds, such as the socialist work unit (*danwei*) system and the urban-rural dichotomy. These characteristics include a flatter density curve, very limited low-density sprawl, and less segregated land uses because of the socialist legacy (see detailed discussions in Wang 2010a). Mixed land use dominates the central cities, but a growing number of residential communities, often in the form of high-density "superblocks," have been located at the fringe or outside the central city, usually along radial corridors connected to the central city (see, e.g., Monson 2008).

Given the preceding discussions of critical city size and structural characteristics, this study presumes that a typical large Chinese city is a circular city with a mixed-use core surrounded by a suburban belt. Most jobs and a significant share of residents are located in the core. The surrounding suburban belt consists of residential areas developed along radial corridors (see figure 6.1).

Within the critical population range of 1.5 to 3 million, specific assumptions are made about the size of the city in order to estimate reasonable traffic volumes and

**FIGURE 6.1**

Representation of a Large Chinese City and Its Corridors

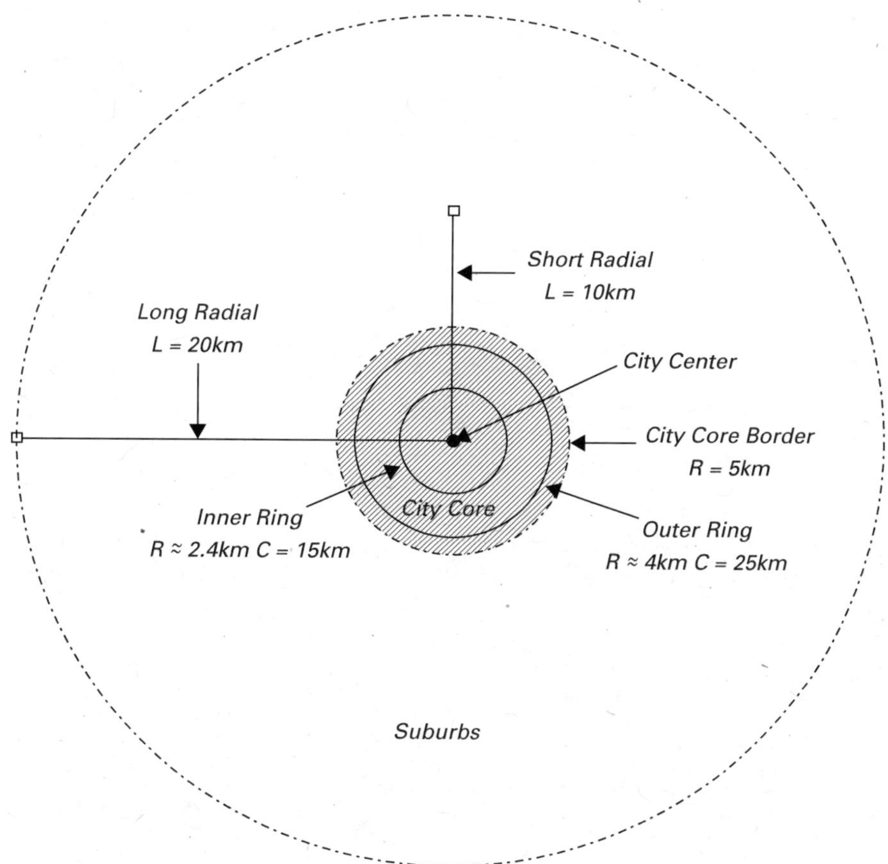

to calculate costs precisely. The population of the city is set at 2.36 million, which translates into a total built-up area of 236 km$^2$ and a central-city radius of 5 km on the basis of the typical Chinese urban population density (also consistent with the Chinese national planning guideline) and the assumption that on average, the area of a central city is one-third of the total built-up area. The city in figure 6.1 has four typical commuting corridors, two radial and two circumferential. The radial corridors serve suburban residents working within the central city, and the circumferential ring corridors serve workers living in the central city. The two radial corridors examined are 10 and 20 km in length and connect the city center to suburban residential areas. The two circumferential corridors are a 15 km inner ring approximately 2.4 km from the city center and a 25 km outer ring about 4 km from the city center. The average trip length on a radial corridor is assumed to be half the corridor length. The inbound morning traffic volume along the corridor increases linearly from zero at its suburban end to its maximum at the boundary of the central city and then decreases linearly to zero at the city center. The ring corridors have constant traffic volumes along the route during peak hours, and the average trip length on the circumferential direction is assumed to be one-fifth of the corridor length.

Four passenger modes are evaluated on each corridor: (1) heavy rail transit that uses electrically propelled multiple-unit trains operating on a fully grade-separated right-of-way that is underground within the central city and elevated outside; (2) buses that use diesel fuel and operate in mixed motor vehicle traffic on urban arterial streets; (3) gasoline cars that use urban expressways as trunk lines and local streets for collection and distribution; and (4) human-powered two-wheel bicycles operating on urban arterial and local streets. All transit modes drop off and pick up passengers over the entire route without short-term or express service. Because of the high density of Chinese cities, commuters travel between transit stations and their homes by either bicycling or walking, a choice determined by comparing the total costs of the two access modes. Also because of the high job density in the central city, it is assumed that all transit users walk between stations and their workplaces.

## A Comparison of Greenness and Full Costs of Alternative Systems

Capital, operation, user time, safety, and environmental costs are estimated for major commuting modes in a representative large Chinese city.[2] Optimal investment and operation of the modes are modeled in a more realistic fashion (e.g., through

---

[2] However, cost variations due to service reliability and levels of comfort and convenience, as reflected by the alternative-specific constants (ASCs) in discrete demand analysis, are difficult to measure. Because of the lack of good estimates of ASCs from Chinese data and the well-known difficulty in transferring estimates of ASCs (see, e.g., Small and Winston 1999), such cost variations are not explicitly accounted for. Instead, two types of measures are taken to reduce the inequality of unmeasured costs across the modes. First, vehicle specifications and loading levels are chosen so that the comfort levels of the automobile and transit modes are as close as possible. For example, all vehicles are air-conditioned, and about 70 percent of transit passengers have seats during peak hours. In addition, intermodal differences in convenience, such as the walking distance between bus and rail stations, are quantified by detailed assumptions of typical station size varying with capacity.

variable vehicle size and frequency and spatially variable highway width) than the methods applied by the previous studies such as Keeler and Small (1975).

The different costs are estimated from a variety of primary and secondary sources. Land costs are calculated according to Wang (2010b), where land prices in Chinese cities are estimated as a function of distance from the urban center, population size, and average per capita local gross domestic product (GDP) on the basis of benchmark land prices published by Chinese city governments. Capital and operating costs are estimated from actual costs for Chinese road and transit systems. Environmental and safety costs are estimated largely by adjusting estimates from the Western cities to account for higher densities and lower per capita incomes in China, as calculated by Wang (2008b). In accordance with ALMEC and Chodai (2001), Small and Verhoef (2007), and others, travelers' value of time (VOT) of riding on rail, buses, and automobiles is assumed to be 50 percent of riders' gross wage rate, while walking and waiting time are valued at 1.8 times in-vehicle time. The typical urban gross wage for large Chinese cities is roughly 12 yuan per hour (2005 prices). Given that bicycles are driven by human power and that bicyclists, like pedestrians, are directly exposed to the ambient environment, per unit time spent riding a bicycle is assumed to have the same value as walking and waiting. A real social discount rate (SDR) of 8 percent is assumed. This rate takes into account the prevailing rates of bank savings and return on investment (Tongji University and RISN 2004), as well as the common discount rate used in public project evaluations.

For transit modes, capital costs are allocated to peak-direction traffic during peak hours. An exception is the cost of road capacity used by buses operating in mixed traffic on expressways or arterial streets, which is calculated using the congestion cost caused by the buses. Cars and bicycles are typically purchased for multiple purposes and depreciate primarily with use rather than with the passage of time, so vehicle capital costs are allocated on the basis of the distance driven, assuming a fixed vehicle life in distance driven and a typical distance driven per year. By contrast, car and bicycle parking spaces depreciate little with use. The cost of a parking space at work is clearly attributable to commuting, because it would not be needed unless the employee commuted by automobile or bicycle. Because decisive motives for purchasing cars are not known, half of total residential parking costs is allocated to commuting trips. Finally, road capacity costs of automobiles are calculated using congestion costs, while those of bicycles are allocated to major-direction peak-hour travel, because the number of bicycle lanes is determined by peak demand.

Because there are insufficient data to calculate the life-cycle GHG emissions of urban passenger modes, the ratios between life-cycle and operational GHG emissions in the United States, estimated by Chester (2008), are assumed to be transferrable to China.[3] Under this assumption, relative magnitudes of carbon emissions per vehicle mile traveled among car, bus, and rail are roughly the same between

---

[3] Life-cycle environmental impacts vary by region, so it can be very difficult to compare products made in different countries. However, it would be difficult to imagine that the ratios between life-cycle and operational energy consumption and GHG emissions in China would be dramatically different from those in the United States for similar transportation technologies.

**TABLE 6.3**

Operational Versus Life-Cycle GHG Emissions per Vehicle Mile

|  | Operational Emissions (gCO$_2$e/VMT)[a] | GHG$_{life\ cycle}$ / GHG$_{operational}$ [b] | Estimated Life-Cycle Emissions (gCO$_2$e/VMT) |
|---|---|---|---|
| Car | 317 | 160.1% | 508 |
| Bus | 2,017 | 137% | 2,763 |
| Rail | 8,211 | 160% | 13,138 |

NOTES: [a]Calculations based on Wang (2008a).

[b] From tables 6.2a, 6.2b, and 6.2c; calculations based on Chester (2008).

**TABLE 6.4**

GHG Emissions per Passenger at Capacity and at Average Occupancy

|  | GHG Emissions per Passenger at Capacity | | GHG Emissions per Passenger at Average Occupancy | | |
|---|---|---|---|---|---|
|  | Capacity[a] | Operational (gCO$_2$e/PMT) | Life cycle (gCO$_2$e/PMT) | Occupancy[a] (peak/off-peak/ avg.) | Operational (gCO$_2$e/PMT) | Life Cycle (gCO$_2$e/PMT) |
| Car | 5 | 63.4 | 101.6 | 1.2/1.6/1.4 | 226.4 | 362.9 |
| Bus | 55 | 36.7 | 50.2 | 55/22/39 | 51.7 | 70.8 |
| Rail | 121 | 67.9 | 108.6 | 121/48/85 | 96.6 | 154.6 |

NOTE: [a]Transit capacity and average occupancies are from Wang (2008a; 2008b).

SOURCE: Author's calculations based on Chester (2008).

the use phase and life cycle, as shown in table 6.3. However, if one takes into consideration the difference in vehicle occupancy (as estimated/assumed in Wang 2008a), the relative magnitudes of carbon intensities change. Buses become the least carbon-intensive mode per passenger-kilometer traveled, while passenger cars are the most carbon-intensive mode at typical occupancy rates, as shown in table 6.4.

Because of the tremendous inherent uncertainty of global climate change, alternative costs of GHG emissions in CO$_2$ equivalence (CO$_2$e) are considered in comparison with the climate-change costs and other economic costs of urban passenger transportation. On the lower end, in accordance with the results of Nordhaus (2006) and Nordhaus and Boyer (2000), which are consistent with many other economic assessments (e.g., Mendelsohn et al. 1998; Pearce 2005), the discounted cost of current carbon dioxide emissions over their expected 100-year atmospheric life is set at $20 per metric ton of carbon ($20/tC in 2005). On the higher end, the cost is set at $300/tC, a number close to the result of Stern (2006), which puts total damages from future warming at 5 percent to 20 percent of global GDP and recommends a current social cost equivalent of $311/tC. A medium value of $50/tC is chosen, as suggested by the meta-analysis of Richard Tol (2005) as a current upper-bound cost. Using the alternative carbon prices and estimates of other costs in Wang (2008b), table 6.5 compares the major types of external costs per Vehicle-kilometers traveled (VKT) by mode. Even with a low carbon price of

**TABLE 6.5**

Comparison of Major Social Costs of Urban Passenger Modes (in 2005 yuan cent/VKT)

| | Air Pollution | Noise | Safety | Climate Change | | | | | |
| | | | | $20/tC | | $50/tC | | $300/tC | |
| | | | | Operational | Life Cycle | Operational | Life Cycle | Operational | Life Cycle |
|---|---|---|---|---|---|---|---|---|---|
| Car | 2.5 | 0.7 | 14.0 | 2.2 | 3.6 | 5.6 | 8.9 | 33.4 | 53.5 |
| Bus | 8.9 | 1.8 | 63.0 | 14.2 | 19.4 | 35.4 | 48.5 | 212.5 | 291.2 |
| Rail | 0.0 | 0.0 | 15.8 | 57.7 | 92.3 | 144.2 | 230.8 | 865.3 | 1,384.5 |
| Bicycle | 0.0 | 0.0 | 63.0 | | | | | | |
| Walking | 0.0 | 0.0 | 75.6 | | | | | | |

NOTE: Air-pollution, noise, and safety costs are from Wang (2008a).

SOURCE: Author's calculations based on Chester (2008).

$20/tC, climate-change cost estimates are significant compared with the costs of air pollution, noise, and accidents.

Table 6.6 breaks down costs per passenger-kilometer traveled (PKT) for three urban passenger travel modal systems: rail, bus, and car. These costs occur on the short radial corridor at a one-way maximum-load-point volume of 10,000 passengers per hour (pph), an intermediate peak volume for major corridors in large Chinese cities.

One can see from table 6.6 that even with a carbon price as high as $300/tC, per PKT social costs of climate change are still far smaller than capital costs of all three modes. The climate-change costs are also smaller than the operating costs and commuters' time costs, though in some cases the life-cycle climate-change costs can be comparable. To understand systematically how life-cycle GHG costs can affect intermodal full-cost comparisons, figures 6.2a through 6.2d simulate the cost curves of four modal systems (rail, car, bus, and bicycle) for the four typical corridors. Demand volumes range from 1,000 to 50,000 pph at the one-way maximum load point.

For modes with significant fixed infrastructure investment, such as rail, the costs per PKT decline with passenger volume because of indivisibilities in capital investments. The results show that an automobile is never the least expensive mode regardless of corridor type or traffic volume. Among the transit modes, rail is always more expensive than buses, especially at lower passenger volumes, because of large fixed capital investments. Overall, the least expensive mode is either bicycles or buses, depending on passenger volume and corridor type.

Results for the ring corridors are somewhat different from those for the radial corridors. Transit modes are more competitive than individual modes on ring corridors. One important source of the differences is that passenger loads are more balanced on the ring corridors than on the radial corridors. On ring corridors, passengers travel in both directions during mornings and evenings. In contrast, on radial corridors, passengers travel mainly inbound in the morning and mainly outbound in the evening. In addition, on ring corridors, passengers can be assumed

**TABLE 6.6**

Baseline Full Commuting Cost on the Short Radial Corridor (in 2005 Yuan/PKT)

|  |  |  | Car | Bus | Rail |
|---|---|---|---|---|---|
| Land |  |  | 0.39 | 0.19 | 0.06 |
| Structure |  |  | 0.62 | 0.13 | 1.29 |
| Parking[a] |  |  | 1.80 | n/a | n/a |
| Equipment |  |  | n/a | 0.10 | 0.84 |
| Vehicle |  |  | 1.16 | 0.61 | 0.69 |
|   Capital |  |  | 3.97 | 1.02 | 2.88 |
|   Operating |  |  | 0.69 | 0.28 | 0.65 |
| Line-haul time |  |  | 0.27 | 0.51 | 0.28 |
| Access time[b] |  |  | n/a | 0.76 | 0.94 |
|   Time |  |  | 0.27 | 1.27 | 1.22 |
| Safety |  |  | 0.12 | 0.04 | 0.01 |
| Air pollution |  |  | 0.02 | 0.00 | 0.00 |
| Noise |  |  | 0.01 | 0.00 | 0.00 |
| Climate change | $20/tC | Operational | 0.02 | 0.00 | 0.01 |
|  |  | Life cycle | 0.03 | 0.00 | 0.01 |
|  | $50/tC | Operational | 0.04 | 0.01 | 0.02 |
|  |  | Life cycle | 0.06 | 0.01 | 0.03 |
|  | $300/tC | Operational | 0.24 | 0.05 | 0.10 |
|  |  | Life cycle | 0.38 | 0.07 | 0.16 |

NOTES: Costs other than those of life-cycle climate change are from Wang (2008a). Life-cycle climate change costs are author's calculations based on Chester (2008).

[a]Only workplace parking costs are included here.

[b]Mode to access transit station is chosen by transit users between walking and bicycling depending on distance. Thus, access costs include mainly time costs and possibly a small share of bicycle capital and parking costs. For downtown distribution from transit stations, walking is presumed to be the only mode. For simplicity, "access time" is used to represent the total access costs.

to get both on and off at uniform rates along the corridor, while on radial corridors passengers board in the suburbs and alight in the city core in the morning, with a reverse pattern in the evening. Such unbalanced loads increase the costs of all modes on radial corridors, but they exert a stronger effect on the costs of rail and buses than on the costs of automobiles or bicycles, because bicycles and automobiles can start and stop where the passenger's trip does, whereas the railcar or bus often operates with many empty seats at the beginning or end of a radial corridor and in the less used direction. As a result, the automobile is sometimes more cost effective than rail at very low volumes on radial corridors, but it is never less expensive than rail on ring corridors. Similarly, a bicycle is the least expensive mode at low to medium volumes on radial corridors, but not on ring corridors.

Given the small costs of GHG emissions relative to other economic costs of urban travel, it is not surprising to find very marginal differences among the simulation results when alternative carbon prices are used, as well as when life-cycle GHG emissions replace operational GHG emissions.

## Full-Cost Comparison on the Inner Ring Corridor

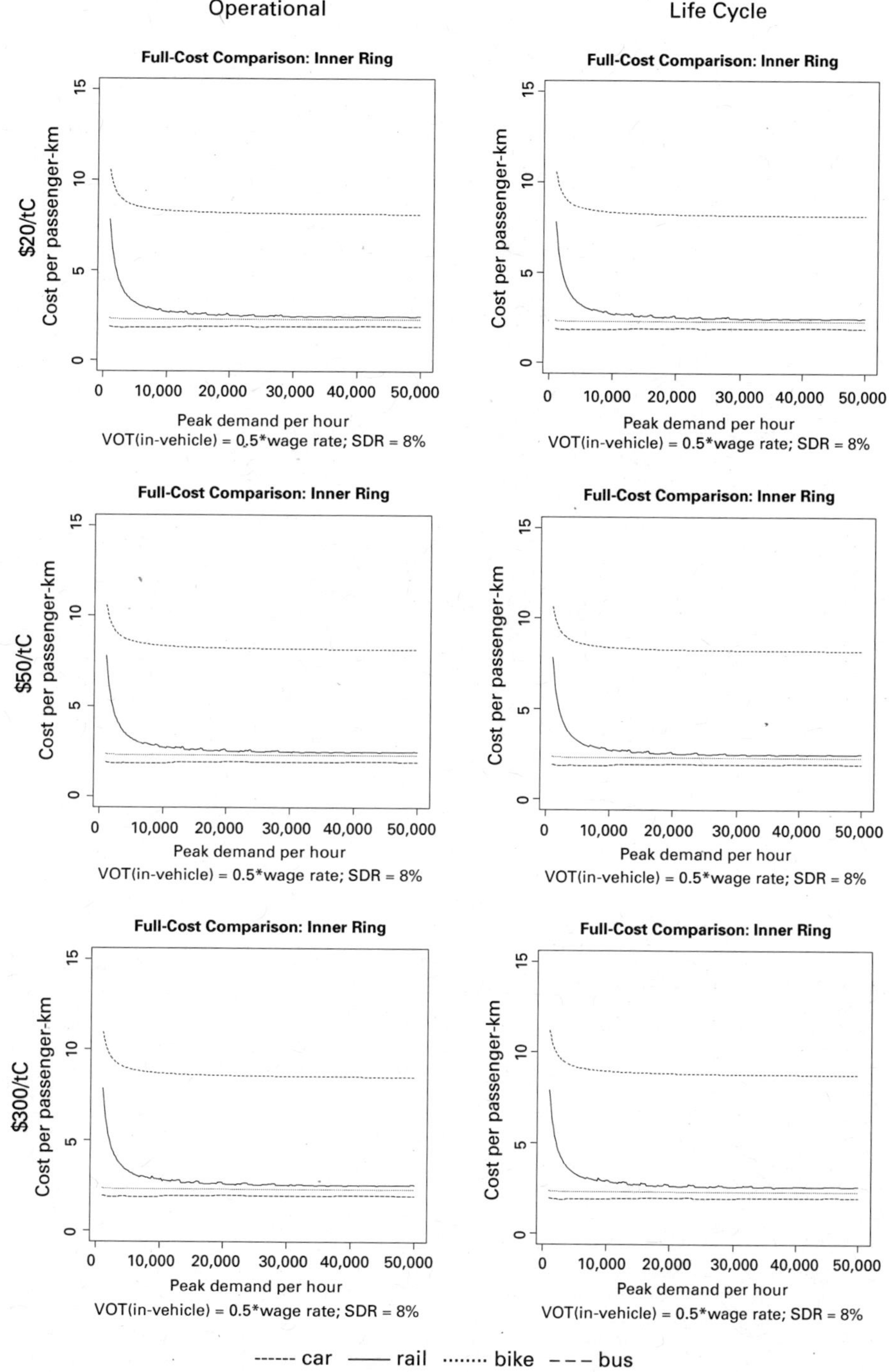


SOURCE: Wang (2008a).

## Full-Cost Comparison on the Outer Ring Corridor

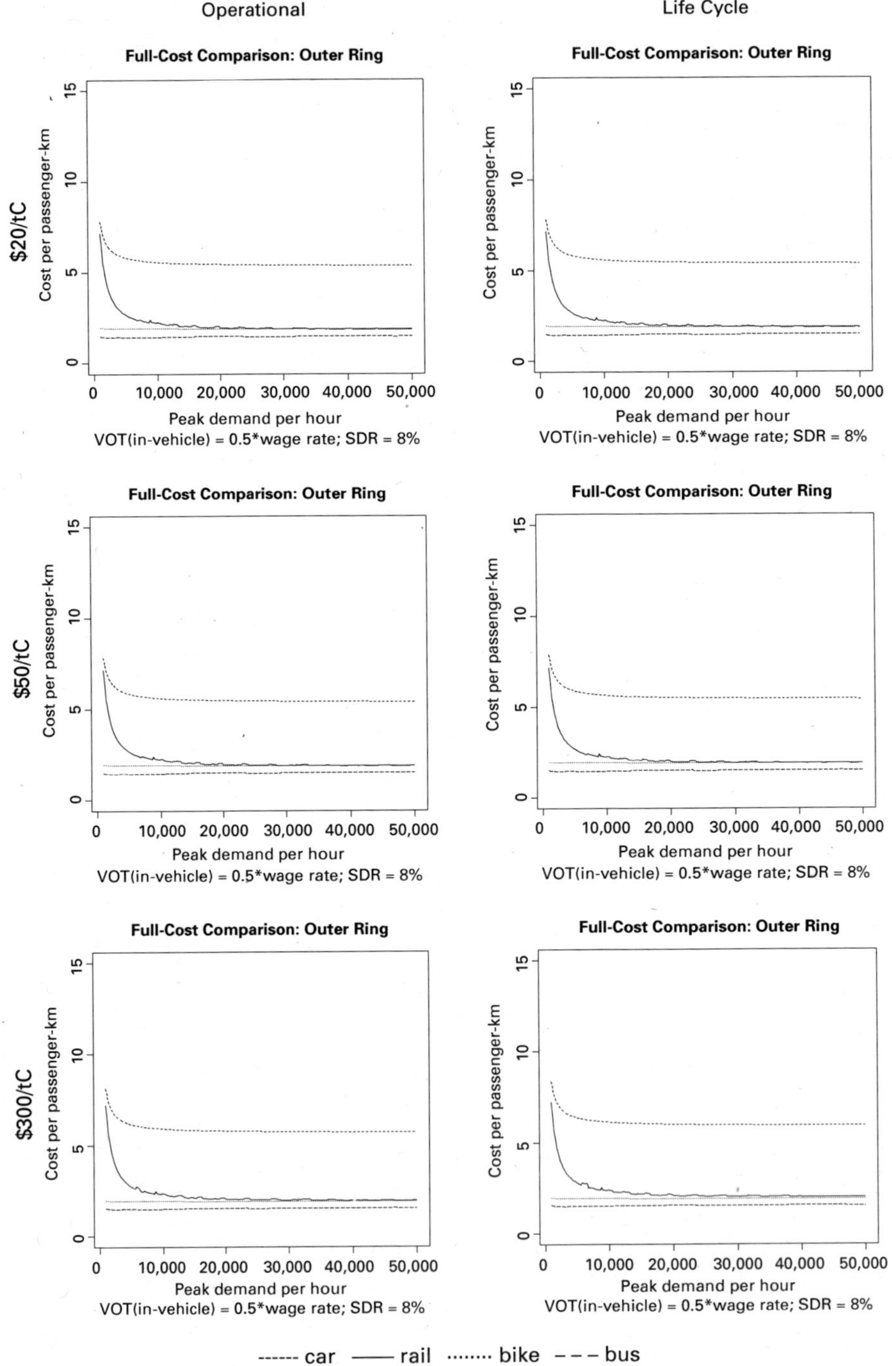


SOURCE: Wang (2008a).

# Full-Cost Comparison on the Short Radial Corridor

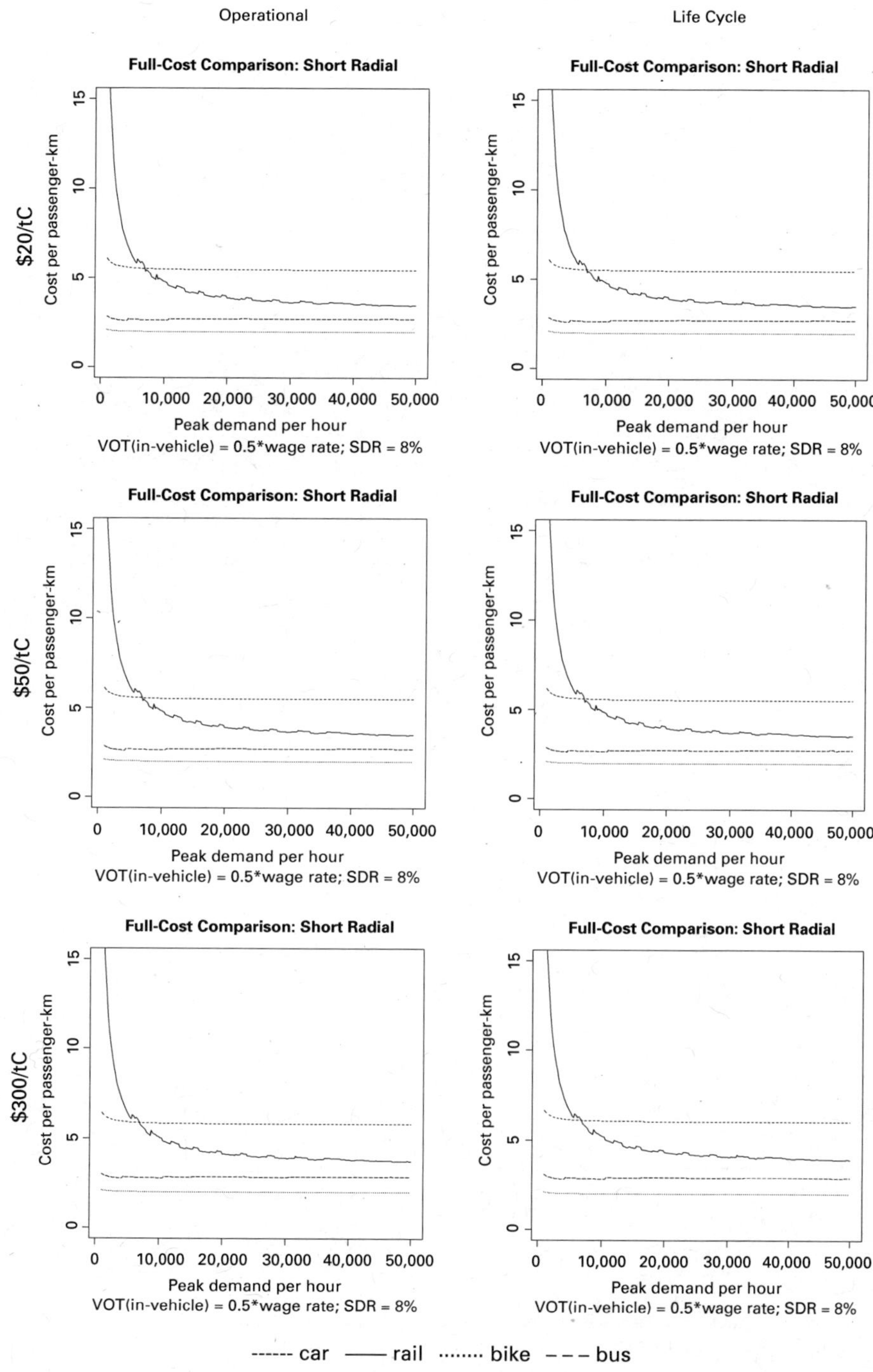


SOURCE: Wang (2008a).

## Full-Cost Comparison on the Long Radial Corridor

Operational | Life Cycle

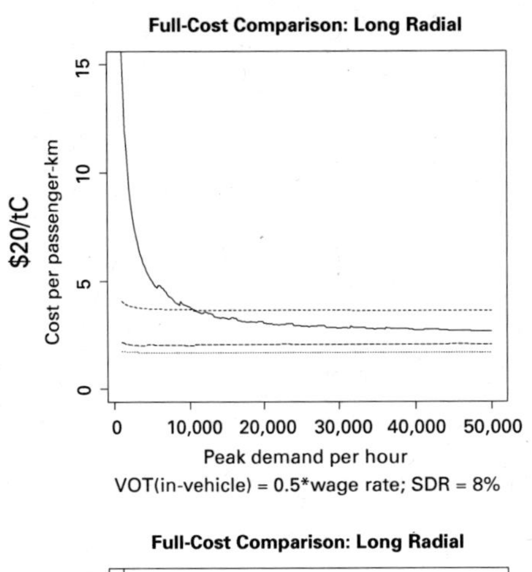
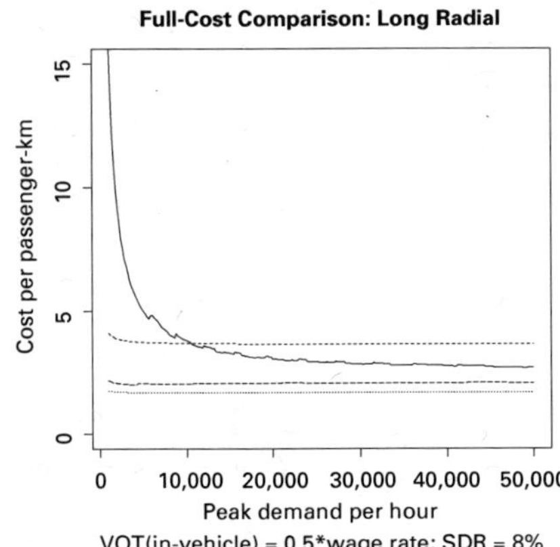
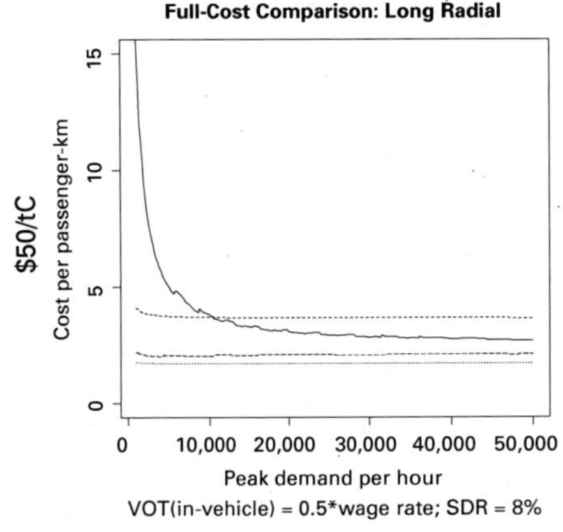
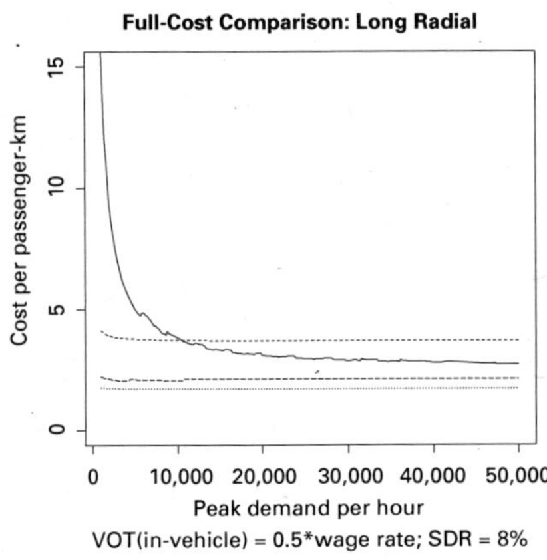
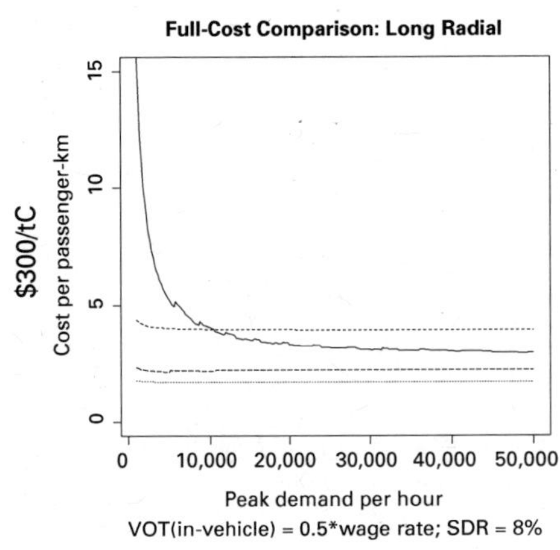
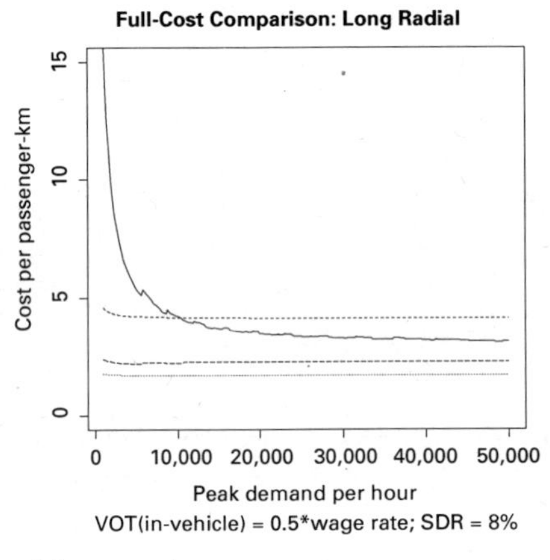



SOURCE: Wang (2008a).

## Do Greener Modes Cost Less?

The full-cost intermodal comparison in a typical large Chinese city shows that in most circumstances, commuting by bus or bicycle has lower social costs than car or rail. Unlike results from similar studies conducted in the United States, passenger-car transportation is not more cost effective than bus transportation at low traffic volumes. In particular, for decision makers, this study shows that (1) neither a high carbon price nor life-cycle accounting is likely to make a difference when the full costs of alternative urban passenger transportation systems are compared; and (2) bicycles are the greenest and most cost-effective option for radial commuting corridors, especially when trip length is relatively short. However, bicycles are not as competitive as buses on ring corridors in the dense central city because of safety issues and parking costs and the balanced loads between the two directions of transit service. To some extent, this supports the policy adopted by some Chinese cities to convert bicycle lanes on congested urban streets into bus priority lanes, because such policies may increase corridor capacity, control safety hazards, and save space occupied by bicycle parking. Buses are the greenest motorized mode and are more desirable costwise than rail in large Chinese cities, a result that echoes that of Keeler and Small (1975) for the United States. Nevertheless, it should be noted that the difference between rail and bus is not always very significant. On ring corridors, the costs of rail and bus modes appear to be much closer than on radial corridors, particularly under medium to high volumes. It is difficult to justify the use of cars as a major commuting mode in large Chinese cities even at volumes well below 5,000 pph.

Because of the lack of a complete transportation life-cycle inventory in China, U.S. results on urban transportation life-cycle energy consumption and GHG emissions have been applied. This is a quick way to test the potential difference that life-cycle GHG accounting can make in intermodal comparisons. These results are likely reliable because climate-change costs are shown to be much smaller than other economic costs of urban travel, even with the assumption of a very high carbon price. However, potential biases exist. Because the carbon intensity of electricity is significantly lower in the United States (especially the San Francisco Bay Area) than in China,[4] using the life-cycle/operational GHG emissions ratios from the United States may overestimate the true ratio for rail in China (Chester 2008). In addition, Chinese urban rail systems are built with many fewer parking spaces than BART. The number of public parking spaces per car is also likely to be fewer in Chinese cities because of higher density. These factors may also contribute to overestimation of the ratios for rail and cars in Chinese cities. However, such adjustments may still be secondary to the differences found for other economic costs among the modes, and it is hard to imagine that a locally constructed life-cycle analysis would be incongruous with the basic results presented in this chapter.

Overall, it seems that the intermodal comparison of full economic costs in this chapter agrees with the carbon-intensity comparison among rail, cars, buses, and

---

[4] It is estimated that $CO_2$ emission factors (internationally, in $gCO_2/MJ$) are 67 for gasoline and 69 for diesel, while the averages for electricity are 80 in the United States, 169 in the Bay Area, and 236 in China. Chester 2008.

bicycles in China. The greenest modes, buses and bicycles, are also the most socially desirable modes in a typical large Chinese city, although rail may rank closely when high passenger volumes on both directions of a corridor exist. This differs from the situation in U.S. cities, where the automobile can be the least socially costly way to travel when travel volume is low, but can hardly be claimed as the greenest mode compared with rail and buses under typical occupancy rates, especially for commuting trips.

## References


ALMEC Corporation and Chodai Co., Ltd (ALMEC and Chodai). 2001. *Study for public transportation improvement in Chengdu City in the People's Republic of China: Final report*. Tokyo: Japan International Cooperation Agency.

Bertaud, Alain, and Steven Malpezzi. 2003. The spatial distribution of population in 48 world cities: Implications for economies in transition. Working Paper. Madison: Center for Urban Land Economics Research at the University of Wisconsin, Madison.

Boyd, J. Hayden, Elliot Wetzler, Norman J. Asher. 1973. *Evaluation of rail rapid transit and express bus service in the urban commuter market*. DOT-P-6520.1. Washington, DC: U.S. Department of Transportation, Institute for Defense Analyses.

———. 1978. Non-technological innovation in urban transit: A comparison of some alternatives. *Journal of Urban Economics* 5:1–20.

Cherry, Christopher R., Jonathan X. Weinert, Yang Xinmiao. 2009. Comparative environmental impacts of electric bikes in China. *Transportation Research, Part D* 14:281–290.

Chester, Mikhail V. 2008. Life-cycle environmental inventory of passenger transportation modes in the United States. Ph.D. diss., University of California, Berkeley.

China Association of Automobile Manufactures (CAAM). http://www.caam.org.cn/

China Daily. 2010. China's Subway Reaches 933 km in 2009. March 19. http://www.chinadaily.com.cn/china/2010-03/19/content_9611211.htm

China's Transport Statistics. http://www.jttj.gov.cn

Delucchi, Mark A. 2003. A lifecycle emissions model (LEM): Lifecycle emissions from transportation fuels, motor vehicles, transportation modes, electricity use, heating and cooking fuels, and materials. Working Paper. Davis: Institute of Transportation Studies, University of California at Davis.

———. 2005. A multi-country analysis of lifecycle emissions from transportation fuels and motor vehicles. Working Paper. Davis: Institute of Transportation Studies, University of California at Davis.

Hackney, Jeremy, and Richard de Neufville. 2001. Life cycle model of alternative fuel vehicles: Emissions, energy, and cost trade-offs. *Transportation Research, Part A: Policy and Practice* 35(3):243–266.

Haddock, Ronald, and John Jullens. 2009. The best years of the auto industry are still to come. *Strategy+Business* 55:2–20.

Kain, John F. 1997. Cost-effective alternatives to Atlanta's costly rail transit system. *Journal of Transportation Economics and Policy* 31(1):25–50.

Karman, Deniz. 2006. Life-Cycle Analysis of GHG Emissions for CNG and Diesel Buses in Beijing, EIC Climate Change Technology Conference, Ottawa, (May 9–12).

Keeler, Theodore E., and Kenneth A. Small. 1975. The full costs of urban transportation, part III: Automobile costs and final intermodal cost comparisons. Berkeley: Institute of Urban and Regional Development, University of California, Berkeley.

Mendelsohn, Robert, Wendy Morrison, Michael E. Schlesinger, and Natalia G. Andronova. 1998. Country-specific market impacts of climate change. *Climatic Change* 45:553–569.

Meyer, John R., John F. Kain, and Martin Wohl. 1965. *The urban transportation problem*. Cambridge, MA: Harvard University Press.

Ministry of Transportation of the People's Republic of China. 2004. National Expressway Network Plan. www.moc.gov.cn

Monson, Kjersti. 2008. String block vs superblock patterns of dispersal in China. *Architectural Design* 78(1):46–53.

National Bureau of Statistics (NBS). Multiple years. *China statistical yearbook*. http://www.stats.gov.cn/english/statisticaldata/yearlydata/

Nordhaus, William D. 2006. Life after Kyoto: Alternative approaches to global warming policies. *American Economic Review* 96:31–34.

Nordhaus, William D., and Joseph Boyer. 2000. *Warming the world: Economic models of global warming*. Cambridge, MA: MIT Press.

Ogden, Joan M., Robert H. Williams, Eric D. Larson. 2004. Societal lifecycle costs of cars with alternative fuels/engines. *Energy Policy* 32(1):7–27.

Pearce, David. 2005. The social cost of carbon. In *Climate-change policy*, ed. Dieter Helm, 99–133. Oxford: Oxford University Press.

Pickrell, Don. H. 1990. *Urban rail transit projects: Forecast versus actual ridership and costs*. Washington, DC: U.S. Department of Transportation.

Small, Kenneth A., and Erik T. Verhoef. 2007. *The economics of urban transportation*. London and New York: Routledge.

Small, Kenneth A. and Winston, Clifford. 1999. The demand for transportation: Models and applications. In *Essays in transportation economics and policy: A handbook in honor of John R. Meyer*, ed. Jose A. Gomez-Ibanez, William B. Tye, and Clifford Winston, 11–55. Washington, DC: Brookings.

Stern, Nicholas. 2006. *Stern review: The economics of climate change*. Cambridge, U.K.: Cambridge University Press.

Tol, Richard S. J. 2005. The marginal damage costs of carbon dioxide emissions: An assessment of the uncertainties. *Energy Policy* 33:2064–2074.

Tongji University and Research Institute of Standards and Norms, Ministry of Construction (Tongji University and RISN). 2004. *Research on governmental investment project economic evaluation method and parameters*. [In Chinese.] Beijing: China Planning Press.

U.S. Environmental Protection Agency (U.S. EPA). Transportation and climate: Tools, analysis and publications website. http://www.epa.gov/OTAQ/climate/publications.htm

U.S. General Accounting Office (U.S. GAO). 2001. *Mass transit: Bus rapid transit shows promise*. Washington, DC: United States General Accounting Office.

Wang, Rui. 2008a. Autos, transit and bicycles: Transportation choices in Chinese cities. Ph.D. diss., Harvard University.

———. 2008b. Environmental and safety costs of urban passenger transportation modes in China. Paper presented at the 87th annual meeting of the Transportation Research Board, Washington, DC (January 13–17).

———. 2010a. Shaping urban transportation policies in China: Will copying foreign policies work? *Transportation Policy* 17:147–152.

———. 2010b. The structure of Chinese urban land prices: Estimates from benchmark land price data. *Journal of Real Estate Finance and Economics* 39(1):24–38.

# Green Urban Planning

# The Greenness of China's Cities

## Air Pollution and Household Greenhouse Gas Emissions

MATTHEW E. KAHN

China's booming economy has attracted worldwide attention. At the same time the international media detail the scale of economic growth in China's cities, there is a steady drumbeat of pessimistic popular articles highlighting the costs of this growth for quality of life (Pomfret and Norton 2009; Spotts 2009). China's cities have some of the highest pollution levels in the world. China's road traffic is notorious, and China's economy now accounts for roughly 25 percent of the world's greenhouse gas emissions. Environmentalists remain concerned that China's sharp growth, urbanization, motorization, and coal endowments all foreshadow worsening pollution challenges.

The claim that urban economic growth damages the quality of life in cities is a recurring theme (Tolley 1974). When Marx and Engels laid out their critique of nineteenth-century industrial British cities, they pointed to the factory towns' long hours, the safety risks, the pollution, and the resulting high levels of infant mortality as evidence that capitalism's high wages overstated the well-being of urban workers. Although economic historians have disputed this "satanic cities" claim (see Williamson 1981), a visit to Pittsburgh in the 1950s would have highlighted the day-to-day consequences for quality of life from relying on steel production as the engine of growth. Today, many of China's cities are grappling with similar issues because their economic growth has been fueled by pollution-intensive manufacturing industries, and electricity is supplied by dirty coal-fired power plants.

The empirical urban economics literature has documented that big cities suffer from more pollution, crime, and traffic congestion than smaller cities (Glaeser 1998; Glaeser and Sacerdote 1999; Kahn 1999; 2010). Much of this literature has focused on estimating cross-sectional relationships by using data from the United States for cities of different sizes. Henderson (2002a) is an exception. He uses a cross-national data set to document that in poorer nations, fast city growth rates raise child mortality rates, reduce access to potable water, and increase school class size. This chapter contributes to this literature by examining the pollution consequences of city bigness in China. It uses city-level data from 2003 to 2007 for 35 major cities to report estimates of the relationship between city size and pollution and to document pollution time trends.

Nonmarket urban amenities are likely to grow in importance to Chinese urbanites as household income and educational attainment rise. Costa and Kahn (2003; 2004) document that the demand for these nonmarket amenities increases with household income. Zheng, Kahn, and Liu (2010) present some evidence that across China's cities, the hedonic price premium for clean air is rising.

Ambient air pollution is only one measure of a city's greenness. Given the paramount importance of climate change, production of greenhouse gas emissions is an important indicator of environmental performance. At the national level, it is well known that the United States produces far more greenhouse gas emissions per capita than China, but that China's amazing growth has closed this gap. This chapter also presents new evidence on how the size of the average Chinese household's greenhouse gas footprint differs across major cities.

## Air Pollution in Major Chinese Cities

A city's emissions level at a point in time is a function of scale, composition, and technique effects. Scale refers to a city's population size and per capita income. Composition and technique refer to the types of activities in which the local economy specializes. A heavy-manufacturing city with one million people will have a higher emissions level than a high-tech city of the same size. Technique refers to the quality of the capital stock. All else equal, cities with a newer vehicle fleet, newer buildings, and newer power plants are likely to have lower pollution levels. Vernon Henderson's world cities database covering the years 1960 to 2000 to highlight the growth of China's cities during this period. Coastal cities have experienced most of the growth (Henderson 2002b).

Because of the ongoing population and income growth of China's cities, urban air pollution can improve only if there is a major composition shift and an improvement in techniques. If nearby power plants transitioned from using coal to natural gas or if the economic activity in cities switched from manufacturing industries to service industries, these composition shifts would significantly contribute to improving local air quality. If one controls for a city's scale and composition of economic activity, the introduction of new cleaner capital can offset much of the pollution impact (Chow 2010). Using a sample of 35 major Chinese cities (the same ones used in this chapter), Zheng, Kahn, and Liu (2010) document a negative correlation between per capita foreign direct investment (FDI) and local air pollution. An explanation for this negative correlation might be that such investments lead to a modernization of the capital stock and hence a greener technique.

To provide some new information about urban ambient air pollution in China, this chapter examines city-level data from 2003 to 2007 for 30 major Chinese cities. Pollution levels of particulate matter less than 10 microns in diamater ($PM_{10}$) and

**FIGURE 7.1**

Ambient Sulfur Dioxide Levels Across China's Major Cities

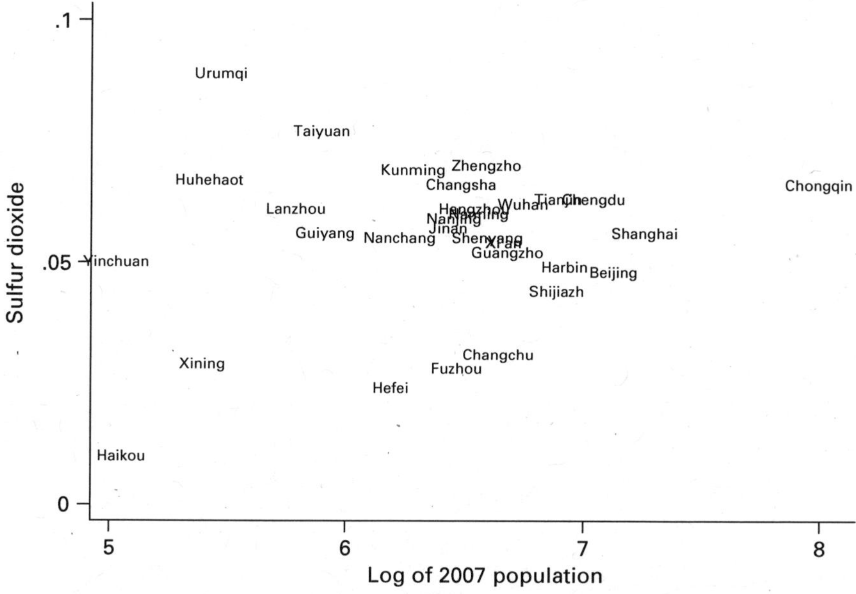




sulfur dioxide ($SO_2$) are noted in figure 7.1. The data are from the *Chinese Statistical Yearbook.* The estimation equation for city $j$ in year $t$ is

$$\text{Log (Ambient Pollutant}_{jt}) = c + b_1 * \log(\text{Population}_{jt}) + b_2 * X_j + U_{jt} \tag{1}$$

Table 7.1 reports two ordinary least squares estimates of equation (1). The table reports the regression coefficients and the t-statistics for each coefficient. The public health literature has documented that exposure to particulate matter and sulfur dioxide raises both morbidity and mortality risks. As shown in table 7.1, the particulate elasticity with respect to population is .16 and is .23 for sulfur dioxide. This indicates that if a city's temperature and the calendar year are held constant, a city with a 10 percent higher population has 2 percent worse local air-pollution levels. All else equal, warmer cities have lower air-pollution levels. A standard deviation increase in average city temperature is associated with a 15 percent reduction in particulate matter. Such warmer cities are likely to be burning less coal for winter heating. If one controls for a city's temperature and population size, the time trend reveals good news. Particulate matter is declining by 5.9 percent per year, and sulfur dioxide is declining by 3.2 percent per year (these estimates are not statistically significant).

Although China's cities have high absolute levels of air pollution, this progress is especially notable in comparison with the United States. Kahn (2010) uses U.S. data for monitoring stations in urban counties and a sample covering the years 1973 and 2000. The sample includes counties in metropolitan areas that have at

**TABLE 7.1**
Urban Exposure to Pollution and Climate
by Calendar Year

| Year | $PM_{10}$ | $SO_2$ | Temperature |
|---|---|---|---|
| 1996 | | | 13.734 |
| 1997 | | | 13.745 |
| 1998 | | | 13.807 |
| 1999 | | | 13.810 |
| 2000 | | | 13.875 |
| 2001 | | | 13.918 |
| 2002 | | | 13.999 |
| 2003 | 0.123 | 0.059 | 14.005 |
| 2004 | 0.119 | 0.060 | 14.037 |
| 2005 | 0.110 | 0.057 | 14.082 |
| 2006 | 0.111 | 0.054 | 14.331 |
| 2007 | 0.106 | 0.055 | 14.268 |

NOTE: This table uses information on 30 major Chinese cities' ambient pollution and average celsius temperature levels. In each calendar year, a weighted average is calculated using the city's population as the weight. Pollution is measured in milligrams per cubic meter.

SOURCE: National Bureau of Statistics of China (NBS) (Mutiple Years).

**TABLE 7.2**
Ambient Pollution Levels as a Function of City Characteristics

| | log ($pm_{10}$) | | log($so_2$) | |
|---|---|---|---|---|
| | Beta | t-stat | beta | t-stat |
| log (temperature) | −0.034 | −3.010 | −0.025 | −0.910 |
| log (city population) | 0.155 | 2.580 | 0.228 | 1.750 |
| time trend | −0.059 | −5.200 | −0.032 | −0.990 |
| constant | −2.498 | −10.020 | −3.882 | −6.660 |
| observations | 150 | | 150 | |
| $R^2$ | 0.419 | | 0.111 | |

NOTE: The sample include 30 Chinese cities and covers the years 2003 to 2007. The unit of analysis is a city/year. The *t*-statistics are adjusted for city-level clustering.

least one monitoring station operating. When population levels of counties are controlled for, ambient urban $PM_{10}$ levels have fallen by 3.2 percent.

China's local air-pollution progress during a time of sharp economic growth represents the ultimate test of the environmental Kuznets curve (EKC) hypothesis. As introduced by Grossman and Krueger (1995), this hypothesis posits a non-monotonic inverted U such that economic development first damages the environment, but past some turning point, economic development contributes to a cleaner environment (Grossman and Krueger 1995; Harbaugh, Levinson, and Wilson 2002). The conventional wisdom, based on cross-national studies such as those of Grossman and Krueger (1995); Harbaugh, Levinson, and Wilson (2002); and Hilton and Levinson (1998); is that the turning point differs by pollutant, but averages roughly US$8,000 in 1990s dollars.[1] As highlighted by Harbaugh, Levinson, and Wilson (2002), the very existence of a turning point based on cross-national data continues to be debated.

Although per capita income levels in China's cities are not close to the traditional turning-point estimates, Zheng, Kahn, and Liu (2010) use data for 30 major Chinese cities and find that the income turning point for the $PM_{10}$ curve is RMB15.95 thousand yuan per year per capita (roughly US$2,500), and that for $SO_2$ it is RMB16.58 thousand yuan. As of the year 2006, eight Chinese cities had per capita incomes that exceeded these turning points. This is encouraging evidence that ongoing growth in Chinese cities may help improve urban air pollution levels.

Effective government regulation is likely to have played a key role in generating this recent progress. Chow (2010) provides specifics about China's recent environmental policy initiatives. He emphasizes that the Chinese government seeks to mitigate local pollution problems because damage is localized. He is optimistic about the implementation of China's environmental policies because he sees a strong resolve of the central government, which has the power to enforce such laws and the willingness to offer incentives to green the economy. Future work should attempt to separate the individual causal roles of different regulatory initiatives.

As discussed in Chow (2010), China's 11th Five-Year Plan introduced explicit financial incentives to encourage coal-fired power plants to reduce their emissions. The policy was called the "desulfurized electricity price premium." After installing an $SO_2$ scrubber, a coal power plant was allowed to sell its electricity to the electric grid at a price of RMB15 yuan per megawatt hour higher than the original price if its $SO_2$ was under normal operation, but it would be fined RMB75 yuan (roughly US$10 per megawatt hour) if its $SO_2$ scrubber were shut down (Chow 2010). The price premium was introduced in 2004, and the penalty was introduced in July 2007.

This deregulation was introduced during a time of sharp economic growth. Perhaps surprisingly, a communist government turned to pollution pricing mechanisms rather than more traditional command-and-control regulations that require that specific technologies be deployed. The J curve for environmental regulation (Selden and S. Daqing 1995) posits that richer nations will enact more effective regulations because of the median voter's rising demand for public goods. China offers a fascinating test case of this claim. Rising educational attainment in China is likely to lead the urban middle class to demand a greening of cities. The beautification of Beijing in preparation for the 2008 Olympics Games may represent an ongoing trend.

Changes in the Chinese land and housing markets also create interest groups with a stake in promoting green cities. As more urban Chinese households become

---

[1] The definition of this turning point is the level of income such that the slope of the relationship between pollution and per capita income equals zero (the top of the hill). One of the simplest examples of this phenomenon is presented in Hilton and Levinson's (1998) compelling study of lead emissions across nations. As poor nations get richer, they consume more gasoline, but they drive with leaded gasoline, so total lead emissions rise. However, beyond a per capita income of US$8,000, nations enact laws mandating unleaded gasoline, and declining lead emissions per gallon offset continued increasing gasoline consumption. The net effect of this quality upgrade is that lead emissions decline in richer nations.

property owners, they will have a financial stake in policies that improve quality of life because the theory of compensating differentials predicts that real estate will sell for a premium. Given that local government officials in China collect a significant portion of their revenues from land auctions, they will also have an incentive to provide green cities because those parcels that are the most desirable will sell for higher prices in the auction.

Anticipated improvements in the quality of life of Chinese cities should have immediate benefits by making these cities stronger. Attracting and retaining skilled workers is the key to urban growth. Skilled workers value quality of life, and environmental quality is a key components of quality of life.[2]

It is interesting to note that China's cities appear to be following a roughly similar path to that of U.S. cities in fighting the battle against urban air pollution. During the twentieth century, urban air pollution in the United States increased and reached its peak in the 1960s before starting to fall sharply in the early 1970s. Beijing has enacted tough Euro IV emissions standards for new vehicles. Such command-and-control regulation has played a role in sharply reducing U.S. emissions from transportation. Under the Clean Air Act, new vehicles faced stringent emissions standards starting in the early 1970s. As vehicles built before 1975 have been scrapped, the average vehicle on the roads has become so much cleaner that many major cities, such as Los Angeles, have experienced significant progress in reducing smog despite ongoing growth in population and miles driven (Kahn and Schwartz 2008).[3]

The deindustrialization of big cities has played a major role in greening U.S. cities. China's efforts to move industries out of Beijing in advance of the 2008 Olympics have been well documented. The level of urban manufacturing was an important factor driving urban pollution levels in the twentieth century. The rise of Pittsburgh as a steel capital had the unintended consequence of sharply increasing particulate levels. An unintended silver lining of the U.S. Rust Belt's decline in the 1960s and 1970s was a sharp improvement of environmental quality in heavy industrial cities, such as Pittsburgh and Gary, Indiana (Kahn 1999). Between 1969 and 2000, the number of manufacturing jobs in New York County (Manhattan) declined from 451,330 to 146,291. Similar declines in manufacturing have taken place in London, England. There are large public health gains from removing older polluting manufacturing plants from heavily populated areas.

Although the U.S. trends just listed have contributed to greening cities, other trends have had the opposite effect. In China's major cities, a significant amount of economic activity takes place in the city center, and even people with private vehi-

---

[2] In the United States, there is a robust correlation that more skilled cities grow more (Glaeser and Saiz 2004). Moretti (2004b) shows that, conditional on observable worker characteristics, wages are higher in high-human-capital cities. An increase of 1 point in the percentage of a local economy's population that is college educated increases local population growth over a 10-year period by half a point (Glaeser and Saiz 2004) and increases real wages of non-college-educated local residents by 1.4 percent and real wages of local college graduates by 0.3 percent (Moretti 2004a). From 1940 to 1990, a 10 percent increase in a metropolitan area's concentration of college-educated residents was associated with a .8 percent increase in subsequent employment growth (Shapiro 2006).

[3] Los Angeles County's population grew by 29 percent between 1980 and 2000, while total automobile mileage grew by 70 percent, but the number of days per year in which the federal one-hour ozone standard was exceeded declined from about 150 days per year at the worst monitoring stations in this metropolitan area during the early 1980s to 20 to 30 days per year today (Kahn and Schwartz 2008).

cles do not drive very much. In contrast, U.S. cities are well known for their sprawl and their resulting consumption of private vehicles and single-family homes. Such privately beneficial consumption activities have environmental implications for both local air pollution and greenhouse gas production. It remains an open question whether Chinese cities will maintain their compact, monocentric form as per capita incomes rise. Future research should investigate employment suburbanization trends and the rise in demand for private vehicles and single-family homes.

## Household Carbon Emissions by City

A second important measure of a city's greenness is greenhouse gas production. Zheng et al. (2011) use micro data to estimate household carbon emissions across China's major cities. The majority of China's greenhouse gas emissions are now produced by its industrial sector, but the household sector's share of total emissions will increase with further economic development. Estimating how standardized Chinese household emissions vary across major cities helps evaluate the impact of current regional policies on carbon emissions, such as those that now bolster employment growth in some regions in the Northeast and West. Policies that favor the growth of particular areas will tend to increase carbon emissions if the marginal resident in that area is associated with more energy usage; they will decrease carbon emissions if the marginal resident emits a lower level of carbon.

Zheng et al. (2009) calculate household carbon emissions by using several data sources, including the 2006 Chinese Urban Household Survey. This survey provides information on energy usage for 25,000 households across 74 cities. Relative to U.S households, transportation represents a smaller share of Chinese urban household emissions, and household heating represents a much larger share. A poorer country can do without air conditioning and cars, but not without winter warmth. Zheng et al. calculate a predicted level of carbon emissions in different places for a standardized household with a fixed size and level of income. In China, carbon emissions are particularly high in places with cold Januarys because of centralized home heating. For example, Shanghai (without centralized home heating) is much greener than Beijing (with centralized home heating). The prominent role played by the central production of heat indicates that carbon emissions could fall significantly if greener sources of energy were used by the government for that purpose.

Figure 7.2 and table 7.3 summarize some of the key findings of Zheng et al. (2009). As shown in figure 7.2, colder cities have much higher average household carbon footprints. This suggests that current regional economic development policies that bolster the growth of China's northeastern cities are likely to increase emissions. As shown in table 7.3, they find that the greenest cities on the basis of this criterion are Huaian and Suqian, while the dirtiest cities are Daqing and Mudanjiang. Even in the dirtiest city (Daqing), a standardized household produces only one-fifth the carbon emissions of America's greenest city (San Diego).

The reliance on coal for winter heating in cold cities helps create a positive correlation of roughly .4 between ambient $PM_{10}$ levels and household carbon levels. Given current fuel sources, this says that China's green cities are toward the south, while the brown cities are located in the North.

Cross-City Relationships Between Winter Temperature and Household Carbon Emissions

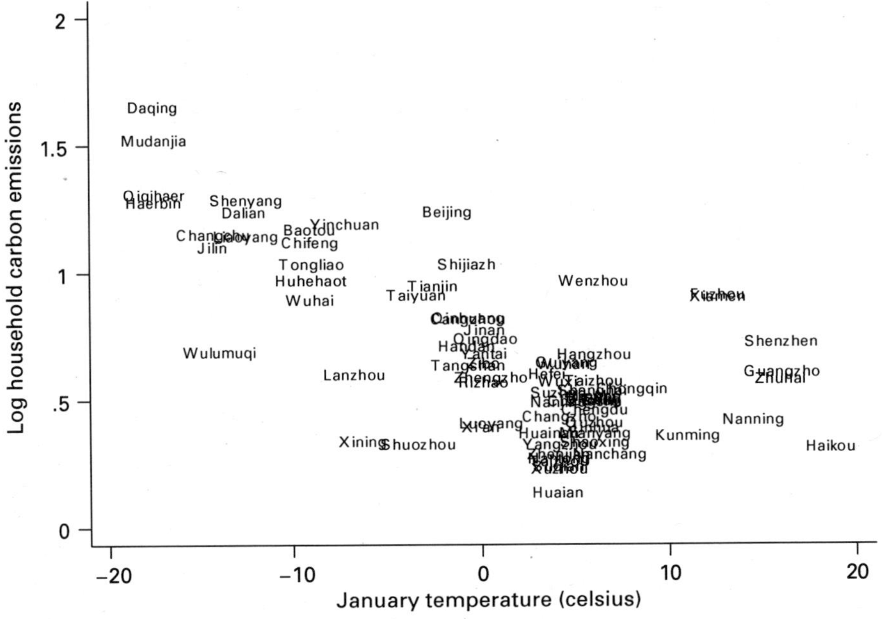


SOURCE: National Bureau of Statistics of China (NBS). (Multiple years).



Major Chinese Cities Ranked by Household Carbon Dioxide Emissions

| Dirty Ten | Tons | Clean Ten | Tons |
|---|---|---|---|
| Daqing | 5.115 | Xuzhou | 1.401 |
| Mudanjiang | 4.827 | Xining | 1.371 |
| Beijing | 3.997 | Shaoxing | 1.365 |
| Qiqihaer | 3.614 | Zhenjiang | 1.331 |
| Yinchuan | 3.543 | Taizhou | 1.307 |
| Shenyang | 3.528 | Nanchang | 1.305 |
| Haerbin | 3.508 | Nantong | 1.281 |
| Dalian | 3.371 | Haikou | 1.252 |
| Baotou | 3.309 | Suqian | 1.231 |
| Liaoyang | 3.237 | Huaian | 1.23 |

SOURCE: Zheng et al. (2009).

This city research at a point in time contributes to work on comparing carbon footprints. Schmalensee, Stoker, and Judson (1998) estimate national panel data using data from 1950 to 1990 and examine the relationship between a nation's per capita income and its per capita carbon dioxide emissions. They estimate a 10-segment spline model to allow the relationship between income and emissions to vary flexibly for poor, middle-income, and richer nations. Such a statistical model allows for a non-linear relationship between pollution and per-capita income. Controlling for nation fixed effects, they focus on using within-nation economic growth and testing how this affects emissions. For nations whose income lies between US$1,283 and US$4,467 in 1985 dollars (including China), the average income elasticity equals .77. Auffhammer and Carson (2008), using Chinese provincial data from the *China Statistical Yearbook* for 25 provinces over the period 1985 to 2004, report a set of income elasticities of greenhouse gas emissions ranging from .2 to 1. Both studies predict that China's greenhouse gas emissions will sharply increase under the business-as-usual scenario.

## Conclusion

China offers an excellent test case of the optimistic claim that effective government regulation and new cleaner capital can offset the pollution consequences of a rising scale of economic activity. An optimist can point to recent air-pollution gains in China's major cities, but a pessimist can point to the convergence in greenhouse gas emissions between China's cities and U.S. cities. Motorization is just beginning in China. Electricity demand will soar as newly middle-class households demand electronic equipment that people in the United States take for granted. For China's local air pollution and greenhouse gas emissions to decline, electricity demand must be met by power plants that do not rely on coal as their primary energy source.

Consider a comparison of Shanghai and Los Angeles. In 2007 Shanghai's average $PM_{10}$ level was 88 micrograms per cubic meter, while the 2009 $PM_{10}$ level of Los Angeles was 29.2. This indicates that Shanghai's local air pollution is three times worse. But 2006 data on household carbon dioxide production show that the average Chinese household would produce 1.796 tons of carbon dioxide if it lived in Shanghai. In contrast, the average household in the United States would produce 19.5 tons of carbon dioxide if it lived in Los Angeles (Glaeser and Kahn 2010). Which is the greener city? If one focuses on air pollution, Los Angeles wins, but if climate change is the major concern, Shanghai wins.

In both $PM_{10}$ and household carbon dioxide production, China's northern cities are ranked as dirty. If their reliance on coal declines, then these cities will rise in the green-city rankings. A city's landowners and politicians have an explicit incentive to promote local greenness that improves local air and water quality, but little incentive to reduce greenhouse gas emissions.

City greenness is just one part of the bigger picture of a city's quality of life in the face of ongoing growth. A more ambitious study would look at more dimensions of nonmarket goods indicators. Data limitations have precluded examination of urban commute times and crime levels across China's cities in this chapter. As the value of time rises for Chinese commuters, commute differentials across and within cities will become even more important for pricing real estate and determining community and city quality of life.

## References


Auffhammer, Max, and Richard T. Carson. 2008. Forecasting the path of China's $CO_2$ emissions using province level information. *Journal of Environmental Economics and Management* 55(3):229–247.

Chow, Gregory. 2010. China's environmental policy: A critical survey. Paper prepared for the Lincoln Institute's Conference on "Urban Development and the Environment in China," Cambridge, MA (May).

Costa, Dora, and Matthew Kahn. 2003. The rising price of non-market goods. *American Economic Review Papers and Proceedings* (May):227–232.

———. 2004. Changes in the value of life, 1940–1980. *Journal of Risk and Uncertainty* 29(2):159–180.

Glaeser, Edward. 1998. Are cities dying? *Journal of Economic Perspectives* 12(2):139–160.

Glaeser, Edward, and Matthew Kahn. 2010. The greenness of cities: Carbon dioxide emissions and urban development. *Journal of Urban Economics* 67(3):404–418.

Glaeser, Edward, and Bruce Sacerdote. 1999. Why is there more crime in cities? *Journal of Political Economy* 107(S6):S225–S229.

Glaeser, Edward, and Albert Saiz. 2004. The rise of the skilled city. *Brookings-Wharton Papers on Urban Affairs*, 47–94.

Grossman, Gene, and Alan Krueger. 1995. Economic growth and the environment. *Quarterly Journal of Economics* 110(2):353–377.

Harbaugh, William, Arik Levinson, and David Wilson. 2002. Reexamining the empirical evidence for an environmental Kuznets curve. *Review of Economics and Statistics* 84(3):541–551.

Henderson, Vernon. 2002a. Urban primacy, external costs, and quality of life. *Resource and Energy Economics* 24(1–2), 15:95–106.

———. 2002b. World cities data. http://www.econ.brown.edu/faculty/henderson/worldcities.html

Hilton, H., and Arik Levinson. 1998. Factoring the environmental Kuznets curve: Evidence from automotive lead emissions. *Journal of Environmental Economics and Management* 35(2):126–141.

Kahn, Matthew. 1999. The silver lining of Rust Belt manufacturing decline. *Journal of Urban Economics* 46(3):360–376.

———. 2010. New evidence on trends in the cost of urban agglomeration. In *Agglomeration economics*, ed. Edward L. Glaser, 339–354. Cambridge, MA: National Bureau of Economic Research.

Kahn, Matthew, and Joel Schwartz. 2008. Urban air pollution progress despite sprawl: The "greening" of the vehicle fleet. *Journal of Urban Economics* 63(3):775–787.

Moretti, Enrico. 2004a. Estimating the social return to higher education: Evidence from longitudinal and repeated cross-sectional data. *Journal of Econometrics* 121(1–2):175–212.

———. 2004b. Human capital externalities in cities. In *Handbook of Urban Economics*, vol. 4, ed. H. Vernon and J. Thisse. Amsterdam: North-Holland.

National Bureau of Statistics (NBS). Multiple years. *China Statistical yearbook.* http://www.stats.gov.cn/english/statisticaldata/yearlydata/

Pomfret, James, and Jerry Norton. 2009. Hong Kong Air pollution worsens, but China is blamed less. *Reuters.* http://www.reuters.com/article/idUSTRE56E10320090715

Schmalensee, R., T. M. Stoker, and R. A. Judson. 1998. World carbon dioxide emissions: 1950–2050. *Review of Economics and Statistics* 80(1):15–27.

Selden, Thomas M., and S. Daqing. 1995. Neoclassical growth, the J curve for abatement, and the inverted U curve for pollution. *Journal of Environmental Economics and Management* 29(2):62–168.

Shapiro, Jesse. 2006. Smart cities: Quality of life, productivity, and the growth effects of human capital. *Review of Economics and Statistics* 88(May):324–335.

Spotts, Peter N. 2009. Study: China's Olympic effort to curb smog had little effect. *Christian Science Monitor.* http://www.csmonitor.com/Environment/Bright-Green/2009/0623/study-chinas-olympic-effort-to-curb-smog-had-little-effect

Tolley, George S. 1974. The welfare economics of city bigness. *Journal of Urban Economics* 1(3):324–345.

Williamson, Jeffrey. 1981. Urban disamenities dark satanic mills, and the British standard of living debate. *Journal of Economic History* 41:75–83.

Zheng, S., M. Kahn, and H. Liu. 2010. Towards a system of open cities in China: Home prices, FDI flows and air quality in 35 major cities. *Regional Science and Urban Economics* 40:1–10.

Zheng, Siqi, Rui Wang, Edward Glaeser, and Matthew. Kahn. 2011. China's green cities: Household carbon emissions and urban development. *Journal of Economic Geography* 11(5):761–792.

# Urban Planning

## The Road to Low-Carbon Cities in China

JUAN JING AND YUN QIAN

Climate change is one of the most serious threats facing people today. It is not just an environmental challenge. It threatens the sustainability of our economies, our societies, and our very existence (Stern 2007). Government officials and scholars in many countries have made tremendous progress in addressing the causes of this global environmental challenge. But the impacts of human activities in modern society can never be overestimated. One official report by an English government agency stated: "Out of 928 peer-reviewed studies on climate change published in reputable scientific journals, not a single one cast doubt on the existence of the human-caused greenhouse effect" (English Partnerships 2006, 2).

Human activities take place most intensively and frequently in cities. Evidence shows that urban areas have significantly affected climate change by contributing at least 70 percent of carbon dioxide emissions, although they occupy no more than 5 percent of all land (Gu et al. 2009; Ove Arup and Partners 2007; Qiu 2009). Glaeser and Kahn (2008) demonstrated that the greatest challenge of climate change is the expansion of urban areas, because evidence shows that people in newly developed urban areas emit more carbon dioxide per person than people in existing urban areas. This explains why the world witnessed a dramatic growth in carbon emissions as the proportion of the population living in cities increased from 29 percent in 1950 to 49 percent in 2010 (United Nations 2007).

Before the 1990s, the volume of carbon emissions in China was very limited, but in the past 20 years China's emissions have skyrocketed. China is becoming the largest carbon dioxide emitter in the world, and per capita emissions have doubled since 1990 (figure 8.1). The growth in urbanization (figure 8.2) is likely to be the best explanation for this increase.

**FIGURE 8.1**

Growth of $CO_2$ Emissions in China

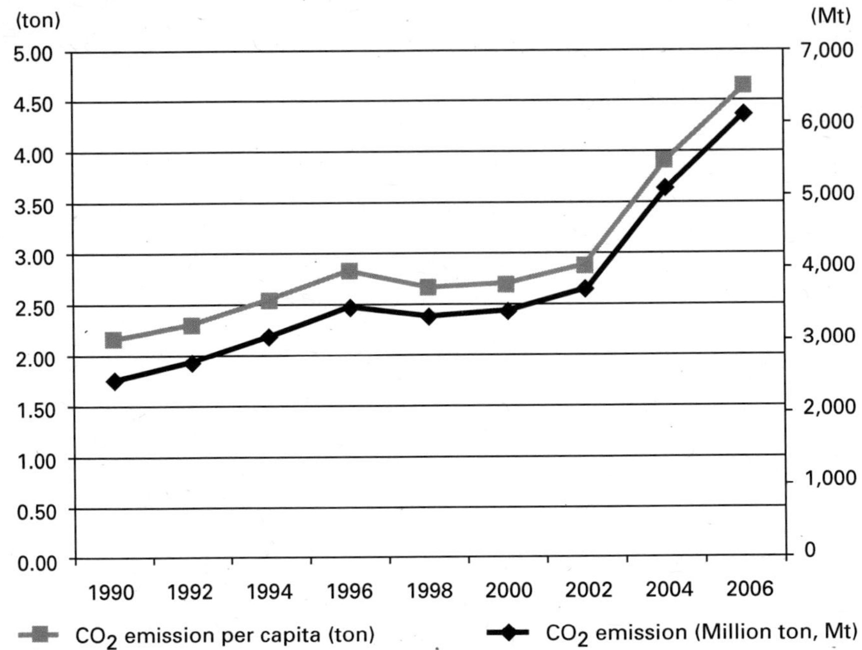


SOURCE: National Bureau of Statistics (2009).

The China Academy of Social Science (2012) estimates that China's urbanization process will continue at present rate until 2030, and the urban population will increase by at least 50 percent. This poses unprecedented challenges for the Chinese government. In the past ten years, the Chinese central government has promised to take on significant international responsibilities in combating global climate change and to try every possible approach to strictly curb and gradually reduce carbon emissions in the future. Therefore, since the end of the 1990s conventional urban development policies have led to high growth in carbon emissions must be abandoned, and effective measures to achieve lower carbon emissions with urban growth are urgently needed.

The use of urban planning tools can be regarded as a very effective approach to controlling pollution. China has a long history of urban planning, which has been relatively strong and effective. Through a well-established urban planning system approved by almost every tier of local governments, policies on many key issues of urban form, including land use, the traffic system, density, and even architectural style, as well as the locations of infrastructure systems (especially energy providers), can be enforced. Glaeser and Kahn (2008) have demonstrated that all these issues can affect carbon emissions. For example, cities with lower density have longer travel distances and thus produce more carbon emissions. Glaeser and Kahn also suggest that stricter planning regulations can reduce emissions more effectively, but the concept of a low-carbon city must be correctly understood and must be the key ideology of multidimensional planning strategies.

**FIGURE 8.2**

Growth of Urban Population in China

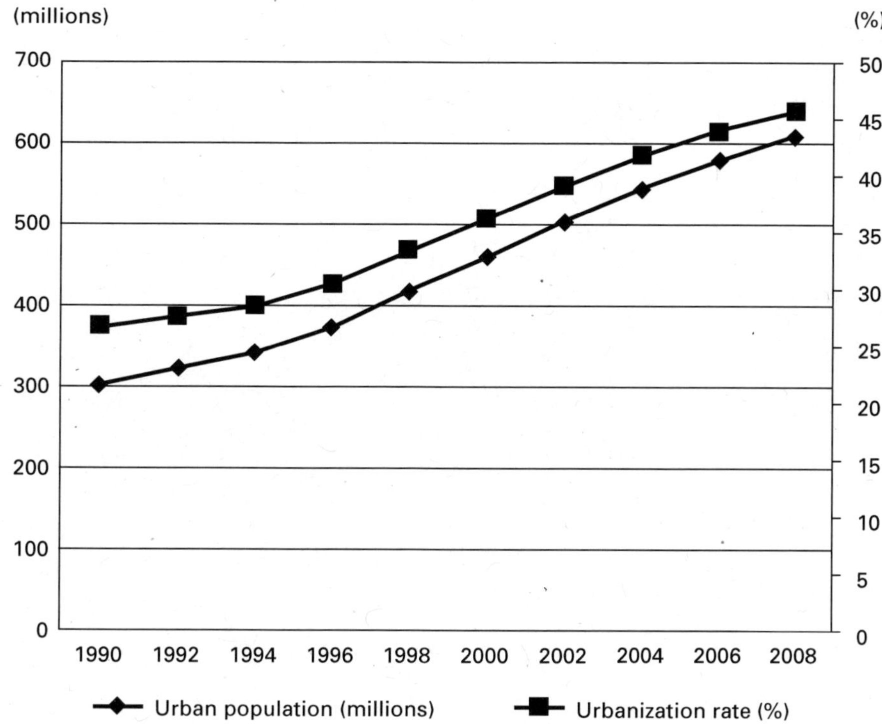


SOURCE: United Nations (2011).

This chapter presents discussions about how to use planning tools to realize the path toward a low-carbon city. By looking at the details, this chapter will answer the following questions: What is the traditional planning system in China? How did this planning system play a big role in influencing urban development? How can low-carbon strategies be realized through urban planning tools in China? How can these strategies be made effective in practice? In addition to a literature review and theoretical analysis, a case study in Nantong will provide more practical answers to all these questions.

## Urban Planning in China in Historical Context

### The Presocialist Era

China is the oldest Oriental civilization in the world and is famous for its long and sustained agrarian culture. However, the role of cities or towns has always been crucial. Few ancient Chinese cities were military forts or trade hubs; the majority of them were the seats of a tier of local governments that ruled the surrounding rural areas. Usually, national, regional, or local political centers were built strictly by bureaucrats, which regularly had common spatial features (Dong 2006; Wang, De Hua 2005).

Map of Beijing Old Town

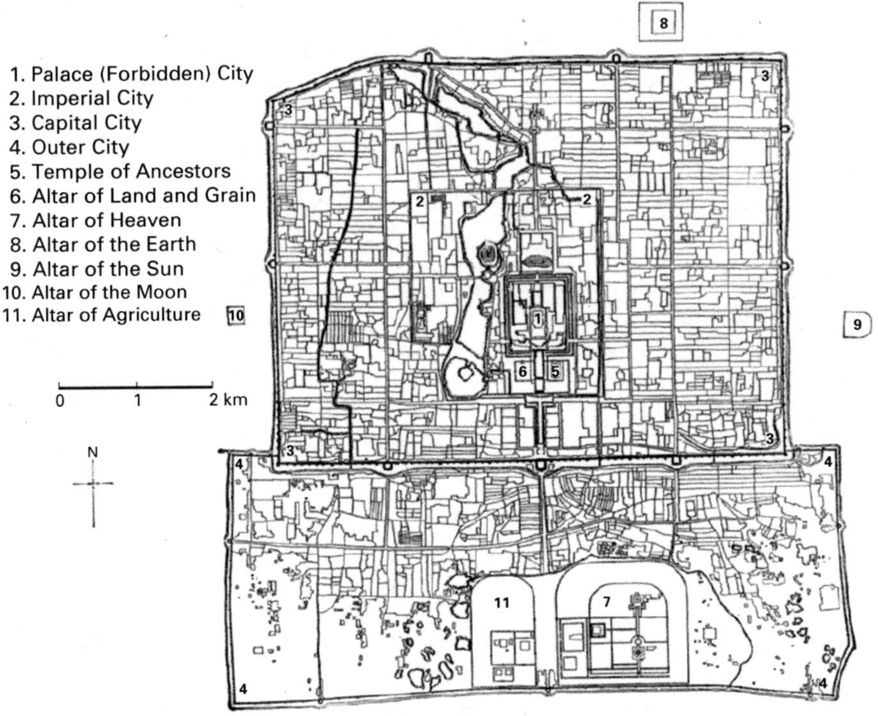


SOURCE: Liu, Dun-Zhen (1980, 280).

Beijing old town is the best example of a planned ancient Chinese town or city (figure 8.3). As the national capital of the last two Chinese dynasties, the city was first completed in 1420 AD and was the largest Chinese city at the time (the urban area enclosed by the city wall is about 62 km$^2$). The city took the shape of a rectangle, and almost all major streets and minor alleys went either north-south or east-west. This arrangement formed a chessboard-like road system that separated rectangular neighborhoods from one another. The Forbidden City (the emperor's palace) was located in the central area, facing south (the direction of the sun) to show the emperor's authority. Altars occupied the other significant points of interest. The homes of key officials were just outside the Forbidden City. The size and architectural style of their homes (normally consisting of one or more courtyards) were decided according to the owner's political grade. Markets were restricted to very small areas in insignificant locations far from the political center (Wang, Ya Ping 1992).

The planning tools could be seen as the instrument to present mainstream Confucian values and political ideology, which emphasized the centralized power structure (Zhu 2004). Under Confucian theory, the emperor and central government ruled the whole empire through a well-established, top-down system, and ordinary people were not allowed to participate in political discussions. Therefore, according to the plans, many houses with similar size and architectural style formed monotonous streetscapes, but they effectively enhanced the impression of the grand architectural structures that represented strong state power over the citizens. Therefore, many key projects were completed by the government. More important, there was also no open space in cities for public gatherings, which were considered to be a threat to the empire's stability (Sit 1995). This plan was used to strictly control the key elements of the urban form, which included the scale of the urban area (enclosed by walls), the basic framework of road systems, the locations and architectural styles of all key buildings, the function of some special plots, and the size and architectural styles of some residential houses.

In the middle of the nineteenth century, Western colonists began to settle in China and engage in market activities. The Chinese government gradually lost control of some coastal areas, and colonists gained development right in these areas instead. In the first half of the twentieth century, most Western-ruled cities underwent quick development and no longer served as administrative centers. The role of planning was still significant, and many newborn Western planning ideas, such as the garden-city, were imported and experimented with in China. Compared with the plans of traditional Chinese cities, the plans made by the colonists still focused on the spatial layouts, but the plots of land involved were much larger. First, buildings such as palaces and temples were replaced by buildings with diverse modern functions, including churches, schools, colleges, hotels, sporting clubs, hospitals, banks, and even railway stations. Second, the layout of many features of modern infrastructure became another important task of the plans. Paved roads, water pipes, electric wires, and sewage systems had to be included in the master-plan drawings. Tsingtao, Dalian, and Harbin are typical examples of the new generation of planned cities.

Of course, modern planning tools were no longer used to realize spatial layouts with Chinese traditional values, but to modernize urban lives and create more beautiful urban images. In practice, although Western-led urban development took place in very limited areas in China, the influence of modern planning ideas was significant in China's later urban development (Wang, Ya Ping 1992).

In the following years, Chinese officials learned how to use Western planning tools to "modernize" other Chinese cities. In 1929 the first Western-style master plan was completed in Nanjing, then the national capital. This plan did not call for a new city to be constructed, but for upgrading the old city with new projects. All urban areas were zoned into specialized functional areas, for example, the central government district, the city administration district, industrial districts, shopping districts, cultural and education districts, and residential districts. The Chinese style of architecture was emphasized, but the whole distribution of land use could not avoid the pattern created in Western countries to promote industrial development.

This style of planning was stalled by the Japanese invasion from 1937 to 1945 and was not followed again until much later. Nonetheless, it clearly showed the improvement of Chinese planning practices. Here the plan focused not only on the key buildings and infrastructure systems, but also on the control of land use of every area. The government hoped to use planning control to adjust the spatial structure of the city and to make sure that the new spatial framework with upgraded infrastructure could support the operation of the city with many modern functions.

## The Planned-Economy Era

The year 1949 marked a new starting point of China's national history. The planned-economy model was imported from Soviet Union, in which the powers of the government were enhanced to control the whole national economic system. Almost all urban construction projects were decided by local economic plans, and urban planning was reduced to using a blueprint master-plan drawing for urban construction projects. In 1952 the Construction Industry Ministry was established to take charge of national urban construction and management, and its local agencies were given responsibilities to draft local plans. Later, in many cities, new versions of master plans were completed. They usually included detailed proposals of land use for every plot, modern road and infrastructure systems, and architectural visions of key buildings (Sit 1995).

The role of urban planning in the socialist state was actually similar to the Nanjing plan of 1929. However, in order to enhance governmental power, the plans became more ambitious. Not only did they include more details, but also they were on a much larger scale than had been seen previously. In addition, the purpose of planning control was also developed. The desire for urban modernization was still strong, but in order to show the socialist ideology, new cities had to be made more equal for all their residents, especially low-income families. Thus, many projects for social well-being, such as the creation of leisure parks, slum-clearance projects, and the development of public housing estates, were also part of the plans.

However, the government quickly realized that the overambitious master plans could hardly be followed because of the lack of sufficient public financing. As a result, only part of the proposed projects could be put into practice, and under the strategy of "production first, life later," "nonproductive projects," including new housing estates, social service facilities, and infrastructure systems, had to give way to some "key" projects. These key projects were new industrial estates and the buildings to accommodate national or local administrative bureaus. In order to direct these projects, detailed plans of the areas to be constructed were introduced to give clearer visions of local development.

In July 1956 the Construction Industry Ministry promulgated *Provisional Regulations for Urban Planning Compilation*, which officially prescribed the two-tier urban planning system (master plan and detailed plan) in the People's Republic of China for the first time (Wang, De Hua 2005).[1] In this system, the master plans were required to give basic principles and some qualitative indexes of urban developments, which included at least the following:

1. The nature of the city, the population size, and the land use scale for short and long terms, which usually followed the requirements of local economic plans.
2. The land use category of every plot, with functional zoning.
3. The spatial structure of traffic system.
4. The spatial allocation of key public amenities and infrastructure systems.

---

[1] According to this document, urban planning should be carried out in three phases: initial plans, comprehensive plans, and detailed plans. In the early stage, those cities that faced difficulties in collection of basic data and materials could first generate the initial plans instead of comprehensive plans. By and large, the initial and comprehensive plans are the same in nature.

In these detailed plans, land use, traffic systems, and infrastructure were still the key issues to be considered, but under the direction of the master plans, the planning controls went further by using a series of quantitative indexes that usually included at least the following:

1. The borders between buildings, green spaces, waterways, roads, and other structures in the area and every plot.
2. The construction density (floor-area-ratio), green land-area-ratio, maximum height limit, minimum parking spaces in every plot.
3. The architectural style and colors of the buildings in every plot.
4. The spatial positioning and section design of every road and the location of some service facilities, such as gas stations or bus stops.
5. The spatial allocation of public amenities and facilities of all kinds of infrastructure systems, such as substations or refuse dumps.

In this way, as an extension of economic plans, the authority of the urban planning system guaranteed that urban forms would be developed under strict state control in the following three decades (Hao 2005), except during a few years because of political chaos. In practice, many plans, particularly the detailed plans, were drafted by architects and engineers so the ideas in the plans could be realized in the follow-up practical works.

## The Reform Era

The national policy "reform and open up" started at the end of the 1970s. Since then, the planned-economy system has been replaced gradually by the socialist market-economy system. As one of the milestones of progress, the land and real estate market was established in the early 1990s. Private developers were allowed to purchase development rights of urban land and gained profits from the market. In later years, all sorts of commercialized projects increased dramatically, and public-led projects were quickly sidelined. These new projects consist of many new functional zones and districts, such as central business districts (CBDs), high-tech research parks, low-rise villa areas, shopping malls, and luxury hotels and tourist districts. Facing rapid urban growth, local governments had to renew urban plans frequently.

The majority of new urban construction projects were no longer completed by public agencies, so the role of urban planning had to be changed again. It could no longer be seen as the spatial reflection of economic plans, because more and more urban construction projects were private led. In this new era, plans became authoritative regulations that projects undertaken by all developers had to follow. Thus, urban development could proceed under relaxed economic regulations, but could still follow the general development vision of local governments. These plans were enacted in laws rather than in administrative regulations.

*The Law of Urban Planning*, the first and only law in the field of urban planning, was issued on 16 December 1989 and became effective on 1 April 1990. A new urban system with legal status was thereby formed. The main contents of master plans were kept, and their significance in directing urban development was reemphasized. In some larger cities, divisional plans were introduced. Their role was similar to that of master plans, but they applied to only a small part of the city and could provide more detailed instructions about urban development in fast-growing areas.

In the lower tier, the detailed plans were divided into regulatory plans and action plans.[2] The former were required to provide very strict quantitative indexes to control land use, construction density, traffic capacity, and infrastructures. The latter, action plans, provided a series of criteria of architectural and landscape designs, but many of them were just advisory plans and were not mandatory to the governmental framework. In the legal framework, master plans and regulatory plans should be implemented legally, while it is not compulsory to produce the divisional and action plans. The new urban planning system aimed to continue the effective state control of urban development, particularly urban spatial form, amid fast urbanization, but also to encourage the creation of customized urban images on smaller scales (Hao 2005; Ren 2000; Tan 2005; Tongji University 1991; Wang, De Hua 2005).

In practice, the ideas of planning control, especially at the local level again, changed significantly. In the marketizing economy, fast urban property development has become the strongest driving force for the prosperity of local economies, and fees from land leases and taxes on large-scale real estate development have become the major extrabudgetary income of local governments. Thus, the frequent renewal of urban plans eventually became an effective tool for local governments to accelerate profitable urban development, and many features of controlled urban development have clearly shown the money-first planning strategy.

Many planners and officials have recognized that the urban forms recommended by current planning ideas are generating a great amount of unnecessary carbon emissions. Therefore, some very large areas have now been designated as single-function areas that will consist of industrial, commercial, or residential areas larger than several square kilometers. This makes it easier for developers to reduce the costs of construction, but it will inevitably lead to longer commuting distances and more traffic congestion. Also, the new traffic systems were usually built with many broad streets and overpasses but ignored public transport facilities and the needs of pedestrians. These will attract more rich people with private cars, but will also increase energy consumption and carbon emissions. Another significant problem is that many low-density buildings were erected close to the green spaces; these buildings wasted land and blocked more people from the landscape system. In short, in quickly urbanizing China, a more sustainable strategy of urban development is needed.

## Low-Carbon Cities and Planning in China

### Low-Carbon Development in the Chinese Context

Low-carbon development has become a concept well recognized by politicians and academicians. However, the understanding of this concept is somewhat ambiguous. It aims to reduce or at least control greenhouse gas emissions and, at the same time,

---

[2] In some cities, such as Shenzhen, regulatory plans were also called statutory plans.

to promote continued social and economic growth. There is much debate about the reality of this goal, and many development models have been generated in an attempt to reach it. The so-called Plan A and Plan B have been the most frequently discussed models in the international context (Qiu 2009; 2010).

Plan A, an American-style plan, represents the form of development prevalent in the United States, the largest carbon emitter in the world. The United States has just 5 percent of the world's population, but it consumes 20 percent of the world's energy and generates 20 percent of the world's carbon emissions. American development is usually oriented toward the principle of "consumption first," which means more consumption of fossil-fuel energy and more car-oriented traffic, low-rise houses, and other industrial goods to improve urban living standards. Meanwhile, it gives little attention to the control and reduction of emissions. Obviously, in the face of global climate change, Plan A should be regarded as a very unsustainable way of life and development. President Barack Obama has admitted that if Chinese urban development followed this development pattern, the high energy consumption and resulting carbon emissions would soon be disastrous for the world. Many researchers have pointed out that Plan A is a failure and is inappropriate for most countries in the world.

The Brown model (Plan B) (Brown 2006) was proposed as a shortcut way to reach the target of carbon reduction by recategorizing the roles of different countries in the world. This idea requires all developing countries to stop development through industrialization and urbanization, to stop carbon emissions, and thus to become the backyard garden of developed countries in order to provide space for carbon emissions for these countries. In practice, this idea can hardly be followed. It produces extreme inequality for industrializing countries like China. Per capita carbon emissions in China are still below the world average, and most developing countries have historically been responsible for only a small part of carbon emissions. Also, the idea is unrealistic because it asks developing countries to stop industrializing and urbanizing, which will ultimately harm the current global economy. Plan B will not be widely accepted.

The Chinese government is now exploring a third plan (Plan C) that will contrast heavily with both Plan A and Plan B and produce a more balanced development model with Chinese characteristics to accomplish low carbon and development simultaneously. Plan C aims to achieve economic prosperity and emissions reduction at the same time, and then to improve living conditions and reinforce national competitiveness. This development principle has been presented in published national strategies in European countries and Japan. These documents have pointed out that new economic development should be based on higher productivity, more business opportunities and employment, improvement of living conditions, and reduction of unnecessary consumption of natural resources and of environmental pollution, but not reduction of the scale of growth. Technical and institutional innovations should be the main approaches to reach low-carbon targets, and a series of detailed strategies have been introduced ("2050 Japan Low-Carbon Society" Scenario Team 2008; Department of Trade and Industry 2003). These international experiences have provided very valuable references for China in establishing its framework for Plan C.

Meanwhile, the differences in national contexts cannot be ignored. In European countries and Japan, the fast urbanization process has almost finished, and cities can hardly be changed physically in the future. Therefore, strategies to direct new development of urban forms are seldom considered. In China, as discussed earlier, the new socioeconomic structure (with competitiveness and health) will be established through the process of rapid urbanization, and the physical growth of new urban areas will definitely continue. A series of specific strategies is urgently needed to supervise the construction of new urban areas in a low-carbon way. These low-carbon strategies for new urban areas are the most innovative parts of Plan C in comparison with the experience in European countries.

## Understanding the Term "Low-Carbon City"

Exploration of the path toward the low-carbon city in China is still at an early stage. Many Chinese cities have announced pioneer proposals to initiate some campaigns to promote low-carbon living (table 8.1). These campaigns usually aim to popularize some emissions-reduction technical innovations in a short period. However, they are almost all on one way to reduce emissions, and no reliable institutional system has been established to oversee these campaigns and monitor their progress. A few governmental agencies have issued standards to encourage the integrated use of a series of low-carbon technical innovations. For example, the Green Building Design Criteria have been put into practice for years and provide an evaluation system to measure the energy efficiency and carbon emissions of buildings in cities. Buildings with better performance are awarded higher national honors. Nevertheless, these technical standards are not mandatory regulations, so their real effects in emissions reduction are very limited.

Theoretical findings are more helpful in understanding the concept of the low-carbon city. The Research Group of Sustainable Development Strategies of the China Academy of Sciences (2009) put forward a series of development strategies for low-carbon cities on a macro scale and established an index system with economic, social, and environmental aspects (table 8.2). Fu, Wang, and Li (2008) also analyzed approaches to develop low-carbon cities from the perspective of systematic theories, which could be summarized as a wide-ranging framework including economic, social and technical issues. Their findings make it clear that the reduction of carbon emissions should rely not only on individual campaigns, but also on a series of strategies to respond to all causes of carbon emissions.

**TABLE 8.1**

Low-Carbon Practices in Several Cities

| City | Practice of Low-Carbon Development |
| --- | --- |
| Shanghai | Free distribution of 1 million energy-saving bulbs to families and enterprises |
| Hangzhou | Free bicycle rental to pedestrians, and advocacy of low-cost public transport |
| Beijing | Distribution of 5 million energy-saving bulbs at one-tenth of the market price |
| Guangdong | Distribution of 3 million energy-saving bulbs at one-fifth of the market price |

SOURCE: Liu, et al. (2009).

**TABLE 8.2**

Low-Carbon Strategies in China, 2009–2020

| Objectives | | Index | Unit | National Level | Level in Top 100 Cities[a] |
|---|---|---|---|---|---|
| Economic | To optimize industrial structure and to improve economic efficiency | GDP per capita | 10,000 yuan | 6 | 12 |
| | | Growth rate of GDP | % | 8 | 10 |
| | | Proportion of service industry output value | % | 50 | 60 |
| | | Proportion of tertiary industry employment | % | 55 | 65 |
| | To recycle natural resources and to improve energy efficiency | Energy consumption per 10,000 yuan of GDP | Tons of standard coal | 0.5 | 0.45 |
| | | Elasticity coefficient of energy consumption | | 0.5 | 0.3 |
| | | $CO_2$ emissions | Tons per unit of GDP | 0.75 | 0.5 |
| | | Proportion of energy from new sources | % | 15 | 20 |
| | | Proportion of combined use of heat and power | % | 100 | 100 |
| | To increase research and development investment and to promote technological innovation | Proportion of research and development investment in financial expenditure | % | 3 | 5 |
| Social | To improve housing affordability of low-income families | Proportion of affordable housing | % | 20 | 30 |
| | | Housing space per capita | Square meters | 20 | 30 |
| | | Proportion of land transfer fee used for public rented housing projects | % | 20 | 30 |
| | To improve living conditions | Disposable income per capita | 10,000 yuan | 2.5 | 4 |
| | | Engel coefficient[b] | | 0.3 | 0.25 |
| | | Urbanization rate | % | 50–55 | 55–60 |
| | To develop Bus Rapid Transit (BRT) and to advocate public transport | Average walking distance to BRT station | Meter | 1,000 | 50 |
| | | Number of buses per 10,000 residents | | 15 | 20 |

*(continued)*

**TABLE 8.2** (*Continued*)

| | Objectives | Index | Unit | National Level | Level in Top 100 Cities[a] |
|---|---|---|---|---|---|
| Environmental | To raise carbon sink capacity | Percentage of land covered by Forest | % | 35 | 40 |
| | | Green space per capita | Square Meters | 15 | 20 |
| | | Percentage of land covered by Green space in built-up areas | % | 40 | 45 |
| | To reduce pollutant emissions and to improve the urban environment | Harmless treatment rate of garbage | % | 100 | 100 |
| | | Urban sewage treatment rate | % | 80 | 100 |
| | | Industrial wastewater treatment rate | % | 100 | 100 |
| | To reduce the effect on climate change through low-carbon design | Proportion of low-carbon buildings | % | 50 | 70 |
| | | Carbon Capture and Storage rate of greenhouse gases | % | 10 | 15 |

SOURCE: Research Group of Sustainable Development Strategies, China Academy of Sciences (2009, 229).

NOTES: [a]Top 100 cities refer to their rank by population. [b]Engel coefficient means the proportion of income spent on food. As the Engel coefficient increases, the country or region is by nature poorer, conversely a low Engel coefficient indicates a higher standard of living.

Many researchers have examined the main causes of the increase in carbon emissions when urban areas keep growing. In general, the growing emissions come from three main sources: (industrial) production, mobility of persons and goods, and the operation of buildings (Chen and Zhu 2009; Gu et al. 2009). Industrial production refers mainly to traditional manufacturing and mining industries, which were seen as the symbols of modern cities in the past. Most traffic emissions result from the popularization of private cars, which primarily consume fossil fuels. The emissions of buildings can be attributed to central heating, air conditioning, and other electrical equipment, which are used extensively in modern society.

Figure 8.4 shows the current carbon-emissions structure in three Western metropolises: New York, London, and Paris. Data show that most emissions in these cities are from traffic and buildings, while emissions from production are now not very significant. Historical data from cities in Organisation for Economic Co-operation and Development (OECD) and European Union (EU) countries (table 8.3) show a clear trend that carbon emissions from traffic and buildings are growing rapidly, while the proportion of emissions from production keeps shrinking. This indicates the arrival of the postindustrial economy: traditional manufacturing industries are being replaced by service-based industries. These new industries are mostly office based and thus contribute to the significant growth of carbon emissions of buildings. However, data from the three largest Chinese cities (figure 8.5) show great differences. Because China is an industrializing country, emissions from production in Chinese cities are still much higher than in OECD or EU cities and are more than 50 percent of total carbon emissions in Shanghai and Tianjin. Since the 1990s, carbon emissions from traffic and buildings have grown very fast because of urban sprawl and economic restructuring upgrades.

The total volume of urban carbon emissions also depends on the performance of the local carbon sink system (Zhao and Liu 2010). In general, this carbon sink system includes urban green spaces, waterways, wetlands, and all other undeveloped natural land, as well as the vegetation and microbes within them. This system mainly contributes to emissions reduction in two ways: (1) it absorbs carbon dioxide and other greenhouse gases locally; and (2) it changes the local microclimate, for example, by reducing the urban heat-island effect, so that the use of central heating or air conditioning can be reduced.

The use of renewable energy has been regarded as another possible way to reduce carbon emissions. However, because of technical barriers and economic inefficiency,

**TABLE 8.3**

Proportion of Emissions from Nonindustrial
Production in OECD and EU Countries (percent)

|  | 1971 | 1980 | 1990 | 2000 | 2005 |
|---|---|---|---|---|---|
| OECD | 54 | 56 | 61 | 62 | 64 |
| EU-25 | 48 | 54 | 59 | 62 | 64 |

SOURCE: Kennedy et al. (2009).

Structure of Carbon Emissions in Three Western Metropolises

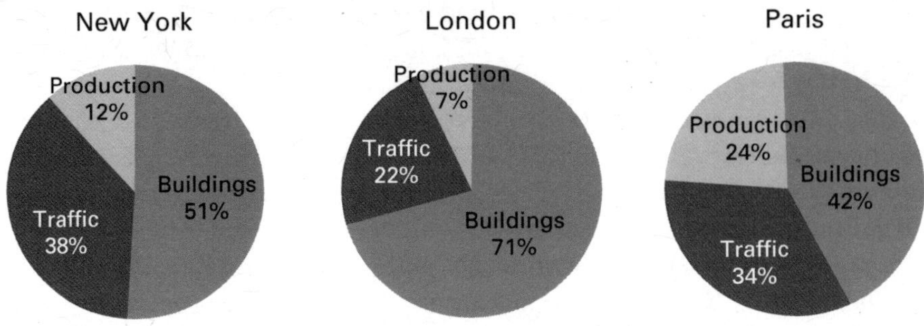



SOURCES: Kennedy et al. (2009); Long et al. (2009).


Structure of Carbon Emissions in Three Chinese Metropolises

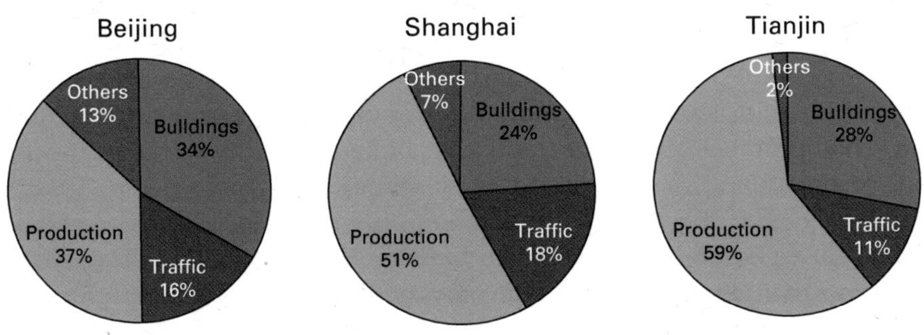



SOURCES: National Bureau of Statistics (2007; 2008).

renewable energy can hardly replace the use of fossil fuels at present and is suitable only for some purposes.

Principles to develop low-carbon cities should have wide and clear coverage. They should restrict unnecessary emissions from production, traffic, and buildings, increase the capacity of the carbon sink system, and promote the use of renewable energy in appropriate cases. The reduction of emissions from two major sources, production and traffic, has the greatest potential.

## The Role of Low-Carbon Planning

Many research studies have recognized that planning tools can be the best approach to realize the principles of low-carbon cities in a pragmatic perspective (Fong et al. 2008; Glaeser and Kahn 2008). In China, a country with very strong planning control and an authoritative planning system, the contribution of planning control could be extremely significant in reaching low-carbon targets. Also, China's well-established planning system provides the possibility to integrate technical and institutional innovations and to form multidimensional indexes to regulate and monitor future urban development effectively.

Glaeser and Kahn (2008) concluded that in many cities, effective planning control, for example, adjusting land use or increasing density, could optimize the way urban development achieves both lower carbon emissions and a more prosperous urban economy. But this effective tool is a two-edged sword as well. Low-density urban development in the United States is a negative case. Compared with most European countries with similar living standards, cities in the United States were usually developed with much lower density. This is partly because urbanization preceded motorization in Europe, while they occurred simultaneously in the United States, the so-called urbanization at the wheel. More importantly, the planning tradition in U.S. cities seldom restricts land-consuming development. As a consequence, U.S. urban traffic relies heavily on private cars, so current U.S. carbon emissions from travel per capita are five times the European level and seven times the Japanese level. Unfortunately, since the end of 1990s this American-style urban development became prevalent in Chinese urban growth when private car ownership in China grew exponentially. Therefore, planning controls to regulate future development of Chinese cities should follow a new planning ideology to pursue the path toward low-carbon cities.

Some experiments have been put into practice in drafting regulatory detailed plans of some new towns in the Yangtze River delta. A series of strategies were proposed to respond to every issue of planning controls: land use patterns, construction density, and traffic systems and capacity, as well as the volume and layout of infrastructure systems. More attention has been given to reduction of traffic emissions, and these plans have proposed all the low-carbon strategies simultaneously, including changes in practices of industrial production and building operation, the establishment of a carbon sink system, and the use of renewable energy. The experiment in Nantong is a typical example of exploring and realizing a series of low-carbon strategies through their application in the local detailed plan.

## Case Study of Nantong

The city of Nantong is located on the north side of the Yangtze River near the East China Sea (figure 8.6). It is not far from Shanghai, the largest city in China, and the surrounding metropolitan areas is one of the richest and earliest-industrialized regions in China. Because crossing the Yangtze River was very difficult, the economy in Nantong grew very slowly for a long time. In 2009 the Su-tong bridge was constructed to connect Nantong and Shanghai by a one-hour car trip. Because of the great improvement in accessibility, Nantong immediately attracted mass investment. A large-scale new town, named Su-tong New Town, was constructed at the north end of the bridge (figure 8.7).

The plan of this new town (with an area of about 50km$^2$) was prepared by a joint team with Chinese and Singaporean planners in efficient but cautious ways. The site of the new town used to be a state-owned farming firm with high productivity. This project was contracted by the local government with stipulations that it be constructed as "a model of low-carbon urban development" and "reduce its threats to the natural ecological system as much as possible."(Tsinghua Institute of Urban

Location of Nantong

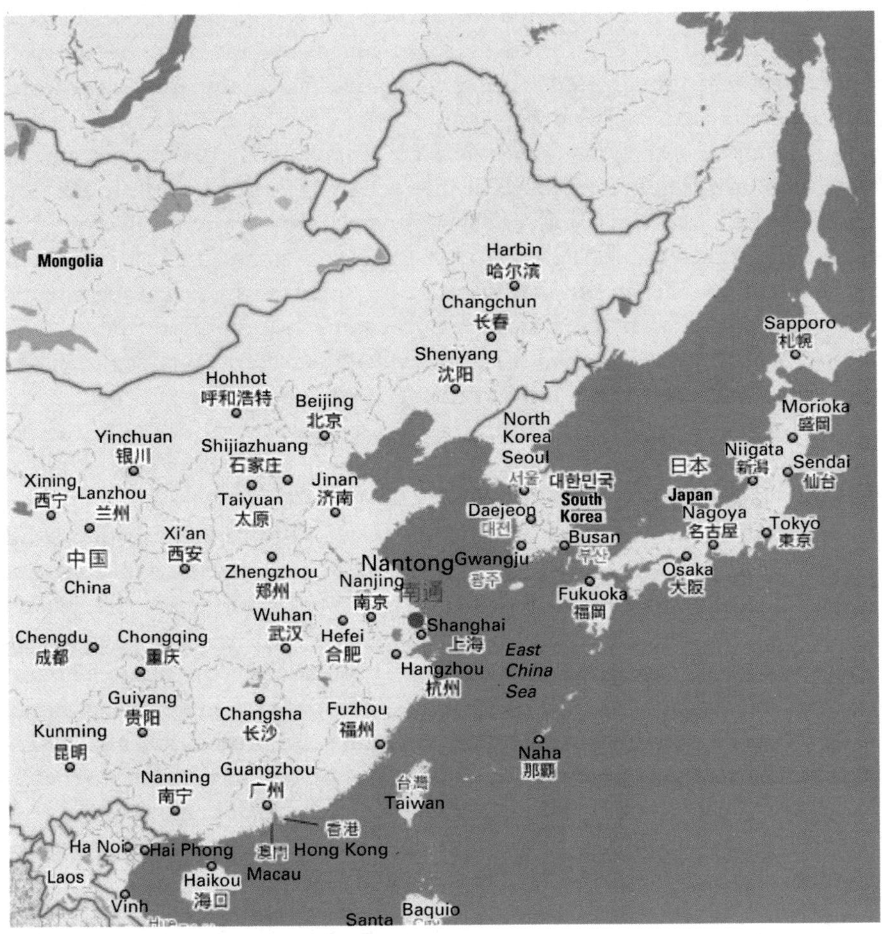




Planning and Design 2009) For the planners, this was a valuable experience that allowed them to put ideas for creating a low-carbon city into practice.

A series of new ideas were introduced in the detailed plan that distinguished it from traditional plans. The new ideas focused on five key issues: more compact land use, greener traffic, more original landscape and ecological system, more efficient energy use, and optimized technologies for water recycling. For every issue, the plan gives detailed guidance to regulate future development.

## Land Use: Compact and Mixed

In order to conserve land, the most important natural resource in China, higher construction density was encouraged in most plots. After a careful survey of the whole area, planners chose those plots with the highest ecological capability to construct the CBD of this new town, which will have the tallest buildings to host headquarters of new firms and enterprises. Most plots were designed for mixed develop-

**FIGURE 8.7**

Location of Su-tong New Town

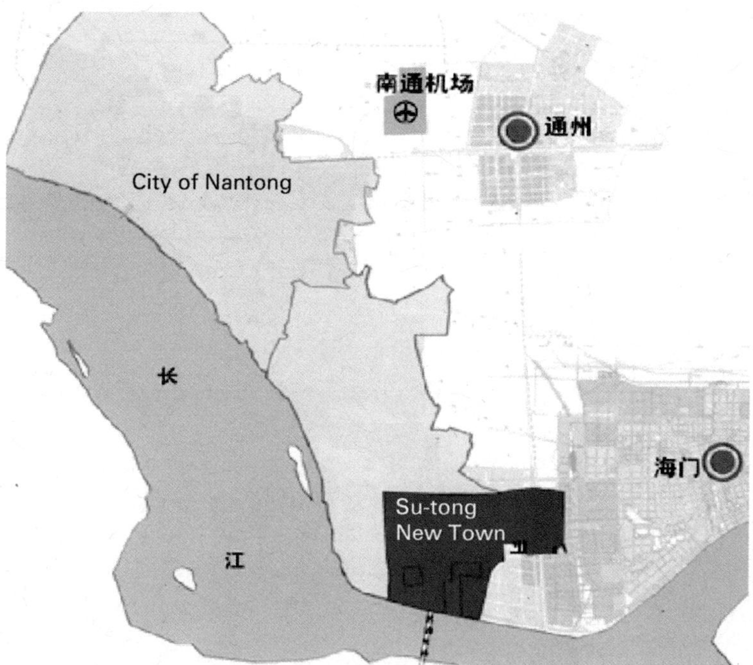


SOURCE: Drawn by author based on Google Earth.

ment. The residential, commercial, and nonpolluting industrial blocks are adjacent; this is expected to reduce daily traffic greatly.

## Traffic System

The first important idea is to implement the transit-oriented development strategy. All plots near the light-rail stations are given the highest floor-area-ratios. For other plots, the permitted construction volume decreases in proportion to the increase in distance to public transport hubs.

This plan also provides a complete low-speed road system for zero-emission traffic (pedestrians and bicycles). The low-speed road system can be reached easily from every block. Many of its parts are designed to cross beautiful woods, grasslands, or waterfront areas and therefore to encourage residents to choose this low-speed system for commuting. The public transportation and low-speed road systems are expected to accommodate approximately 85 percent of the traffic of the whole town.

## Landscape and Ecological System

The original natural landscape is highly emphasized in this plan. About 80 percent of the trees, grassland, wetlands, and waterways in the site are preserved. New trees are carefully chosen to increase local botanic diversity. In many large-scale industrial buildings, vegetation is required to be planted in the walls and roofs of buildings so that the green system could be continuous. Some special facilities, like stepping stones, have been installed to provide more suitable places for birds to rest.

## Energy Use

Very detailed guidance is provided to decide the applications of different central heating and air-conditioning facilities and technologies in every plot. In the densest areas, 100 percent of buildings are required to reach the national low-emissions building standard. The use of recycled energy is also encouraged in plots where the economic cost is considered to be lower.

## Water Recycling

More than 80 percent of original waterways have been preserved. They can be reached easily by residents after appropriate landscape design. Many new facilities for water supply have been introduced in appropriate areas in order to collect and clean rainwater for daily use. Because of very frequent rain in Nantong year-round, the use of rainwater could increase the water supply by 15 percent very inexpensively. The wetlands system is used to clean a part of wastewater, thus a smaller portion of wastewater cleaning facilities need to be used, which greatly reduces energy consumption.

On the basis of the principles in these five areas, the largest permitted volume of energy use and carbon emissions of every plot is decided. Energy use and carbon emissions can also be calculated if traditional ways were still used to regulate future development as usual, without any use of low-carbon technologies and facilities. Then energy savings and reductions in carbon emissions can be estimated for each plot and for the whole city (figures 8.8 and 8.9). Through the statutory power of the planning system, the ideas of the low-carbon city can be put into practice effectively.


Estimated Energy Saving in Every Plot

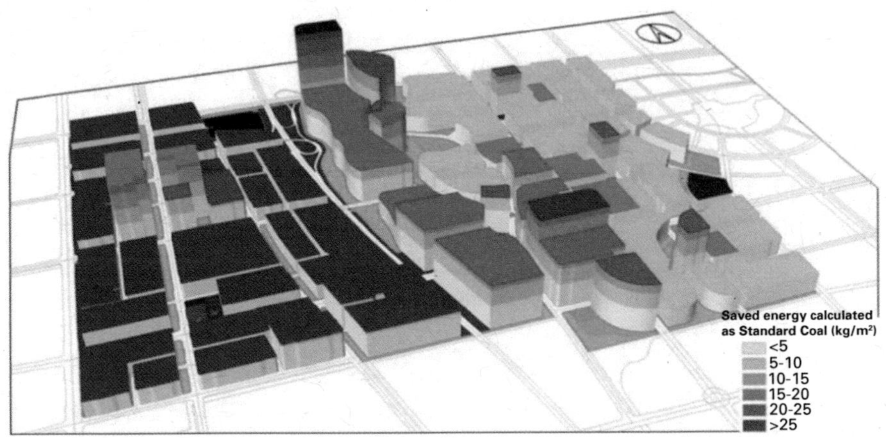


SOURCE: Tsinghua Institute of Urban Planning and Design (2009).

Estimated $CO_2$ Emissions Reduction in Every Plot

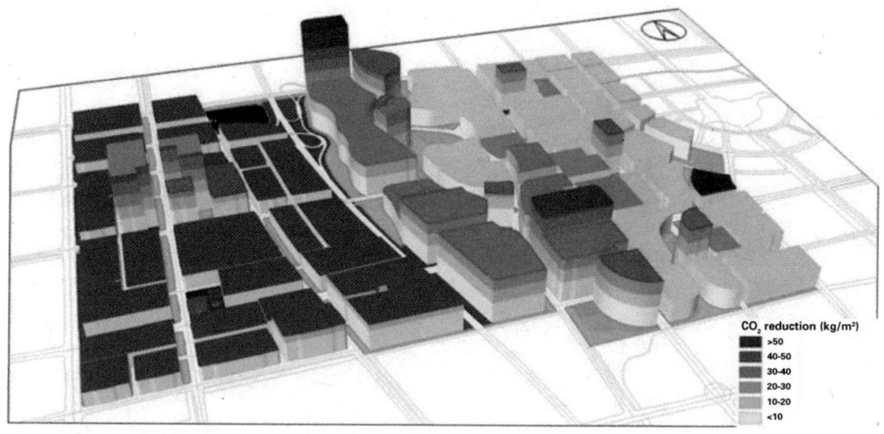


SOURCE: Tsinghua Institute of Urban Planning and Design (2009).

## Conclusion

A well-designed urban planning system can be an effective way to direct and monitor the development of low-carbon cities. The development of urban planning control has a very long history in China. Since the end of China's agrarian society, the planning system has been well-established and its authority is always maintained to regulate urban development effectively. Different planning ideas have been put into practice in every historic period. In the planned economy era, the Soviet urban planning system was introduced into China; as a result, urban planning was a reification of the national economical plan. Since the "reform and open" policy in 1978, the urban planning system changed sharply along with the economics system transformation. Under the market-oriented economics system, there is more and more guiding outline instead of control indexes in the urban planning. Economic reforms became the prime principle in implementing planning control. As a consequence, fast urban sprawl, similar to the American-style, has led to higher and higher carbon emissions. Although the high-speed urban growth in China can still go on in future years, the Chinese government still chooses to follow a more sustainable way toward "low-carbon cities" as a response to global climate change. The planning system then becomes the most effective way to direct and monitor the development of "low-carbon cities."

In recent practice, particularly the case in Nantong, many new attempts have been introduced distinguishing from the "traditional" plans in land use, traffic system, landscape and ecological system, energy use, and water cycle. All these attempts focus on five key issues: more compact land use, greener traffic, more original landscape and ecological systems, more efficient energy use, and optimized technologies for the water cycle.

Although China has recognized the importance of low-carbon urban planning and some cities have begun to institute low-carbon practices, most of them are still at the stage of macro aims and have not started implementation and operation. More research about both the low-carbon city and low-carbon urban planning is needed before the low-carbon ideology can be applied efficiently in urban planning practice and implementation.

## References


"2050 Japan Low-Carbon Society" Scenario Team. 2008. Japan scenarios and actions towards low-carbon societies. http://2050.nies.go.jp/material/2050_LCS_Scenarios_Actions_English_080715.pdf

Brown, Lester. 2006. *Plan B 2.0: Rescuing a planet under stress and a civilization in trouble.* Washington, DC: Earth Policy Institute.

China Academy of Social Science. 2012. China Urban Blue Book 2012. [In Chinese.] Beijing: China Academy of Social Science.

Chen, Fei, and Da Jian Zhu. 2009. Theory of research on low-carbon cities and Shanghai empirical analysis. [In Chinese.] *Urban Studies* 16(10):71–79.

Department of Trade and Industry. 2003. U.K. energy white paper: Our energy future—Creating a low carbon economy. London: The Stationary Office.

Dong, Jian Hong. 2006. The epic of 57 years: The development of urban planning since the establishment of the PRC. [In Chinese.] *Beijing Planning Review* 5:13–16.

English Partnerships. 2006. *A climate of change: English partnerships' response to the environmental agenda.* London: English Partnerships.

Fong, Wee-Kean, Hiroshi Matsumoto, Chin-Siong Ho, and Yu-Fat Lun. 2008. Energy consumption and carbon dioxide emission considerations in the urban planning process in Malaysia. *Journal of the Malaysian Institute of Planners* 6:101–130.

Fu, Yun, Yunlin Wang, and Ding Li. 2008. Research on low carbon city development. [In Chinese.] *Effect of Science on Society* 2:5–10.

Glaeser, Edward, and Matthew Kahn. 2008. The greenness of cities: Carbon dioxide emissions and urban development. NBER Working Paper No. 14238. http://www.escholarship.org/uc/item/2pk7j5cp

Gu, Chaolin, Zongbo Tan, Chunqiang Han, Zhilin Liu, Yixin Dai, Siqi Zheng, Yuan Liu, Taofang Yu, and Qing Han. 2009. *Climate change and low carbon urban planning.* [In Chinese.] Nanjing: Southeast University Press.

Hao, Shou Yi, ed. 2005. *Urban planning system in the rapidly urbanizing China.* [In Chinese.] Wuhan: Science and Technology University of Central China Press.

Kennedy, Christopher A., Anu Ramaswami, Sebastian Carney, and Shobhakar Dhakal. 2009. Greenhouse gas emission baselines for global cities and metropolitan regions. http://www.urs2009. net/

Liu, Dun-Zhen. 1980. *History of Chinese ancient architecture.* [In Chinese.] Beijing: China Construction Industry Press.

Liu, Zhilin, Yixin Dai, Changgui Dong, and Ye Qi. 2009. Low-carbon city: Concepts, international practice and implications for China. [In Chinese.] *Urban Studies* 16(6):1–12.

Long, Weiding, Wei Bai, Hao Liang, and Rui Fan. 2009. Energy system in low-carbon city. [In Chinese.] *Heating, Ventilating & Air Conditioning* 39(8):79–84.

National Bureau of Statistics. 2007. *China energy statistical yearbook.* [In Chinese.] Beijing: China Statistics Press.

———. 2008. *China energy statistical yearbook.* [In Chinese.] Beijing: China Statistics Press.

———. 2009. *China energy statistical yearbook.* [In Chinese.] Beijing: China Statistics Press.

Ove Arup and Partners. 2007. *A review of planning and climate change.* London: English Partnerships.

Qiu, Baoxing. 2009. The urbanization mode of the towns with Chinese features—mode C: Surpassing the enticement of mode A and the trap of mode B. [In Chinese.] *Urban Studies* 16(1):1–7.

———. 2010. From green building to low-carbon ecocity. [In Chinese.] *China City Planning Review* 19(1):8–16.

Ren, Zhiyuan. 2000. *The management of urban planning in the 21st century.* [In Chinese.] Nanjing: Southeast University Press.

Research Group of Sustainable Development Strategies, China Academy of Sciences. 2009. *Report of sustainable development strategies in China 2009.* [In Chinese.] Beijing: Science Press.

Sit, Victor F. S. 1995. *Beijing: The nature and planning of a Chinese capital city.* West Sussex, U.K.: John Wiley and Sons.

Stern, Nicolas. 2007. *The economics of climate change: The Stern review.* Cambridge, U.K.: Cambridge University Press.

Tan, Zongbo. 2005. *Introduction to urban planning and design.* [In Chinese.] Beijing: Tsinghua University Press.

Tongji University. 1991. *Urban planning principles.* [In Chinese.] Beijing: China Construction Industry Press.

Tsinghua Institute of Urban Planning and Design. 2009. Conception planning for Nantong Science Park. [In Chinese.] Report to Nantong Municipal Govenment.

United Nations. 2007. *World population prospects: The 2006 revision and world urbanization prospects: The 2007 revision.* http://esa.un.org/unup

United Nations. 2011. Millennium Development Goals Indicators. http://mdgs.un.org/unsd/mdg/SeriesDetail.aspx?srid=749&crid=

Wang, De Hua. 2005. *Outline of the city planning history of China.* [In Chinese.] Nanjing: Southeast University Press.

Wang, Ya Ping. 1992. Private sector housing in urban China since 1949: The case of Xian. *Housing Studies* 7(2):119–137.

Zhao, Caijun, and Xiaoming Liu. 2010. The role of the urban green space system in the low-carbon city. [In Chinese.] *Chinese Landscape Architecture* 6:23–26.

Zhu, Jianfei. 2004. *Chinese spatial strategies: Imperial Beijing, 1420–1911.* London: Routledge Curzon.

# Carbon Footprint in the Least Developed Regions

## A Case Study of Guangyuan City

DABO GUAN

In addition to the long-standing environmental concern about industrial air pollution, the sheer quantity of resources consumed by the world economy is recognized today as the overarching threat to planetary health. In spite of increasing efficiency levels and better management of hazardous materials, human demand for resources continues to grow (Peters et al. 2007). Thus, maintaining a balance between socioeconomic goals and environmental sustainability requires not only an understanding of economic resource flows but also knowledge of how much biological capacity is needed to support resource flows and absorb waste streams. The international community has become aware of the urgent need to combat global climate change, which is mainly the result of greenhouse gas (GHG) emissions, particularly carbon dioxide ($CO_2$) emissions.

The term "carbon footprint" in this chapter refers to the total amount of $CO_2$ emissions that result directly and indirectly from the individual consumption of goods and services. The carbon footprint can be used as an environmental indicator to study low-carbon development in Guangyuan. Direct emissions arise from heating, cooking, electronic appliances, daily commutes, and personal traveling, among other sources. Indirect emissions arise from the production and distribution of food, drinks, clothes, and all other products made for purchase.

China has been enjoying the world's fastest economic growth, with a 9.6 percent average annual growth rate of gross domestic product (GDP) since Deng Xiaoping implemented the "open-door policy" in 1978, in comparison with the world's average of 3.3 percent during the same period (National Bureau of Statistics 2007). By 2005 China's GDP reached US\$1.13 trillion (Hubacek et al. 2009), which puts China among the world's four largest economies and makes it the second-largest economy in purchasing power parity. The latest statistics have shown that China has overtaken Japan and become the world's second-largest economy after the United States in 2010. However, Deng's "ladder-up" strategy of economic development has increased regional income inequality between the more affluent coastal urban areas and rural western China and also between southern and northern regions (Hubacek et al. 2009; Hubacek et al. 2007).

The great regional socioeconomic disparity has led to different levels of $CO_2$ emissions. China has been the world's top emitter since 2007 (Gregg et al. 2008; Guan et al. 2009) and will continue to be the leading contributor to global carbon emissions over the next few decades. However, Chinese per capita $CO_2$ emissions are still far below those of many developed countries, especially in the lagging regions such as rural China. Chinese per capita $CO_2$ emissions (carbon footprint) increased from 1.8 tons/year in 1981 to 5.1 tons/year in 2007 (figure 9.1). The Chinese figure is less than one-fourth the U.S. level and one-third the European Union's average or Japanese level, but almost twice the Latin America and Carribean average and four times the South Asia average (figure 9.2). The per capita urban Chinese carbon footprint was 8 tons/year of $CO_2$ emissions in 2009 (Feng et al. 2012), which was almost similar to the EU average. Every rural Chinese resident generated 2.3 tons/year of $CO_2$ emissions in 2009 (Liu et al. 2012), which was similar to the Latin American countries.

China has shown a determination to collaboratively tackle climate change after 2012. For example, China made a commitment to reduce energy intensity by 20 percent from 2005 to 2010 in its 11th Five-Year Plan (NDRC 2006) and, before the Copenhagen Climate Summit meeting, expanded its commitment to achieve a 40 to 45 percent reduction of carbon intensity by 2020 relative to 2005 levels, partly through its rapid increase in electricity-generation capacities from low-carbon energy sources. For example, China has doubled its installed capacity for wind power annually since 2005 (Guan and Hubacek 2010). However, there are significant

**FIGURE 9.1**

Per Capita Carbon Footprint in China (1981–2007)

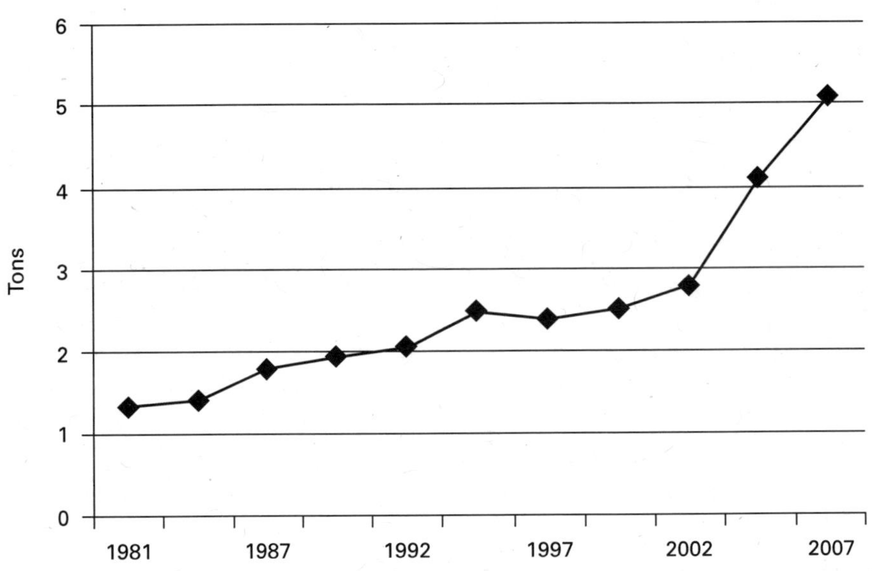


SOURCE: Guan et al. (2008).

**FIGURE 9.2**

Per Capita Carbon Footprints, 2008

| The trend of per capita carbon footprint | 2008 (Tons) | Trends 1990 to 2008 |
|---|---|---|
| Region 1: North America | | 20.00 |
| Region 2: Europe & USSR | | 11.76 |
| Region 3: Pacific OECD | | 12.06 |
| Region 4: Centrally planned Asia & China | | 4.41 |
| Region 5: South Asia | | 1.20 |
| Region 6: Other Pacific Asia | | 1.75 |
| Region 7: Sub-Saharan Africa | | 0.57 |
| Region 8: Middle East & North Africa | | 6.28 |
| Region 9: Latin America & the Caribbean | | 2.89 |

SOURCE: Author's own calculation based on datasets from Peters et al. (2012).

disparities in technology level among Chinese regions. For example, the relatively wealthier regions in China, such as the coastal provinces, usually possess relatively advanced production technologies, and there are no effective domestic technology spillovers within Chinese provinces. Therefore, China faces great challenges in helping the country's least developed regions move away from a carbon-intensive modernization path.

This chapter explores current trajectories and scenarios for the development of Guangyuan, one of the least developed cities, located in Sichuan Province in southwestern China, until 2020. This case study can provide information for designing low-carbon development of the least developed regions or countries. The scenarios include analyses of population growth, per capita income growth, urbanization, and lifestyle changes, as well as structural economic changes, technical changes, and changes in resource efficiency. The implications of these changes are analyzed and measured by adopting the carbon footprint. The approach is based on input-output (I/O) analysis extended by these resource-consumption indicators.

## Scenario Analysis Based on Input-Output Methodology

Scenario analysis has become very popular with researchers because it provides an indispensable tool for analyzing large-scale interactions among social, economic, and environmental systems with long-term horizons (Hubacek et al. 2007). Its coherent framework of analysis can show the development of and interaction among the relevant systems and can guide discussion on points of interest (Clark and Munn 1986; Prieler et al. 1998; Toth et al. 1989).

In order to compare different development paths or scenarios in a society, a framework for evaluation is needed. I/O tables extended by sustainability indicators provide such a framework (Duchin 1998). I/O analysis emphasizes the structure, interrelationship, and state of ecological-economic systems during a certain interval of time, usually a year. The fundamental purpose of the I/O model is to analyze the interdependence of economic sectors. Its extensions include social institutions (e.g., Stone 1970) and the environment (see e.g. Duchin and Lange 1994;

Leontief 1970; Victor 1972). I/O analysis has often been criticized on the grounds that the basic input-output relations are represented by fixed coefficients, given a certain period of time. The assumption behind input-output analyis is that the physical structure does not automatically respond to changes in prices. Input-output assumes fixed-proportion (Leontief-type) production functions, which also means that input functions are linear. On the other hand, input-output analysis does allow one to deal with discrete and explicit changes in structures (Duchin 1998, 80). These changes in structure are derived from scenarios developed around each question to be explored. Structural changes include the technology used in different sectors, the proportion of industrial outputs from different sectors contributing total economic output, changes in the composition and extent of the different final demand sectors, and the availability and quality of different environmental resources. Technical literature and expert knowledge are important sources of information on current and potential future production processes, population and other social trends, and the environment.

## The Basic Input-Output Model

Input-output models can be used to show income and trade relationships among sectors within an economic region and among regions. They are also useful as a policy tool for analyzing the interaction between land use change and economic and social systems.

The basic I/O equation is

$$(I - A)\, x = y, \tag{1}$$

where the exogenous variable, final demand ($y$), appears on the right-hand side, and the endogenous variable, sectoral output ($x$), appears on the left of equation 1. The ratio of input to output, $x_{ij}/x_j$, is denoted by $a_{ij}$, where $x_j$ is defined as the total output of sector $j$:

$$a_{ij} = \frac{x_{ij}}{x_j}. \tag{2}$$

These technical coefficients $a_{ij}$ are assumed to be fixed within a certain specified period. This means that each sector uses inputs in fixed proportions, with the assumption that the average expenditure propensities are equal to marginal ones, and economies of scale in production are ignored.

Economic effects are estimated by an analysis of the impact of changes in the exogenous factors. Effects on total output ($\Delta x$) of the economy are calculated by multiplying the matrix inverse $(I - A)^{-1}$ by the vector $\Delta y$ representing the change in final consumption:

$$\Delta x = (A - A)^{-1}\, \Delta y, \tag{3}$$

where the term $(I - A)^{-1}$ is usually written as $M$, the matrix of multipliers or Leontief coefficients. Changes over time in the matrix $M$ reflect the effects of technical change, changes in product mix, and changes in input prices.

## Extension of the Input-Output Model: Accounting for the Environment

Over the past decades, one of the most frequent applications of I/O analysis has been examination of the interaction of the economy and the environment (Rose and Miernyk 1989). However, the application of I/O analysis to environmental problems seems surprising at first sight because there is often a lack of market prices, and there are nonlinear relationships that govern the interactions between economic and ecological systems. But environmental inputs and outputs can be made consistent with I/O accounting. A number of different approaches to incorporate the environment have been developed. We follow the tradition developed by Leontief (1970), who focused on the flows from the economy to the environment. "The technical interdependence between the levels of desirable and undesirable output can be described in terms of structural coefficients similar to those used to trace the structural interdependence among all the regular branches of production and consumption into the conventional input-output framework" (Leontief 1986, 242).

Leontief introduced pollution coefficients to relate pollution to the activity of each industry. This basic idea can be extended to account for all types of pollution or resource-consumption coefficients and is here applied to carbon footprints (CFs).

In order to link an environmental indicator, for example, the CF, here denoted by $L$, to economic sectors, the vector representing changes in output ($\Delta x$) is premultiplied by a diagonal CF coefficient matrix ($\hat{C}$). The CF-requirement coefficient vector ($c_j$) is calculated by dividing total CF in each sector ($L_j$) by the total sectoral output ($x_j$):

$$c_j = \frac{L_j}{x_j}. \tag{4}$$

The CF-requirement coefficient vector ($c_j$) represents the CF in tons per 10,000 yuan or dollar of output of sector $j$ (see also Wiedmann et al. 2006). The derived coefficients are then used to calculate the total CF requirements, $CF_{2020}$, for 2020 by premultiplying the new output vector for 2020 ($x_{2020}$) by the diagonalized emission coefficients:

$$CF_{2020} = \hat{C} \times x_{2020}. \tag{5}$$

## Scenarios

In order to make the projection of the total CF required in Guangyuan for the year 2020, five main factors are determined, and widely accepted scenarios for these major driving forces are applied (see Garbaccio et al. 1999; Hubacek and Sun 2001; 2005; Wu et al. 2005).

*Economic Growth and Consequent Per Capita Income Growth.* Since 1978 China's GDP has expanded at an average annual rate of nearly 10 percent. Since 2005, the growth has achieved double digits. However, GDP growth in Guangyuan has been slower than the national average. Its per capita GDP increased at an average annual rate of 7.8 percent from 1978 to 2007 (Guangyuan Statistics Bureau 2009). The Guangyuan Development and Reform Commission established a 12 percent GDP increase per year until 2010 and an annual 10 percent increase during its 12th Five-Year Plan (2011–2015) (Guangyuan Development and Reform Commission 2009b). For the period 2006–2010, the national average GDP growth rate projected by the World Bank is used. Assuming the continuance of high savings rates that support high investment rates, of the market-oriented reforms, and of high factor-productivity growth, the World Bank projected an average annual GDP growth rate of 6.6 percent until 2020 (World Bank 1997). It is assumed that the pace of GDP growth will slow over time, from about 10 percent today to 7 percent in 2020, because of a slowdown in the growth of the labor force, diminishing marginal returns, and lower gains from structural change (Hubacek et al. 2009). Furthermore, separate growth rates for urban and rural areas are used because of the huge inequalities in growth and governmental investment between the two areas. Hubacek et al. (2009) stated that the per capita income level of urban residents has been growing to 3 times higher than that of their rural counterparts since 1980s.

*Population Dynamics and Urbanization.* China's population increased from about 540 million in 1949 to more than 1.3 billion by 2006 (National Bureau of Statistics, 2007). The high share of Chinese of reproductive age has created a strong population momentum that drives China's population growth despite low levels of fertility (Heilig et al. 2000). China is confronted with two counteracting trends: although economic growth, urbanization, and associated lifestyle changes may lead to lower fertility rates, modernization and the opening of society may lead to opposition to the government's strict one-child policy in family planning. Guangyuan's population growth has been in line with the national trend. Guangyuan's population was about 3.1 million in 2007, and the population growth rate has been around 1 percent per year since 2000. Furthermore, Guangyuan's urbanization rate was only 21 percent in 2007 (Guangyuan Statistics Bureau 2009). In order to predict Guangyuan's population in 2020, a 1 percent growth rate is used, and therefore, the population will reach 3.5 million by 2020. In its most recent projection, the Population Group of the International Institute for Applied System Analysis in Austria estimated that China's population will be 1.43 billion in 2020 (Cao 2000), and the urbanization rate will be about 50 percent. In this chapter, it is assumed that the urbanization rate in Guangyuan will reach the national average of 50 percent by 2020.

*Changing Consumption Patterns.* For 2007, people's consumption patterns in urban and rural households are taken from the derived Guangyuan input-output table for 2007 (details of the construction of this table are presented later). For the year 2020, estimates of income elasticities of demand and per capita income are used (Hubacek and Sun 1999; 2001).

*Technical and Structural Change.* The RAS technique is adopted to estimate the Leontief technical coefficients matrix (*A* matrix) for 2020, $\mathbf{A}_{2020}$. The RAS method is widely used to update an I/O table over a certain period or to adjust a national table in order to derive a regional table. The basic method is outlined in Miller and Blair (1985). The base-year technique matrix is denoted by $\mathbf{A}_{2007} = [a_{ij}]$. Each coefficient $a_{ij}$ is subject to two intertemporal effects: the substitution effect, which measures the extent to which the output of the $i$th sector has been replaced by other sectoral outputs intermediate production; and the fabrication effect, which measures the extent to which the ratio of intermediate to total inputs changed in the $j$th sector. As a result of these two effects, the technical coefficient matrix in 2020 can be computed as $\mathbf{A}_{2020} = \hat{r}\,\mathbf{A}_{2007}\,\hat{s}$. The information in the two diagonal matrices, $\hat{r}$ and $\hat{s}$, can be obtained from estimations of the total output in 2020, $x_{2020}$. In order to obtain $x_{2020}$, it is assumed that the ratio of final demand in 2020 ($y_{2020}$) to total output ($x_{2020}$) is the same as in the base year 2007.

*Carbon intensity.* In this chapter, one scenario is set up to meet the target of carbon intensity for Guangyuan to achieve by 2020: 40 percent, which complies with China's national requirement "to achieve 40%–45% of carbon intensity reduction by 2020 relative to 2005 level" (Qiu 2009, 551).

## Data

### Guangyuan Input-Output Table

In this chapter, environmental input-output techniques are used to assess Guangyuan's carbon footprint. The core is an input-output table. China regularly publishes national and provincial input-output tables every five years. However, city-level tables rarely exist. Many studies in the literature use the production technology matrix (the *A* matrix) from other sources. For example, either the national average or the Sichuan provincial production technology matrix can be used as a proxy. However, Guangyuan is at an early stage of industrialization, which agricultural and primary industrial activities are the main economic contributor. This is different from the Sichuan provincial or the national economy. In other words, the *A* matrix obtained from either the Sichuan or the national input-output table can be used as a reference base, but it requires appropriate adjustments to fully represent Guangyuan's production structure.

In order to understand Guangyuan's economic structure, the first step was to interview key officials in the Guangyuan Development and Reform Commission, the Guangyuan Statistics Bureau, and the Guangyuan Agriculture Bureau to obtain necessary production and consumption information for Guangyuan. These interviews provided important information about the dominant economic sectors and key production and export commodities in Guangyuan. Three focus-group interviews were conducted at each governmental agency. Each focus group consisted of six to eight people, including a director or deputy director of the agency and supervisors of different executive offices. Second, national accounts, GDP composition, industrial outputs, and consumption data were obtained from the *Guangyuan Statistics Yearbook 2008* (Guangyuan Statistics Bureau 2009) to generate the final-demand and value-added sections of an input-output table for the year 2007. Third, the Sichuan production technology matrix obtained from the Sichuan input-output table for 2005 (Sichuan Statistics Bureau 2007) was adapted by using the RAS technique to generate a Guangyuan-oriented production technology matrix for 2007.

The Guangyuan input-output table is presented at 42 by 42 economic sectors. This is a commodity-by-industry table based on the assumption of homogeneous sector output. This means that each commodity is produced by only one industry, and each industry produces only one product. The value-added categories in the table include capital depreciation, labor compensation, taxes, and profits. "Final use" comprises six categories: rural households, urban households, government consumption, fixed investment, inventory changes, and net exports.

### Energy-Inventory and $CO_2$ Emissions Data

An energy-balance table is essential for $CO_2$ emissions accounting. China conducts a regular energy inventory and publishes annual energy-balance tables at both national and provincial levels every year. However, city-level tables are not always available. Guangyuan, one of the least developed regions in China, does not possess a complete energy-inventory system; in other words, the local statistical authority has never compiled an energy-balance table for Guangyuan. In order to guarantee the quality of the data, key officials were interviewed with the approach and procedures described earlier, but this time from the Guangyuan Development and Reform Commission, the Guangyuan Statistics Bureau, the Guangyuan Electricity Bureau, and the Guangyuan Agriculture Bureau, to obtain the necessary information and some raw statistics. This information was used to generate the energy-balance table for Guangyuan 2007 that is used in this chapter.

Furthermore, industrial final energy-consumption data at the sectoral level are needed in order to apply the environmental I/O analysis to assess the carbon footprint. The *Guangyuan Statistics Yearbook 2008* (Guangyuan Statistics Bureau 2009) provided sectoral industrial final energy-consumption data for large and medium-size enterprises. The Guangyuan Development and Reform Commission estimated that large and medium-size enterprises account for approximately 80 percent of final energy consumption. This estimate was used to generate industrial final energy consumption for Guanyuan.

$CO_2$ emissions from combustion of fuels and industrial processes were calculated using the Intergovernmental Panel on Climate Change's emissions-accounting methodology (IPCC 2006). The energy and emissions data for both years cover 38 production sectors and 2 household sectors (urban and rural). Due to different sectoral specifications between emission (38 sectors) and I/O datasets (42 sectors), a normalization process is required between energy data and input-output tables follows our previous work (Guan et al. 2008).

## Guangyuan's Carbon Footprint in 2007

Guangyuan's production-related $CO_2$ emissions within its territorial boundaries in 2007 were 5.72 million tons of $CO_2$. The per capita carbon footprint (in terms of in-territory inventory accounting) was 1.86 tons, which is approximately one-third the national average.

**TABLE 9.1**

Top 5 Sectors in Share of Direct $CO_2$ Emissions in
Guangyuan, 2007

| Sector | Million Tons | Share of Total Emissions (%) |
|---|---|---|
| Coal mining and processing | 3.33 | 58 |
| Coking | 0.86 | 15 |
| Electricity generation | 0.50 | 9 |
| Nonmetal mineral products | 0.25 | 4 |
| Agriculture | 0.17 | 3 |

Table 9.1 shows the major sources of Guangyuan's direct $CO_2$ emissions in 2007. Primary and secondary energy-processing industrial sectors are the dominant sources and together accounted for over 70 percent of the total emissions. For example, of the 5.72 million tons of $CO_2$ emissions, 3.3 million tons (58 percent) were from coal mining and processing, and 0.86 million tons (15 percent) were from coking and its refining sector. The power-generation sector accounted for about half a million tons of total $CO_2$ emissions, or 9 percent. The remaining 1 million tons of $CO_2$ emissions, or 18 percent, were shared among nonmetallic-material processing, such as cement production (0.25 million tons, 4 percent), agriculture (0.17 million tons, 3 percent), construction (0.01 million tons, 2 percent), and other sectors.

If both direct and indirect emissions are accounted for from the perspective of the entire production supply chain, $CO_2$ emissions caused by Guangyuan's economic activities are primarily driven by the construction and petroleum-refining sectors. As shown in table 9.2, the construction and metal-processing sectors were the main driving forces of $CO_2$ emissions in Guangyuan in 2007, at 8.80 million and 3.95 million tons, respectively. On the other hand, the consumption of imported petroleum by urban households was responsible for 8.73 million tons of $CO_2$ emissions generated in other regions (outside Guangyuan territory) (table 9.3). Similarly, the net imports (imports minus exports) of nonmetallic materials (e.g., cement and glass) for construction purposes caused 1.14 million tons of $CO_2$ emissions in other regions. The net imports of apparel, leather, furs, down, and related products mainly consumed by urban households were responsible for 1.06 million tons of $CO_2$ emissions in other regions.

## Guangyuan's Carbon Footprint in 2020

This section first introduces the projected economic conditions for Guangyuan in 2020 according to the projection parameters described earlier in this chapter. Second, Guangyuan's projected 2020 $CO_2$ emissions and carbon footprint are calculated, and the main driving forces under the 40 percent carbon intensity reduction target described earlier are analyzed.

**TABLE 9.2**

Top 5 Sectors in Share of Both Direct and Indirect $CO_2$ Emissions in Guangyuan, 2007

| Sector | Million Tons |
| --- | --- |
| Construction | 8.80 |
| Metals smelting and pressing | 3.95 |
| Electricity generation | 1.85 |
| Food processing | 0.89 |
| Agriculture | 0.84 |

**TABLE 9.3**

Top 5 Sectors in Share of $CO_2$ Emissions in Other Regions Due to Guangyuan's Imports, 2007

| Sector | Million Tons |
| --- | --- |
| Wearing apparel, leather, and related products | 1.06 |
| Petroleum processing | 8.73 |
| Nonmetal mineral products | 1.14 |
| Metal products | 0.65 |
| Electric equipment and machinery | 0.52 |

## Guangyuan's Economic Condition in 2020

Guangyuan's annual GDP growth is projected to be an average of 9.8 percent from 2008 to 2020. The level of GDP will reach 7.7 billion yuan by 2020, up from 2.3 billion yuan in 2007 (constant 2007 prices). The population will grow from 3.1 million in 2007 to 3.5 million by 2020. The urbanization process will be accelerated to achieve a rate of 50 percent in 2020, up from 21 percent in 2007. Urbanization will significantly influence people's consumption patterns and economic final-demand distributions. Current great disparities in income levels and consumption expenditure patterns between rural and urban households will increase further. As a result, per capita consumption in rural households will increase from 1,773 yuan in 2007 (Guangyuan Statistics Bureau 2009) to 2,622 yuan in 2020, while per capita consumption in urban households will increase from 7,572 yuan to 11,802 yuan during the same period (Guangyuan Statistics Bureau 2009). Households consumption patterns will also shift from agricultural and primary industrial products to services. For example, the share of agricultural products will decrease from 36 percent in 2007 to 28 percent by 2020, while the share of industrial goods and services will increase slightly from 34 percent and 30 percent to 37 percent and 35 percent, respectively, during the same period.

Consumption patterns in urban households will also change significantly. The share of agricultural products will decrease from 18 percent to 13 percent, and the share of industrial goods and services will increase from 44 percent and 38 percent to 46 percent and 41 percent, respectively.

## Carbon Footprint in the 40 Percent Carbon-Intensity-Reduction Scenario

China's energy-consumption structure is dominated by coal, which accounted for almost 70 percent of total energy use in 2007. Although coal is still the dominant energy source for Guangyuan's economy, the proportion is much less, 62 percent of total energy use. Renewable energy (e.g., hydropower) accounts for 17 percent, compared with the Chinese national average of 7 percent (Guangyuan Statistics Bureau 2009; National Bureau of Statistics 2008). Furthermore, Guangyuan has great potential to enlarge the development and use of natural gas (which produces much lower carbon emissions than coal) and renewable energy, particularly hydropower and biogas.

Guangyuan's production-related coal consumption in 2007 was 4.3 million tons. The coal-mining and dressing sector accounted for 64 percent, the coking sector for 14 percent, and the electricity-generation sector for 12 percent (Guangyuan Statistics Bureau 2009). Hydropower accounts for about 80 percent, or 2.1 terawatt-hours, of total electricity generation in Guangyuan, while the remaining 20 percent, or 560 gigawatt-hours, is produced by coal-fired power plants. The electricity production generated by Guangyuan itself can satisfy only 60 percent of total industrial and household consumption demands. The gap is filled by importing electricity from other regions, which is usually produced by coal-fired plants. Guangyuan local authoritites will continue using renewable energy and will develop fossil fuels with lower carbon emissions (e.g., natural gas) in order to gradually self-supply its electricity consumption. By 2015 Guangyuan will complete the construction of 1.5 gigawatts hydropower plants, 1.1 gigawatts – 600 millonwatts natural gas plants, and 5 × 1 millionwatts biogas electricity generators for rural households' consumption (Guangyuan Development and Reform Commission 2009b).

Furthermore, Guangyuan aims to take advantage of low-carbon development to promote the concept of circular flows for its economic growth. Guangyuan traditionally has had a good reputation for tea, forestry products, and kiwi fruit, which are high-value-added agricultural products. However, the planting scale is relatively small and is based on the family unit. Guangyuan local authorities have invested in and encouraged centralized and large-scale planting (Guangyuan Agriculture Bureau, 2009), which could potentially benefit local employment and accelerate change of the production structure toward low-carbon but high-value-added industrial development. In other words, many economically least developed regions or countries have unique characteristics that usually involve low carbon emissions and can maintain their economic growth, and policy makers should try to build on these characteristics and not mimic the industrialization and modernization patterns of developed regions.

If Guangyuan were to achieve a 40 percent reduction in carbon intensity relative to the 2005 level by 2020 (the Chinese national target presented at the Copenhagen meeting), Guangyuan's production-related $CO_2$ emissions would decrease by 4 percent to 5.52 million tons because of its continuously rapid economic development. Furthermore, the per capita carbon footprint would significantly decline, from 1.86 tons per year in 2007 to 1.59 tons per year by 2020.

Under this scenario, energy mining and processing sectors would still be the major drivers of Guangyuan's direct $CO_2$ emissions, as in 2007. Coal-mining and coking sectors will account for 42 percent (2.3 million tons) and 11 percent (0.6 million tons) of $CO_2$ emissions, respectively. The share of $CO_2$ emissions from the power-generation sector will increase from 9 percent (0.5 million tons) to 17 percent (0.95 million tons). Other major drivers, such as chemicals and nonmetallic production, are shown in table 9.4.

If both direct and indirect $CO_2$ emissions are considered from the perspective of entire product life cycles, construction will be responsible for 8.58 million tons of $CO_2$ emissions, while electricity generation will be responsible for 2.25 million tons of $CO_2$ emissions (table 9.5). On the other hand, Guangyuan will import 231 million yuan worth of petroleum products to drive its economy, and these imports will result in the emission of 5.24 million tons of $CO_2$ in other regions. Other major imports, such as nonmetallic products, coal, and metal products, will result in emissions of 1.27 million tons, 0.63 million tons, and 0.56 million tons of $CO_2$, respectively, in other regions (table 9.6).

**TABLE 9.4**

Top 5 Sectors in Share of Direct $CO_2$ Emissions in Guangyuan in 2020 for the 40% Carbon-Intensity-Reduction Scenario

| Sector | Million Tons | Share of Total Emissions (%) |
|---|---|---|
| Coal mining and processing | 2.32 | 42 |
| Electricity generation | 0.95 | 17 |
| Coking | 0.60 | 11 |
| Nonmetal mineral products | 0.34 | 6 |
| Chemicals | 0.31 | 6 |

**TABLE 9.5**

Top 5 Sectors in Share of Both Direct and Indirect $CO_2$ Emissions in Guangyuan in 2020 for the 40% Carbon-Intensity-Reduction Scenario

| Sector | Million Tons |
|---|---|
| Construction | 8.58 |
| Electricity generation | 2.25 |
| Metal smelting and pressing | 0.64 |
| Chemicals | 0.60 |
| Wholesale and retail trade | 0.31 |

**TABLE 9.6**

Top 5 Sectors in Share of $CO_2$ Emissions in Other Regions Due to Guangyuan's Imports in 2020 for the 40% Carbon-Intensity-Reduction Scenario

| Sector | Million Tons |
| --- | --- |
| Petroleum processing | 5.24 |
| Nonmetal mineral products | 1.27 |
| Coal mining and processing | 0.63 |
| Metal products | 0.56 |
| Paper and printing | 0.30 |

## Conclusion

The analysis in this chapter gives an overview of only one possible low-carbon economic future Guangyuan may have. One of the prerequisites to allow technology significantly reduce the emission led by economic growth is that Guangyuan maintain a production pattern and development path similar to that of the past. Production activities that are low in energy intensity, such as agriculture and services, will still need to play the dominant role in Guangyuan's economic development. In other words, Guangyuan to will have to leapfrog from preindustrialization to postindustrialization. However, the reality is that many of the least developed regions in northwestern and southwestern China, including Guangyuan, are being urged to develop their economies, and energy-intensive industrialization is a shortcut to achieve high GDP growth. In order to the latest governmental plan, Guangyuan local authorities are interested in attracting investments via both domestic and foreign channels to build a large-scale production base for electrolytic aluminum and cement. If the newly built energy-intensive factories have the latest technology, their carbon intensity will be significantly less than that of the small-scale production Guangyuan currently has. But the price paid for heavily expanding aluminum and cement production is damage to the environment, which repeats the development path of many Western countries, as well as the economically advanced coastal regions in China. The key driver of local authorities eager for quick success in economic growth is regional competition in economic achievements. Further, GDP is still the main measure of officials' performance. One of the key messages from the Chinese "harmonious development" concept is to avoid the development path of polluting first and dealing with it later. Local authorities in the least developed regions or countries should give careful thought to whether they and their citizens would prefer low-carbon development or only lower-carbon development.

## References

Cao, Gui-Ying. 2000. The future population of China: Prospects to 2045 by place of residence and by level of education. Interim Report. Laxenburg, Austria: International Institute of Applied System Research.

Clark, William C. and Ted R. E. Munn. 1986. *Sustainable development of the biosphere.* Cambridge, U.K.: Cambridge University Press.

Duchin, Faye. 1998. *Structural economics: Measuring change in technology, lifestyles, and the environment.* Washington, DC: Island Press.

Duchin, Faye, and Glenn-Marie Lange. 1994. *The future of the environment: Ecological economics and technological change.* New York: Oxford University Press.

Feng, Kuishuang, Klaus Hubacek, Yim-Ling Siu, and Dabo Guan. 2012. Analyzing drivers of regional carbon dioxide emissions for China. *Journal of Industrial Ecology* 16(4):600–611.

Garbaccio, Roberto F., Mun S. Ho, and Dale W. Jorgenson. 1999. Why has the energy-output ratio fallen in China? *The Energy Journal* 20:63–91.

Gregg, Jay, Robert J. Andres, and Gregg Marland. 2008. China: Emissions pattern of the world leader in $CO_2$ emissions from fossil fuel consumption and cement production. *Geophysical Research Letters* 35.

Guan, Dabo, and Klaus Hubacek. 2010. China can offer domestic emission cap-and-trade in post 2012. *Environmental Science & Technology* 44:5327.

Guan, Dabo, Klaus Hubacek, Christopher L. Webber, Glen P. Peters, and David M. Reiner. 2008. The drivers of Chinese $CO_2$ emissions from 1980 to 2030. Unpublished paper.

Guan, Dabo, Glen P. Peters, Christopher L. Webber, and Klaus Hubacek. 2009. Journey to world top emitter—An analysis of the driving forces of China's recent emissions surge. *Geophysical Research Letters* 36.

Guangyuan Agriculture Bureau. 2009. *Guangyuan's future agriculture development.* Guangyuan: Guangyuan Agriculture Bureau.

Guangyuan Development and Reform Commission. 2009a. *Guangyuan's energy: Current situation and future outlook.* Guangyuan: Guangyuan Development and Reform Commission.

———. 2009b. *Report on economic planning and project investment in 2010.* Guangyuan: Guangyuan Development and Reform Commission.

Guangyuan Statistics Bureau. 2009. *Guangyuan Statistics Yearbook 2008.* Guangyuan: Guangyuan Statistics Press.

Heilig, Gerhard K., Gunther Fischer, and Harrij van Velthuizen. 2000. Can China Feed itself? An Analysis of China's Food Prospects with Special Reference to Water Resources. *International Journal of Sustainable Development and World Ecology* 7:153–172.

Hubacek, Klaus, Dabo Guan, John Barrett, and Thomas Wiedmann. 2009. Environmental implications of urbanization and lifestyle change in China: Ecological and water footprints. *Journal of Cleaner Production* 17:1241–1248.

Hubacek, Klaus, Dabo Guan, and Anamika Barua. 2007. Changing lifestyles and consumption patterns in developing countries: A scenario analysis for China and India. *Futures* 39:1084–1096.

Hubacek, Klaus, and Laixiang Sun, 1999. *Land-Use change in China: A scenario analysis based on input-output modeling.* Laxenburg, Austria: International Institute for Applied Systems Analysis.

———. 2001. A scenario analysis of China's land use change: Incorporating biophysical information into input-output modeling. *Structural Change and Economic Dynamics* 12:367–397.

———. 2005. Economic and societal changes in China and their effects on water use: A scenario analysis. *Journal of Industrial Ecology* 9:187–200.

IPCC. 2006. *2006 IPCC Guidelines for National Greenhouse Gas Inventories.* Hayama, Japan: Intergovernmental Panel on Climate Change.

Leontief, Wassily. 1970. Environmental repercussions and the economic system. *Review of Economics and Statistics* 52:262–272.

———, ed. 1986. *Technological change, prices, wages, and rates of return on capital in the USA economy,* Second Edition. Oxford, U.K.: Oxford University Press.

Liu, Zhu, Yong Geng, Soren Lindner, and Dabo Guan. 2012. Uncovering China's greenhouse gas emission from regional and sectoral perspectives. *Energy* 45(1):1059–1068.

Miller, Ronald E., and Peter D. Blair. 1985. *Input-output analysis: Foundations and extensions.* Englewood Cliffs, NJ: Prentice-Hall.

National Bureau of Statistics. 2007. *China statistical yearbook 2007*. Beijing: China Statistics Press.

———. 2008. *China energy statistical yearbook 2007*. Beijing: China Statistics Press.

NDRC. 2006. *Overview of the 11th five year plan for national economic and social development*. Beijing: National Development and Reform Commission.

Peters, Glen P., Gregg Marland, Corinne Le Quere, Thomas Boden, Joseph G. Canadell, and Michael R. Raupach. 2012. Rapid growth in CO2 emissions after the 2008–2009 global financial crisis. *Nature Climate Change* 2:2–4.

Peters, Glen P., Christopher L. Webber, Dabo Guan, and Klaus Hubacek. 2007. China's growing $CO_2$ emissions—A race between lifestyle changes and efficiency gains. *Environmental Science & Technology* 41:5939–5944.

Prieler, Sylvia, Andres P. Lesko, and Stefan Anderberg. 1998. *Three scenarios for land-use change: A case study in central europe*. Laxenburg, Austria: International Institute for Applied Systems Analysis.

Qiu, Jane. 2009. China's climate target: Is it achievable? *Nature* 462:550–551.

Rose, Adam, and William Miernyk. 1989. Input-output analysis: The first fifty years. *Economic Systems Research* 1:229–271.

Sichuan Statistics Bureau. 2007. *Sichuan input-output table*. Chengdu, China: Sichuan Statistics Press.

Stone, Richard. 1970. Demographic input-output: An extension of social accounting. In *Contributions to Input-Output Analysis*, ed. Anne Pitts Carter and Andras Brody, 293–319. Amsterdam: North-Holland Publishing.

Toth, Ferenc L., Eva Hizsnyik, and William C. Clark. 1989. *Scenarios of socioeconomic development for studies of global environmental change: A critical review*. Laxenburg, Austria: International Institute for Applied Systems Analysis.

Victor, Peter A. 1972. *Pollution: Economy and the environment*. Toronto: University of Toronto Press.

Wiedmann, Thomas, Jan Minx, John Barrett, and Mathis Wackernagel. 2006. Allocating ecological footprints to final consumption categories with input–output analysis. *Ecological Economics* 56:28–48.

World Bank. 1997. *China 2020: Development challenges in the new century*. Washington, DC: The World Bank.

Wu, Libo, Shinji Kaneko, and Shunji Matsuoka. 2005. Driving forces behind the stagnancy of China's energy-related $CO_2$ emissions from 1996 to 1999: The relative importance of structural change, intensity change and scale change. *Energy Policy* 33:319–335.

# Environmental Taxation and Policy Impacts

# Environment-Related Taxes in China

## A Comparative Study

JOYCE YANYUN MAN AND YINGER ZHENG

Since China's economic reform began in 1978, rapid economic growth, industrialization, and urbanization have generated enormous pressure on the environment and have caused tremendous damage to human health and natural resources. Estimates of the economic losses caused by the environmental damage range from 3.05 percent of gross domestic product (GDP) by a Chinese environmental agency in 2004 to 7.7 percent of GDP by the World Bank in 1997 (SEPA 2006; World Bank 1997). As a result, economic instruments, such as taxes and fees, can be effective and efficient measures in promoting a broad spectrum of environmental protections. This chapter provides a comparative analysis of environmentally related taxes in China by applying the Organization for Economic Co-operation and Development (OECD) standard and definition.

In the 1970s OECD countries relied heavily on command-and-control policies to deal with environmental pollution. However, because of rapidly growing industrial development and enforcement difficulties, these policies had limited effects on pollution control. Therefore, at the beginning of the 1980s, the OECD started to question the validity of the direct control policy and resorted to broad uses of economic instruments (Buckley 1991; OECD 1999). Such economic instruments, established on the basis of the polluter-pays principle (PPP), include taxation, emission and user fees, tax incentives and subsidies, tradable permits, deposit-refund systems, and other monetary and financial tools. In order to improve environmental protection and employment rates, the European countries adopted the "double-dividend" environmental tax reform (Li 2002). Pearce (1991) suggested that environmental tax reform could enhance tax efficiency while protecting the environment. The establishment of the double-dividend theory alleviated the resistance to tax reform and at the same time gave confidence to policy makers. Barde argued that environmental taxes had the potential to protect the environment and at the same time could promote greater economic efficiency. Some OECD countries started to levy new taxes for environmental purposes, to raise environmental tax rates, and to reduce income and/or social insurance taxes in order to stimulate employment. As an important part of green tax reform, environmental taxes reflect the new role that economic tools play in environmental protection (Barde 2000).

China's environmental policies have placed increasing emphasis on economic instruments for environmental protection. The PPP was recognized in the mid-1970s and was included in the Chinese Environmental Protection Law (initiated in 1979 for trial implementation and amended in 1989). The pollution-levy system was used to control both the total volume and the concentration of pollutants, and more user charges have been adopted to promote energy conservation. Although there are a limited number of taxes that specifically target environmental purposes, it is hard to deny that some taxes in China are levied on tax bases deemed to be of particular environmental relevance according to the OECD definition and classification. This chapter studies the current uses and structure of environmentally related taxes in China in comparison with OECD countries to provide policy implications for future environmental reform in China.

## OECD Definition of Environmentally Related Taxes

The OECD, the International Energy Agency (IEA), and the European Commission have agreed to define environmentally related taxes as any compulsory, unrequited payment to a general government levied on tax bases deemed to be of particular environmental relevance (OECD 2006). The term "unrequited taxes" indicates that the payments to the government levied on taxpayers are not normally in proportion to services or benefits provided to them. Requited compulsory payments to the government that are levied more or less in proportion to services provided can be labeled as fees and charges. The term "levy" covers both taxes and fees/charges (OECD 2006, 36). According to this definition, the important aspect of environmentally related taxes is the real and potential effects of those taxes on the environment. From an environmental perspective, it is the effect of a tax on behavior patterns that counts, regardless of its name, the alleged purpose of a tax, or how the revenues raised by the tax are used. Environmentally related taxes (often referred to as environmental taxes) are taxes levied on products and activities with a proven negative impact on the environment. For example, energy taxes initiated for a purely fiscal purpose are considered environmentally related taxes because of their beneficial environmental impact. In considering whether a tax is an environmentally related tax, the tax base is what matters most. The relevant tax bases include energy products, motor vehicles, waste, emissions, and natural resources (OECD 2006).

## Environmentally Related Tax Bases in OECD Countries

The database of natural resources management and an environmental policy developed by the OECD and the European Environment Agency (EEA) detail environmentally related taxes in all the OECD member countries. By 2009 the majority of those taxes were in the area of energy products and motor vehicles, including 150 different kinds of taxes on energy products and 125 taxes on motor vehicles. There are also 50 kinds of waste taxes, consisting of 35 taxes on specific products and 15 taxes on final waste disposal, for example, waste incineration and waste burial. In addition, there are 40 other types of environmental taxes, such as taxes on air and water emissions and on chemical refining. The OECD member countries have extensive tax bases that not only are related to environmental pollution, but also are linked to natural resources. As a result, such tax bases cover a wide spectrum, including energy products, transportation devices and services, water and air pollution, ozone-depleting substances, specific non-point-source water pollutants, and waste management and noise. The integrated management of water, land, soil, forests, biodiversity, wildlife and fish also belongs to the environment-related tax bases.

In OECD countries, 64 percent of the environmentally related tax revenues are related to transport fuels, and motor vehicles account for 26 percent of such tax revenues. Heating, fuel for heavy industry, and electricity account for about 8 percent. Tax revenues on the management of waste collection make up only 1 percent. The revenues of other environmental taxes, such as those on pesticides, fertilizers, and natural resources, are almost negligible (Braathen 2009).

The taxes on transport fuels such as unleaded or leaded gasoline, diesel, light and heavy fuel oil, and other transport energy contribute most to the environmental tax revenues. Since 1995, the tax base for leaded gasoline has gradually disappeared from the market, while the taxes on unleaded gasoline and diesel have been drastically increasing. The continuing shift from gasoline-powered to diesel-powered vehicles has increased the share of diesel fuel taxes, which have become especially important component in the total environmentally related tax revenues. Taxes on motor vehicles also generate a significant amount of revenue sources, but the taxes on heating and process fuels and electricity only accounts for a small percentage of environmentally related tax revenues. Although waste management accounts for very little environmental tax revenue, it has experienced considerable growth in the past decade. Some OECD countries have expanded the tax base of waste. Besides levying taxes on the final disposal of waste (incineration or burial) and some special products, such as batteries, tires, and lubricants, they have also levied a waste-management tax. Revenues from waste-management taxes in nine OECD countries (Austria, the Czech Republic, Denmark, Finland, The Netherlands, Norway, Sweden, Switzerland, and the United Kingdom) accounted for about 0.7 percent of total environment tax revenues in 1995, but rose to 2.9 percent in 2003 (OECD 2006).

According to OECD/EEA database in 2010, environmentally related taxes accounted for 2.32 percent of GDP on average based upon arithmetic average calculation, but its weighted average share was 1.65 percent in 2010, down from 1.93 percent of GDP in 1995. In 2010, environmentally related tax revenue as a share of GDP is highest in Denmark, reaching 4.03 percent of GDP. In contrast, environmentally related taxes in the United States account for less than 1 percent of GDP, the lowest figure among all the OECD countries except for Mexico.

## Environmentally Related Taxes in China

The concept of an environmental tax frequently used in China is poorly defined and very confusing. Some people refer to such taxes as taxes on emissions, while others use the term to reflect the fact that there is no tax levied for environmental purposes per se. As a result, this chapter attempts to clarify this issue and terminology and to provide a classification of environmentally related taxes based on China's current tax system using the international standard and definition of the OECD.

The tax system in China is quite different from that in OECD countries because of the different definitions and classifications used for tax bases, tax rates, formulas, fees, and charges, as well as the administrative structures of tax collection. Although China has started in the recent years to levy taxes for the purpose of environmental protection, the existing tax system includes several resource-related taxes and taxes on energy products and motor vehicles that are directly related to environmental protection. Table 10.1 lists the most narrowly defined environment-related taxes, which include only consumption taxes levied on energy products, motor vehicles, taxes on the use of resources and pollution emission charges and fees.

Environmentally related taxes under this narrow definition, which focuses on consumption taxes on energy products and taxes on motor vehicles and resources, generated total revenues of 570.06 billion yuan (about $90.49 billion), accounting for 1.43 percent of China's GDP and 7.37 percent of total government tax revenues in 2010. As shown in table 10.1, nearly 47.4 percent of those tax revenues were collected from motor vehicle related taxes, while taxes on energy products and resources account for 42.15 percent and 7.32 percent, respectively. Pollution emissions are charged in the form of fees by the Chinese government, but these levies imposed

**TABLE 10.1**

Environment-Related Taxes in China Under a Narrow Definition

| Category | Name of Tax Instruments | Revenues 2012 (Billions Yuan) | Revenues 2010 (Billions US$) |
|---|---|---|---|
| Energy related taxes | Refined Oil consumption tax | 240.3 | 38.14 |
| Motor-vehicle-related taxes | Vehicle purchase tax | 179.26 | 28.45 |
|  | Vehicle and vessel tax | 24.16 | 3.83 |
|  | Automobile consumption tax | 65.35 | 10.37 |
|  | Motorcycle consumption tax | 1.44 | 0.23 |
| Other environment-related taxes | Resources tax | 41.75 | 6.63 |
| Emission charges and fees | Emission fees and charges | 17.79 | 2.82 |
| Total |  | 570.06 | 90.49 |
| % of total revenue |  | 7.37 |  |
| % of GDP |  | 1.43 |  |

SOURCE: China's State Administration of Taxation (2011); China's Environmental Yearbook Editing Committee (2011).

NOTES: Emission fees and charges include Wastewater fee, Exhaust (Air) Discharge fee, Noise Emission fee and Hazardous waste & Solid Waste fee.

upon wastewater, exhaust discharge, noise emission and hazardous waste and solid waste are compulsory and non-requited and therefore shall be viewed as one type of environmental taxes according to the OECD definition. In 2010, such levies only account for 3.12 percent of total environmentally related taxes in China.

As in many other countries, taxes on energy and transport fuels in China were designed and levied to increase tax revenue. But research shows that taxes on transportation fuel and other energy products could reduce inefficiency in the use of resources and significantly improve environmental conditions by lowering energy consumption and pollution. Since January 1, 2009, the Chinese government has increased taxes on gasoline from 0.2 yuan per litre to 1.0 yuan per litre and raised taxes on diesel from 0.1 yuan per litre to 0.8 yuan per litre. Taxes on energy and transport fuels calculated according to the sales value of energy products account for nearly 0.6 percent of GDP in 2010.

There are two types of motor-vehicle-related tax bases among OECD countries: (1) motor vehicle taxes as one-time import or sales taxes; and (2) recurrent taxes on transportation registration or use of motor vehicles. In China motor-vehicle-based taxes include vehicle purchase taxes, consumption taxes on automobiles and motorcycles, and the use of vehicles and vessels. The first two types of taxes are one-time excise taxes on the value of transport vehicles, but the latter one is an annual tax on the use of the vehicles according to the cylinder capacities.

Vehicle purchase taxes are based on the No. 294 Interim Regulations of the People's Republic of China on the Vehicle Purchasing Tax, issued by the State Council of the People's Republic of China. The tax became effective on January 1, 2001, and replaced the vehicle purchase surcharge. This tax is now levied on the value of the vehicle purchased at 10 percent rate at the stage of transaction. In 2010, the vehicle purchase tax generated about 179.26 billion yuan ($28.45 billion), the second largest environmental tax in China, accounting for 0.45 percent of GDP. Revenues from the vehicle purchase tax are used to finance construction projects and to stimulate the construction of transportation infrastructure. In order to promote energy conservation and environmental protection, the Chinese government adopted a plan in June 2012 to allow for the exemption of pure electric vehicles or plug-in hybrid electric vehicles from vehicle purchase tax until 2020. This will provide important savings for the consumer and a significant preferable treatment of environment friendly vehicles.

In addition, an annual recurrent tax is levied on vehicles and vessels registered with public security, transportation, agriculture, fisheries, military, and other management departments according to their types. On December 27, 2006, the State Council's executive meeting passed the Interim Rules of the People's Republic of China Concerning the Vehicle and Vessel Use Tax, which went into effect on January 1, 2007. Recently, China's top legislature adopted a law for Vehicle and Vessel Taxation, which aims to encourage the use of smaller engines in vehicles and vessels to reduce pollution and oil dependence. Effective on January 1, 2012, this law taxes cars according to engine size ranging from 300 yuan (or US$46) to 5,400 yuan (or US$821). Tax burden for owners of vehicles with engine capacities of more than 2.0 liters will be dramatically increased in hope of encouraging the use of fuel efficient vehicles in China.

The Chinese government also levies consumption tax on a selective number of consumer goods in addition to VAT starting in 1994. China started to levy a consumption tax on vehicles in 1994 and made a few adjustments in 2006 and 2008. In 2008 it imposed differential tax rates on the basis of the engine size and emission standards. The automobile consumption tax is an excise tax that aims to impose a higher tax burden on larger, energy inefficient vehicles and reflects the government's recent embrace of a "small car policy." In 2008, the automobile consumption tax rate was adjusted to tax the large cars more heavily. According to the revised tax policy, starting September 1, 2008, the rate for small cars with a capacity of 1.0 to 1.5 liters decreases to 3 percent, two percentage points lower than before. Cars of 1.5 to 2.0 liters continue to enjoy a tax rate of 5 percent. The rate for cars of 2.0 and 2.5 liters is 9 percent as before, and cars of 2.5 to 3.0 liters are taxed at an unchanged rate of 12 percent. But the rate for cars of 3.0 to 4.0 liters increases from 15 percent to 25 percent. The cars of 4.0 liters and more are taxed at 40 percent, up by 20 percentage points than before. The empirical evidence shows that this new tax policy results in a skewed sale distribution toward more efficient new cars (Xiao and Ju 2010).

## China's Environmentally Related Taxes in International Comparison

In 2010 China's environmentally related taxes according to the narrow definition as consumption taxes on energy products, motor vehicle taxes, resource taxes and pollution emission generated 570.06 billion yuan in revenues. These taxes were about 1.43 percent of GDP, which is lower than the average level of OECD member countries (the weighted average and arithmetic mean were 1.65 percent and 2.32 percent, respectively, in OECD countries in 2010). However, as figure 10.1 reveals, China's environmental taxes as a share of its GDP were higher than that of Mexico (negative figure), United States (0.79 percent), Chile (1.14 percent), Canada (1.18 percent), and New Zealand (1.37 percent) and very close to that of Japan (1.61 percent) and the weighted average of all OECD member countries. Most importantly, the environmentally related taxes in China have been growing rapidly from about 80 billion yuan in 2002 to 570 billion yuan in 2010, up by 600 percent. The revenues from the environmental taxes as a share of GDP increased from 0.6 percent to 1.43 percent between 2002 and 2010, more than doubled in less than ten years in China (China's State Administration of Taxation 2003–2011). Contrarily, the weighted average of the environmental taxes as the share of GDP among OECD countries have decreased from 1.85 percent in 2002 to 1.65 percent in 2010.

The revenue from China's environmentally related taxes as a share of tax revenue was 7.37 percent, which was higher than that of the weighted average of all OECD countries in 2010 (5.63 percent) as indicated in figure 10.2. Not surprisingly, this figure was higher than that of United States (3.18 percent), France (4.25 percent), Germany (6.07), United Kingdom (7.34 percent), and many other OECD countries (OECD/EEA database, 2012). These results indicate that Chinese government has been paying more attention to its environmental problems and increasingly

Environmentally Related Taxes as the Share of GDP in China and OECD Countries, 2010

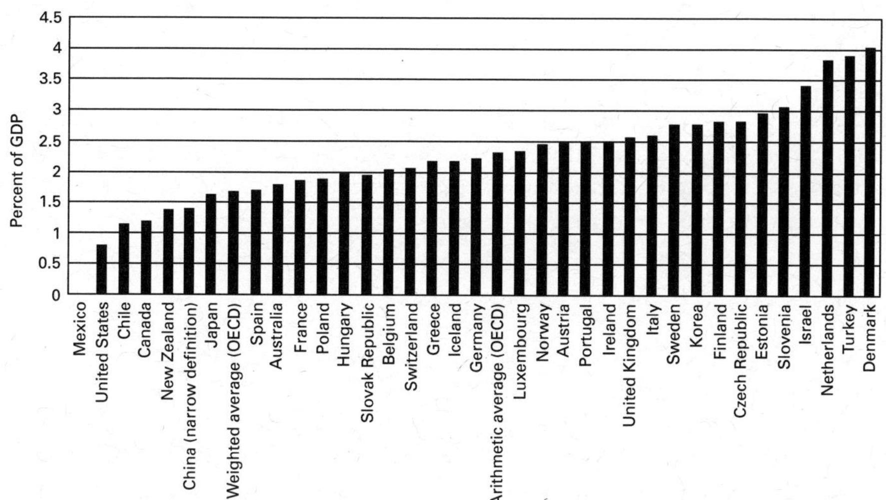


SOURCES: OECD/EEA (2011). Database on instruments used for environmental policy and natural resources management. China's State Administration of Taxation (2011). Tax revenue in China was calculated by the authors.



Share of Environment-Related Taxes in Total Tax Revenue in China and OECD Countries, 2010

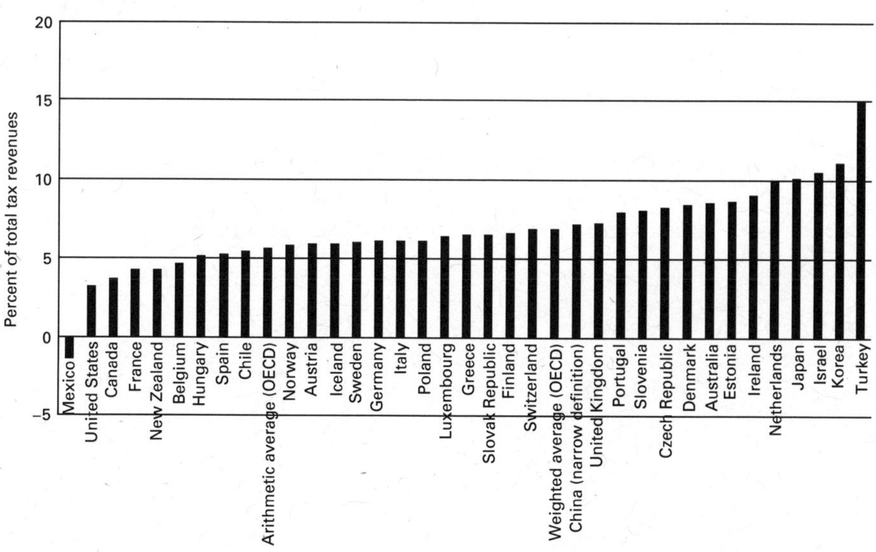


SOURCES: OECD/EEA (2011) Database on instruments used for environmental policy and natural resources management. China's State Administration of Taxation (2011). Tax revenue in China was calculated by the authors.

using environmental taxes as policy instruments to promote environmental protection and energy conservation.

In terms of the environmental tax structure, the Chinese government relies heavily on the motor vehicle related taxes, which accounted for about 47.4 percent of total environmental taxes in 2010. By comparison, OECD countries collected only about 26 percent of their environmental tax from such taxes (Braathen 2009). The data also shows that more than two-thirds of motor vehicle related taxes were generated from the vehicle purchase tax, but the recurrent tax on the use of vehicles was less than 10 percent, indicating that the efficiency can be improved by increasing tax burdens on the users of vehicles to reduce pollution emissions and energy conservation.

## Conclusion

China's environmentally related taxes have become increasingly important as a share of its tax revenue and GDP in the past decade. Even by the narrow definition of the environmental tax, the revenues generated from these taxes as a share of total tax revenues exceeded that of most OECD countries in 2010. The environmentally related taxes as a ratio to GDP in China were also higher than that of United States and Canada and close to the weighted average of all the OECD countries. Most strikingly, environmental tax revenues have been increasing rapidly and its share in GDP was more than doubled by 2010. All these results show that environmental taxes have been attracting attention as policy instruments to deal with environmental issues in China. However, this tool should be used more efficiently and effectively for the direct purpose to change the behavior of individuals and institutions. China still faces enormous challenges in establishing an effective behavior-oriented tax system to deal with pollution and environmental protection. Most taxes are levied on the production side and are not directly related to environmental purposes. As a result, their effect may be limited in encouraging the adoption of environment-friendly technology, business operations, management, and planning among businesses in China. The current tax system in China has also failed to promote conservation because of its limited use of user charges and fees on natural resources. There is an urgent need for China to restructure its existing tax system and establish a fair and effective green tax structure in China.

## References

Braathen, Nils Axel. 2009. Environmentally related taxes in OECD countries. International Conference on Green Taxes, January 29, Copenhagen.

Buckley, Ralf. 1991. Green taxes: Legal and policy issues in using economic instruments for environmental management. *Revenue Law Journal* 2(1):26–31.

China's State Administration of Taxation. 2003–2011. *China taxation yearbook*. Beijing: Chinese Tax Press.

China's Environmental Yearbook Editing Committee. 2011. *China environmental yearbook*. Beijing: China Environment Yearbook Editorial Board.

Environmental Protection Tax Research Group of the State Administration of Taxation. 2006. Environmental protection tax issues. *China Tax Report*:342–363.

Li, Han Yin. 2002. Environmental protection, employment double dividend: The European experience of the green tax reform. *Taiwan Outlook*.

Liu, Zuo. 2010. *Overview of China's tax system.* Beijing: Economics Science Publishing House.

OECD. 1999. *Environmental taxes—Recent Developments in China and OECD Countries.* Paris: OECD, 19–21.

———. 2006. *The political economy of environmentally related taxes.* Paris: OECD, 26–30.

OECD/EEA. 1995–2010. Database on instruments used for environmental policy and natural resources management. http://www2.oecd.org/ecoinst/queries

Pearce, David. 1991. The role of carbon taxes in adjusting to global warming. *The Economic Journal* 101(407):938–948.

State Environmental Protection Administation (SEPA). 2006. China Green National Accounting Study Report 2004.

World Bank. 1997. *Clear water, blue skies: China's environment in the new century.* Washington, DC: World Bank.

Xiao, Junji, and Heng Ju. 2010. The impact of air-pollution motivated automobile consumption tax adjustments of China. Working Paper Series. Shanghai: School of Management at Fudan University.

JING CAO

# The Incidence of Carbon Tax in China

**11**

Driven by booming economic growth and rapid urbanization, China's carbon dioxide ($CO_2$) emissions have risen rapidly and now account for about one-third of the world's carbon emissions. China has edged closer to levying an environmental tax on polluters. At the UNFCCC Copenhagen Climate Conference in 2009, the Chinese government officially committed to reducing carbon intensity by 40 to 45 percent in 2020 compared with the level in the benchmark year of 2005. So far, the Chinese government and academics have emphasized a tax on energy or carbon itself as an important policy option to control both global greenhouse gas emissions and conventional pollutants, such as particulate matter and sulfur dioxide. For instance, the resource tax has been revised to encourage energy efficiency. The resource tax on oil and gas has been raised to 5 percent in Xinjiang Province as a trial experiment, then the tax on crude oil and natural gas was revised from a unit tax to an ad-valorem tax; the next reform is likely to extend the tax reform on coal use. In 2011, several Chinese government agencies, including the Ministry of Finance, the Ministry of Environmental Protection, and the National Tax Bureau, proposed implementing environmental tax reform for the 12th Five-Year Plan (2011–2015). This reform is likely to impose some kind of carbon tax or energy tax to achieve the 40 to 45 percent carbon-intensity-reduction target and to promote the shift toward a low-carbon economy.

Existing studies of the carbon tax are mostly concerned with the effects the policy will have on economic efficiency or the cost-effectiveness of achieving certain pollution-control targets, but an analysis of aggregate costs and benefits is important to evaluate the performance of environmental policies. However, a more interesting question is, who bears the costs, and who gets the benefits? That is, what are the distributional effects of the tax policy, i.e., tax incidence? Public economics has developed theories and tools to analyze the tax incidence of conventional tax policies, such as personal income taxes, corporate income taxes, and property taxes, but such analytical or empirical methodologies are not widely used to examine distributional effects of environmental policies. Among the few studies of environmental policies or taxes (Bento et al. 2009; Hassett, Mathur, and Metcalf 2009; Metcalf 1999; Sterner and Lozada 2012; West and Williams 2004), most focus on the gasoline tax or the carbon tax in the United States and European countries. Except for analyzing the distributional effects of the gasoline tax, very few studies have been conducted to examine the distributional effects of the carbon tax in the developing world, especially China. This chapter attempts to bridge the gap. It uses the tax-incidence literature as a starting point and then combines a computable general equilibrium (CGE) model with household income and expenditure survey data to shed some light on the likely distributional effects of carbon tax policies in China.

In measuring the distributional effects of a tax policy that would affect certain commodity prices, a very simple test of whether the tax is progressive or regressive is to compare whether the budget shares for the consumption of that particular good after the policy shock are higher or lower among rich and poor households. If the tax affects the poor more than the rich, it is regressive; if it affects the rich more than the poor, it is progressive. Theoretically, a carbon tax will affect the prices of energy-intensive commodities because other goods use energy commodities as intermediate inputs. A carbon tax will also affect other commodity prices through a general equilibrium effect and may even raise the inflation level. Besides, a carbon tax may have its own properties with regard to distributional effects, such as reducing environmental externality and capitalization effects due to changes in the market values of certain properties. Overall, the distributional effects are likely to be the following:

1. A carbon tax will make it more expensive to produce energy-intensive commodities, so consumers may bear more of the economic burdens directly (the users' side). In the short run, if Hicksian (compensated) demand for energy is assumed to be inelastic, the burden may fall completely on consumers. However, if the short-run elasticities are large or consumers are more flexible and adapt to the policy change in the long run, the burden on consumers will be smaller.
2. If the supply curve of the taxed energy-intensive commodities is not perfectly elastic, the tax burden will fall on producers as well. A carbon tax will reduce production, decrease returns on energy-intensive sectors, and place burdens on workers and investors (sources' side).
3. A carbon tax policy will also bring substantial cobenefits, which may accrue to some individuals but not others. For instance, if more rich people live in urban areas, which tend to be dirtier, and more poor people live in rural areas, which tend to have better air quality, then if a carbon tax hits the energy-intensive urban manufacturing sectors, the benefits of a cleaner environment may accrue more to urban rich people and less to rural poor people. This policy will then be more regressive.
4. A carbon tax may also bring capitalization effects from changes of market values of certain properties, or change the pre-existing rent seeking structure. Although a carbon tax will affect the manufacturing sectors, because of political

concerns about competitiveness or interest-group lobbying, many powerful sectors, such as the electricity sector, tend to receive free distributive allowances (such as the cap-and-trade system in the European Union Emissions Trading Scheme [EU ETS]) or tax credits to offset the negative impact on production. Thus, existing firms receive such "grandfathering" rents and are better off. Similarly, land and house prices may rise when the air pollution is reduced, so landlords or homeowners may accrue more benefits than individuals with less property. Such a policy is likely to exacerbate regressivity results.

Therefore, an incidence study for a carbon tax is more complicated than for other forms of taxes that have been discussed thoroughly in the public economics literature. Ideally, a complete study of carbon tax incidence should capture all its effects. However, because of limitations on spatial environmental data or the lack of data to measure capitalization effects and scarcity rents of firms most studies up to now have focused predominantly on the direct and indirect effects on users and sources, either making strong assumptions about elasticities and time scale or ignoring environmental and capitalization effects.

In their pioneering works on the carbon tax incidence, Metcalf (1999) and Hassett, Mathur, and Metcalf (2009) measured the lifetime tax incidence of the carbon tax in the United States and suggested that an appropriate carbon tax design can mitigate regressivity in practice. Datta (2011) examined a tax on coal in India using an input-output approach and found that the direct distributional effect is regressive, but if indirect distributional effects on all commodities are captured, the tax on coal is progressive. However, because poor households use kerosene more frequently, a tax on kerosene is regressive. Blackman, Osakwe, and Alpizar (2011) examined the fuel tax incidence in Costa Rica and found opposite results for gasoline (progressive) and diesel (regressive), which can easily substitute each other. Several other studies of developing countries included in Sterner (2011) suggest that gasoline tax incidence is likely to be progressive in developing countries because poor households do not own automobiles and are less affected. However, the carbon tax incidence is still a blank area, especially for China, which is likely to implement some form of energy or emissions tax in the near future.

In order to fill this gap in the literature, a CGE model and microlevel household expenditure and income data are combined to measure the likely distributional effects of a carbon tax in China. As mentioned earlier, a carbon tax is likely to affect the price of almost all commodities; thus, it is important to consider economy-wide effects and to take intersector interactions into account. In China inequality issues have arisen and have attracted much political attention. Because the Gini coefficient is between 42–47 percent, it is important to study the distributional effects of any potential reform, and especially whether it exacerbates inequality and how adverse effects can be mitigated.

In this chapter, instead of the input-output analyses used in Metcalf (1999) and Hassett, Mathur, and Metcalf (2009), a computable general equilibrium (CGE) model is applied to analyze the impacts of two kinds of carbon tax policies in China. The CGE model is superior to input-output analysis because it can better model producers' and consumers' behaviors without the assumption of fixed-technical coefficient before and after policy changes. Next, the CGE results are combined with micro-data from urban household expenditure surveys in China from 2002 to 2007. The results show that a carbon tax would be regressive in China as part of the total tax burden in both an annual-income framework and a lifetime framework, so it would need to be mitigated by using an appropriate revenue-recycling regime to offset the adverse distributional effects.

## A CGE Model Analysis of Carbon Tax Policy in China

A multisector CGE model of China's economy and energy use is employed to assess carbon tax policies in China. In this model, economic growth is mainly driven by labor-force growth, capital accumulation, and productivity growth; additional drivers include improvements in the quality of labor and capital. The main agents are households, producers, the government, and the rest of the world. Household savings and government-funded investment are the main sources of investment, in contrast to developed economies, where the government's role is smaller. The model recognizes the fact that in some sectors, such as the electricity industry, the central plan imposed by the government still plays some role in setting some prices and quantities, or have unexpired plan capital from the former plan economy period. The plan component is modeled inframarginally that we assumed as the exogenous parameters while market components clear the market at the margin.

The household sector maximizes a utility function that consumes 33 commodities. The demand for consumption goods is allowed to change over time to represent the income effect; the share of total expenditures allocated to income-inelastic goods, such as food, falls as income rises, while the share allocated to services rises. Household income is derived from labor, capital, and land and is supplemented by transfers from the government. Labor is assumed to be supplied inelastically by households and is mobile across sectors.

The model is a Solow model where the private savings rate is set exogenously. Total national savings are made up of household savings and retained earnings of enterprises. They also finance the government deficit and the current account surplus. Investment in period $t$ increases the stock of capital that is used for production in future periods.

The capital stock is owned partly by households and partly by the government. The plan part of the stock set by the government is immobile in any given period, while the market part responds to relative returns. Over time, plan capital is depreciated, and the total stock becomes mobile across sectors.

The government imposes taxes on value added, sales, and imports and also derives revenue from a number of miscellaneous fees. On the expenditure side, it buys commodities, makes transfers to households, pays for plan investment of the government, makes interest payments on the public debt, and provides various subsidies. The government deficit is set exogenously and is projected for the duration of the simulation period. This exogenous target is met by making government spending on goods endogenous.

Finally, the rest of the world supplies imports and demands exports. World relative prices are set exogenously. The current account balance is set exogenously in this one-country model, and an endogenous variable for terms of trade clears this equation. On the production side, thirty-three industries are identified, including six for energy. Each of the producers uses capital, labor, and intermediate goods to produce output, and a constant return-to-scale cost function is used to determine the choice of inputs. The production technology changes over time, there is a term for "neutral" productivity growth, and changes in certain parameters represent "biased" growth. Biased technical change refers to changes in input mix that happen over time and are not caused by price changes. Such changes in energy use are often referred to as the autonomous energy efficiency improvement (AEEI) coefficients.

There are 33 markets for the commodities; that is, there are 33 endogenously determined prices that equate supply with demand for the domestic commodities identified in the model. The total supply consists of domestically produced goods and imported varieties, and the endogenous variable for terms of trade clear the international market. There are three markets for the factors of production—land, capital, and labor—and three prices to clear them. Finally, the government budget constraint is met by the endogenous level of government purchases. The model is a standard constant return-to-scale model and is homogeneous in prices; that is, doubling all prices leaves the economy unchanged. Price normalization can be chosen freely, and in the model, labor cost is chosen as numeraire.

The base-case simulation is determined by the projections of the exogenous variables, such as the savings rate, and the initial stocks of debt, capital, and the labor force. The main aim of the model is to study the effect of policy shocks, that is, to estimate the percentage changes in variables of interest between a counterfactual simulation and the base case. The base case itself is not the primary interest, and most of these percentage changes are affected only slightly by the levels in the base case. The main outcomes of the base-case projection are documented for completeness and for those who may have an independent interest in them. Given the initial stock of capital and the labor force, one can solve for the three factor prices and the thirty-three commodity prices that clear the markets in the first period. This gives all the quantities for the first period, including investment, which augments the stock of capital for use in the next period. The solution process is repeated for each period in the simulation horizon.

In the base case, gross domestic product (GDP) is projected to grow at an annual rate of 7.6 percent from 2005 to 2030. During these 25 years, total primary energy use is projected to rise by only 3.7 percent per year, with coal use growing slowly by 3.4 percent per year and oil use by 3.9 percent, but natural gas use by a rapid 7.2 percent. These projections are similar to the International Energy Agency forecasts in the *World Energy Outlook 2008* (IEA, 2008). Because of the change in energy mix, $CO_2$ emissions from fossil fuels are projected to grow slightly more slowly than energy use. Between 1990 and 2006, the carbon intensity in China fell from 179 tons of carbon per million yuan of GDP (constant 2000 yuan) to 95 tons, declining by 4.0 percent per year. The projection gives a similar rate of decline in intensity. The carbon intensities per yuan of output for individual sectors in China are very high compared with those in the United States and indicate prospects for improved carbon efficiency in China's future.

The carbon tax is modeled as a direct unit tax on energy use, and the tax base is the carbon contents of the fossil-fuel use. More specifically, the unit carbon tax rate (U.S. dollars per unit of fuel) is calculated by multiplying the exogenous carbon tax rate $tx^u$ (expressed in U.S. dollars per ton of carbon content) by the carbon content $XU_i$ per unit of fuel $i$. The unit carbon tax is calculated as

$$tc_i^u = tx^u XU_i \ (i = \text{coal, oil, gas}). \tag{1}$$

The carbon tax rate per ton of carbon content $tx^u$ is exogenously set in the model. Carbon prices in the European Trading Scheme were about \$25 to \$30 per ton of $CO_2$ in 2007, or 210 yuan/ton. The U.S. Environmental Protection Agency's analysis of the Waxman-Markey bill projects an initial carbon price of \$13 to \$17/ton. Because the price of coal in China is much lower than the world price, the model starts with a tax of 100 yuan/ton of carbon, about 27 yuan/ton of $CO_2$ (\$4/ton of $CO_2$). Because the mine-mouth price of coal in 2005 was 360 yuan/ton, this is a substantial tax of about 14 percent on the price of China's primary energy source.

The policy simulation consists of imposing a tax of 100 yuan per ton of carbon on the use of coal, oil, and gas, including imported fuels. This tax is imposed every year at the same rate. How the tax revenue is used affects the impact of the policy, as many other analysts have emphasized. The first scenario recycles the revenue in lump sums back to households to maintain the base-case level of government spending. The second scenario uses the revenue to cut existing distortionary taxes, an approach often shown to be better for economic growth. For simplicity, it is assumed that all the tax cuts are at the same fraction $\xi_t$ compared with their benchmark rate. Therefore, the counterfactual tax rates are given by

$$t_t^k = \xi_t t_{t0}^k, \quad t_t^{VAT} = \xi_t t_{t0}^{VAT}, \quad t_t^S = \xi_t t_{t0}^S, \quad \text{and so on,} \tag{2}$$

where $t_t^k$ is the capital income tax, $t_t^{VAT}$ is the value-added tax, and $t_t^S$ is the sales tax. The fraction coefficient $\xi_t$ is endogenously determined by setting government expenditure fixed at base-case government expenditure.

In both revenue-recycling regimes, the constrained revenue-neutrality condition is expressed as

$$GG(t) = GG_{base}(t), \tag{3}$$

where $GG(t)$ is the quantity index of government purchases. In later sections, the fuel tax simulation and the output simulation adopt the same revenue-neutrality condition.

The summary results of the two kinds of carbon tax are given in table 11.1. The lump-sum transfer would boost consumption, but it would reduce investment incentives, while revenue recycling by reducing other preexisting taxes would boost investment, but consumption would decline. The overall impact on GDP would be small, but the reductions in energy use and carbon emissions would be significant. There would be about 14 percent less coal use, with a slight increase in oil and gas use, and overall, carbon would be abated by about 12 percent under both tax regimes.

**TABLE 11.1**

CGE Model Results of Carbon Tax Policy

| | Effect of Carbon Tax Versus Base Case in 5th Year | |
| --- | --- | --- |
| Variable | Lump-Sum Transfer | Reduce Other Taxes |
| GDP | −0.19 | −0.03 |
| Consumption | 0.13 | −0.14 |
| Investment | −0.25 | 0.28 |
| Energy use | −11.5 | −11.3 |
| Coal use | −14.6 | −14.4 |
| $CO_2$ emissions | −12.2 | −12.0 |
| Pollution tax revenue / total tax revenue (%) | 3.07 | 3.09 |

SOURCE: Cao et al. (2010).

In addition, a quite small tax of $4/ton on $CO_2$ would bring the Chinese government 3 percent of its total revenue. Therefore, for both revenue collection and carbon abatement, a carbon tax seems a very effective policy instrument even at a very modest tax rate.

## Measurement of Carbon Tax Incidence in China

### Data

Urban Household Survey (UHS) data are used to calculate average direct and indirect expenditures on energy by both income and expenditure deciles. The UHS survey is conducted by the National Bureau of Statistics and uses a stratified multistage method to select samples. This data set includes information on household disposable income and expenditure for numerous consumption goods. Data are currently available for nine provinces from 1997 to 2006: Beijing, Liaoning, Zhejiang, Anhui, Hubei, Guangdong, Sichuan, Shanxi, and Gansu. These provinces are from different regions of China and represent different economic conditions. Very detailed commodities in the survey data are aggregated into 24 categories of personal consumption items, such as food, clothes, tobacco, alcohol, and furniture.

The microlevel household surveys are used to divide the sample into both income deciles and consumption/expenditure deciles; the latter are used as a proxy for lifetime income. For the annual-income approach, the focus is on household-level income. For the expenditure approach, an equivalence-scale adjustment is adopted that is similar to that of West and Williams (2004), and the incidence calculation is based on the individual level. The argument is that given the same total household income, a household with fewer members clearly has a higher standard of living. The parameter that West and William used is employed to weight adults and children equally, but to allow for economies of scale in consumption.[1] More

---

[1] Alternative OECD equivalence-scale functions were also tried, but the results are all similar. http://www.oecd.org/social/familiesandchildren/35411111.pdf

specifically, total expenditure is divided by (adults + children)$^{0.5}$. All households are then pooled and ranked by equivalence-scale-adjusted total expenditure on gasoline and other goods.

In order to link the CGE model's carbon tax simulation results and the micro-level expenditure data set, especially considering that the input-output definitions of sectors are different from the consumption categories in the expenditure survey, a bridge matrix for China in the benchmark year 2005 is constructed for the conversion of sectors and consumption commodities. Because the National Bureau of Statistics does not provide such a bridge matrix for China, the U.S. bridge matrix is used as the initial value for the China bridge matrix table by regrouping the sector classifications of 600 categories of consumption goods into the 24 Chinese commodity categories. Because of the differences between the U.S. and China tables, the retailing and wholesale margins for China are lowered. Some food is also allocated to the agriculture sector (more direct consumption of unprocessed food), in contrast to the United States, where almost all food comes from the food-processing sector. Survey data on each of these commodity categories and the urban household consumption over 33 industry sectors are fixed as control total. Iteration procedures are then used to obtain an estimate for the bridge matrix of China by employing a Residual Allocation System (RAS) procedure. Table 11.2 gives the estimated bridge matrix for China in 2005 for a subset of consumption goods.

## Tax Incidence: Assumptions and Measurements

To evaluate whether a tax is fair, this question needs to be answered: who bears the burden of a particular tax? The most telling measure is the budget share. Suppose that 50 percent of the budget of a low-income person is spent on energy use, while a rich person spends only 10 percent on energy use. Clearly, a tax that increases the price of energy by 20 percent would take 10 percent of the low-income person's income, but only 2 percent of the rich person's income. Such a tax would be regressive. Therefore, a straightforward method to indicate whether a tax is progressive or regressive is simply to show the budget shares of certain forms of consumption for different income groups. A carbon tax is more complicated than a simple tax, such as a gasoline tax, whose effects may be concentrated in only one or two categories of consumption. Imposing a carbon tax, however, will raise the price of energy and of any commodities that use energy as an input, as well as the overall inflation level. Thus, it is necessary to rely on a general equilibrium model instead of a partial equilibrium model to measure relevant incidence results.

Some studies have used existing research results to generate plausible assumptions about the incidence of specific taxes (e.g., Pechman 1985). Hassett, Mathur, and Metcalf (2009) adopted an input-output approach to evaluate how the effect of a carbon tax is passed through the economy in the United States; in this approach, the factor input substitution is fixed and is not allowed to change as factor prices change. To relax this assumption, a China CGE model is applied here to show how a carbon tax would increase energy prices and cause other changes in factor prices (substitutes or complements), and how these changes would be passed on to consumers. At this stage, a representative-household assumption for the CGE model is

TABLE 11.2

## Bridge Matrix for 2005 for a Subset of Consumption Goods

| Industry Sector | Food | Clothes | Furniture | Indoor Decoration | Home Equipment |
|---|---|---|---|---|---|
| Agriculture | 0.3610 | 0.0000 | 0.0000 | 0.0000 | 0.0000 |
| Coal mining and processing | 0.0000 | 0.0000 | 0.0000 | 0.0000 | 0.0000 |
| Crude petroleum mining | 0.0000 | 0.0000 | 0.0000 | 0.0000 | 0.0000 |
| Natural gas mining | 0.0000 | 0.0000 | 0.0000 | 0.0000 | 0.0000 |
| Nonenergy mining | 0.0011 | 0.0000 | 0.0000 | 0.0000 | 0.0000 |
| Food products and tobacco processing | 0.3855 | 0.0000 | 0.0000 | 0.0000 | 0.0000 |
| Textile goods | 0.0000 | 0.1205 | 0.0000 | 0.1702 | 0.0000 |
| Apparel, leather, furs, down, and related products | 0.0000 | 0.6964 | 0.0000 | 0.0169 | 0.0000 |
| Sawmills and furniture | 0.0000 | 0.0000 | 0.7108 | 0.0873 | 0.0000 |
| Paper and products, printing, and record-medium reproduction | 0.0000 | 0.0000 | 0.0000 | 0.0000 | 0.0000 |
| Petroleum processing and coking | 0.0000 | 0.0000 | 0.0000 | 0.0000 | 0.0000 |
| Chemical | 0.0021 | 0.0000 | 0.0000 | 0.0195 | 0.0111 |
| Nonmetal mineral products | 0.0000 | 0.0000 | 0.0000 | 0.2214 | 0.0000 |
| Metal smelting and pressing | 0.0000 | 0.0000 | 0.0000 | 0.0000 | 0.0006 |
| Metal products | 0.0000 | 0.0000 | 0.0000 | 0.0000 | 0.0000 |
| Machinery and equipment | 0.0000 | 0.0000 | 0.0000 | 0.0000 | 0.0705 |
| Transport equipment | 0.0000 | 0.0000 | 0.0000 | 0.0000 | 0.0000 |
| Electric equipment and machinery | 0.0000 | 0.0000 | 0.0000 | 0.0599 | 0.6875 |
| Electronic and telecommunication equipment | 0.0000 | 0.0000 | 0.0000 | 0.0000 | 0.1118 |
| Instruments, meters, cultural and office machinery | 0.0000 | 0.0000 | 0.0000 | 0.0000 | 0.0000 |
| Other manufacturing products | 0.0000 | 0.0057 | 0.0000 | 0.0624 | 0.0000 |
| Electricity, steam, and hot water production and supply | 0.0000 | 0.0000 | 0.0000 | 0.0000 | 0.0000 |
| Gas production and supply | 0.0000 | 0.0000 | 0.0000 | 0.0000 | 0.0000 |
| Construction | 0.0000 | 0.0000 | 0.0000 | 0.0000 | 0.0000 |
| Transport and warehousing | 0.0205 | 0.0456 | 0.0736 | 0.0322 | 0.0229 |
| Post and telecommunication, computer service | 0.0000 | 0.0000 | 0.0000 | 0.0000 | 0.0000 |
| Trade | 0.0840 | 0.1256 | 0.1949 | 0.3133 | 0.0956 |
| Hotels and restaurants | 0.1458 | 0.0000 | 0.0000 | 0.0000 | 0.0000 |
| Finance and insurance | 0.0000 | 0.0000 | 0.0000 | 0.0000 | 0.0000 |
| Real estate | 0.0000 | 0.0000 | 0.0000 | 0.0000 | 0.0000 |
| Business services | 0.0000 | 0.0000 | 0.0207 | 0.0000 | 0.0000 |
| Education, culture, and other services | 0.0000 | 0.0062 | 0.0000 | 0.0170 | 0.0000 |
| Public administration and other sectors | 0.0000 | 0.0000 | 0.0000 | 0.0000 | 0.0000 |

used instead of a microsimulation that might give different elasticity estimates for each decile or each different household.[2]

Another important issue is how to divide households into different income deciles. Economists have long recognized that annual income may not be a very accurate measure to explain individuals' consumption behavior and have proposed alternatives, such as the permanent-income hypothesis of Friedman (1957). Ideally, individuals should be grouped on the basis of their present discounted value of income, that is, lifetime income (Poterba 1989). For example, retirees have a small annual income, but they may still consume quite a lot by drawing from their retirement fund; using annual income as a measure is likely to understate this capacity substantially. Similarly, the annual incomes of college students are low, but they have large expected future incomes. On the basis of this lifetime-income idea, Poterba (1989) points out that using disposable income may overstate the progressivity or regressivity of a tax. Poterba (1989; 1991) adopts consumption expenditure as a proxy for lifetime income because, according to permanent-income theory, consumers set current consumption proportional to their lifetime income. Poterba (1989; 1991) and Metcalf (1994) find that tax incidence measured in a consumption framework is less regressive than the same tax in an annual-income framework. Although consumption tends to smooth over the life cycle, some empirical evidence suggests that consumption may closely track current income over the life cycle (Bull, Hassett, and Metcalf 1994). Thus, this simple proxy may also impose some bias.

Despite the attractiveness of lifetime-income measures, it is very difficult to conduct such an analysis over individuals' life cycles. Currently, most lifetime-income measures are based on a conventional cohort analysis by linking household earning profiles with households' stages of the life cycle and education, age, and other characteristics. Hassett, Mathur, and Metcalf (2009) classify people into different subsamples on the basis of their education level. For each subsample, they then calculate a "typical" path of consumption through the averages for the age groups and finally compute their lifetime consumption by multiplying the ratio of their current consumption to the average for their age group by the present value of the typical lifetime path. This complicated calculation requires panel data on employment, wages, and individual characteristics, as well as the latent assumption that persons with similar backgrounds and age profiles will have similar earning profiles. However, during the rapid economic transition, salary profiles in China over the past two decades have been quite different even if education, age profiles, and other variables are controlled for. In addition, a college graduate could easily get a high-paying job 20 years ago, but with the increasing rate of college graduation today, only very lucky college graduates can get very good jobs. In addition, it is difficult to collect long-term panel data to elicit lifetime income in China. Therefore, the approach of Poterba (1989; 1991) is adopted, which uses current consumption/expenditure as a proxy for lifetime income instead of the very complicated calculation of correct lifetime income. A comparison of the calculations under both

---

[2] A microsimulation CGE model to measure the tax incidence would require more information on price elasticities of all commodities across deciles that would be difficult to obtain from current empirical evidence.

methods in Hassett, Mathur, and Metcalf (2009) shows that the differences are quite modest, less than 15 percent for the United States, and the trend over time remains relatively constant.

The CGE model has been adopted as an important tool not only to examine the cost-effectiveness or efficiency of environmental policies, but also to evaluate distributional effects of various energy policies. Examples are the studies that examine U.S. climate bills, such as the Waxman-Markey, Kerry-Boxer, and Cantwell-Collins proposals (Jorgenson et al. 2010; Rausch et al. 2010). Jorgenson et al. (2010) show that under an Inter-temporal General Equilibrium Model (IGEM) model with econometrically estimated parameters in both production and consumption equations, when full wealth is considered, an equivalent-variation measure of tax incidence suggests that the U.S. cap-and-trade policy is regressive.[3] Rausch et al. (2010) use the MIT U.S. regional energy policy model, whose structure is similar to that of their MIT Emissions Prediction and Policy Analysis (EPPA) model. They examine the distributional effects of all three climate proposals, Waxman-Markey, Kerry-Boxer, and Cantwell-Collins, and suggest that the first two proposals appear to overcompensate in early years, and that all three policies are slightly progressive in the short and the long term. Similar to these two studies, a China CGE model is adopted here as a major simulation tool to analyze the carbon tax and is combined with the data from the household survey for incidence analysis.

Fullerton and Heutel (2010) point out that many previous incidence studies focus only on users and find that a carbon tax is regressive; that is, poor households spend proportionally more on carbon-intensive commodities, such as gasoline and electricity. They emphasize the importance of incorporating the sources side, such as how climate policies would also affect factor prices and, therefore, overall income and expenditure levels. They do not use simulation or empirical studies but work out an analytical closed-form solution from a simple two-sector model. A dynamic CGE model can be used to examine the tax incidence for both uses and sources sides.

In addition, different revenue-recycling regimes affect the economy differently, so the two revenue-recycling regimes described earlier are examined: (1) a lump-sum transfer that gives the revenue back to households; and (2) reduction of other distortionary preexisting taxes. Because each approach affects factor prices differently, the incidence results differ as well. The next section provides preliminary results for carbon tax incidence under different decile allocation rules and different revenue-recycling regimes.

## Estimates of Carbon Tax Incidence in Urban China

Table 11.3 presents the incidence results for a carbon tax of 100 yuan per ton and a lump-sum transfer to households when annual income is used as the measure of economic welfare. Households are grouped by annual income and sorted into 10

---

[3] In Jorgenson et al. (2010), the climate policy is described in the American Clean Energy and Security Act of 2009 (H.R. 2454). The core scenario has an allowance price beginning in 2012 at $9.65 in 2000 dollars per metric ton of carbon dioxide equivalent ($MTCO_2Eq$). With optimal banking, this price rises at a rate of 5 percent annually through 2050.

**TABLE 11.3**

Distribution of Carbon Tax Burden: Annual Income

| Decile | 2002 | | | 2005 | | | 2007 | | |
| --- | --- | --- | --- | --- | --- | --- | --- | --- | --- |
| | Direct | Indirect | Total | Direct | Indirect | Total | Direct | Indirect | Total |
| Bottom | 0.36 | 0.50 | 0.86 | 0.38 | 0.51 | 0.89 | 0.30 | 0.50 | 0.81 |
| Second | 0.25 | 0.45 | 0.70 | 0.26 | 0.45 | 0.70 | 0.18 | 0.40 | 0.59 |
| Third | 0.21 | 0.44 | 0.65 | 0.22 | 0.42 | 0.64 | 0.16 | 0.36 | 0.52 |
| Fourth | 0.18 | 0.42 | 0.60 | 0.20 | 0.41 | 0.60 | 0.16 | 0.39 | 0.56 |
| Fifth | 0.17 | 0.42 | 0.59 | 0.18 | 0.40 | 0.58 | 0.13 | 0.38 | 0.52 |
| Sixth | 0.16 | 0.41 | 0.57 | 0.16 | 0.38 | 0.54 | 0.12 | 0.37 | 0.48 |
| Seventh | 0.14 | 0.39 | 0.54 | 0.15 | 0.38 | 0.53 | 0.12 | 0.32 | 0.44 |
| Eighth | 0.13 | 0.39 | 0.52 | 0.14 | 0.37 | 0.51 | 0.12 | 0.35 | 0.46 |
| Ninth | 0.12 | 0.38 | 0.50 | 0.12 | 0.36 | 0.48 | 0.10 | 0.29 | 0.39 |
| Top | 0.10 | 0.35 | 0.45 | 0.10 | 0.34 | 0.45 | 0.11 | 0.32 | 0.43 |

NOTE: The table reports the within-decile average ratio of carbon tax burden to annual income.

**FIGURE 11.1**

Distribution of Total Burden: Annual Income

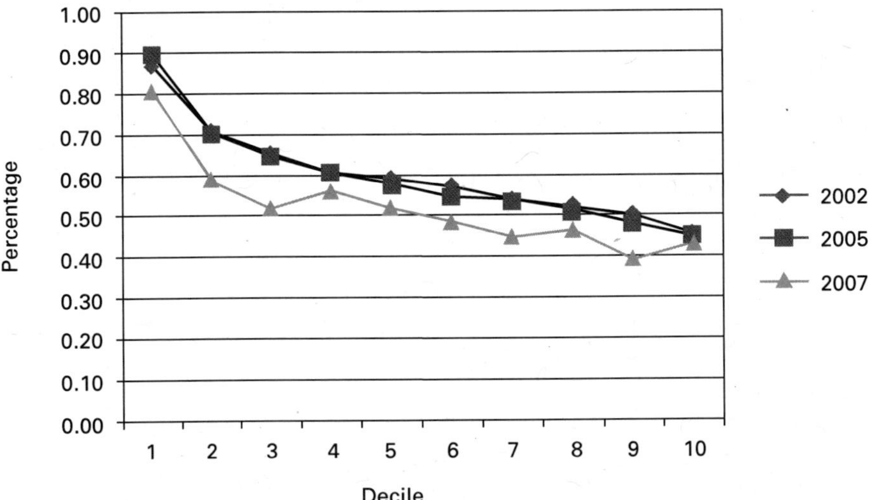


income deciles, from the poorest 10 percent of the population to the richest 10 percent. In agreement with conventional wisdom and Hassett, Mathur, and Metcalf's (2009) study of the United States, the carbon tax is regressive when the measure is current annual income in 2002, 2005, and 2007. The total burden in the bottom decile for all three years is roughly double the burden on the top decile when it is measured as a fraction of annual income, an outcome that is less regressive than the results in Hassett, Mathur, and Metcalf (2009).[4]

---

[4] Hassett, Mathur, and Metcalf (2009) measure the carbon tax incidence in the United States and find that the burden on the lowest decile in 1997 and 2003 was over four times the burden in the top decile when annual income was used as the measure.

Distribution of Direct Burden: Annual Income

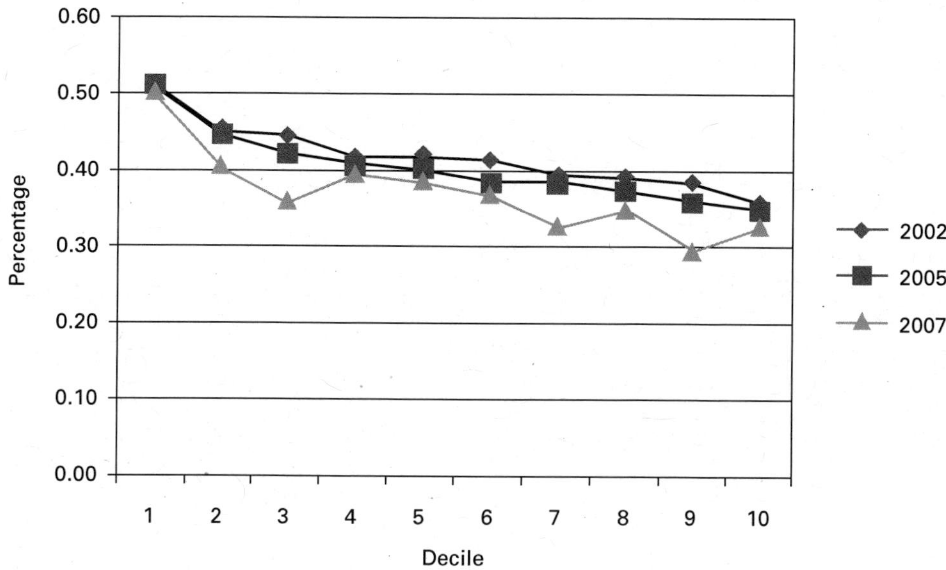



Distribution of Indirect Burden: Annual Income

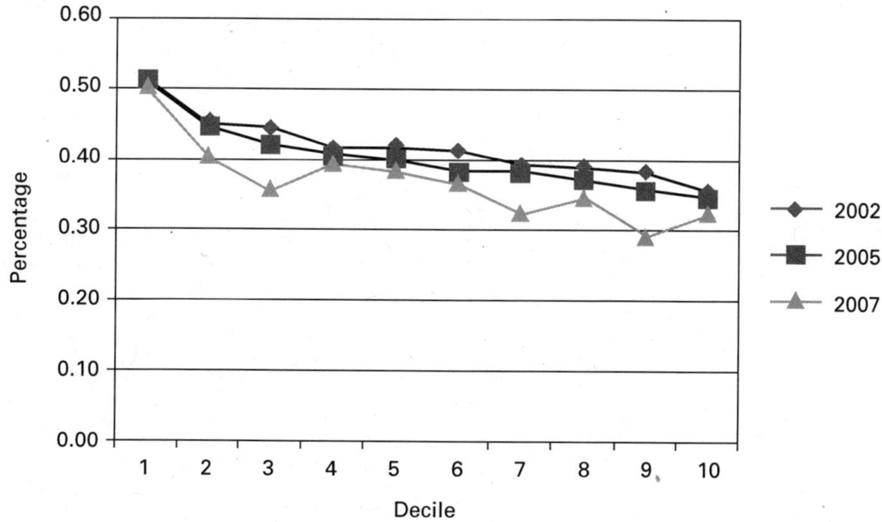


Figure 11.1 displays the overall burden distribution, which is slightly less regressive in 2007 than 2002 and 2005, when annual income is used to rank households. The burden falls very quickly in the lowest deciles, but it falls more slowly in the top deciles. The overall average burden for all deciles declines from 0.60 percent of income in 2002 to 0.52 percent by 2007. This might reflect a modest improvement in

**Distribution of Carbon Tax Burden: Current Expenditure**

| Decile | 2002 | | | 2005 | | | 2007 | | |
|---|---|---|---|---|---|---|---|---|---|
| | Direct | Indirect | Total | Direct | Indirect | Total | Direct | Indirect | Total |
| Bottom | 0.40 | 0.48 | 0.87 | 0.41 | 0.46 | 0.87 | 0.32 | 0.47 | 0.79 |
| Second | 0.30 | 0.48 | 0.78 | 0.33 | 0.47 | 0.80 | 0.26 | 0.48 | 0.74 |
| Third | 0.25 | 0.49 | 0.74 | 0.28 | 0.47 | 0.75 | 0.25 | 0.48 | 0.73 |
| Fourth | 0.24 | 0.49 | 0.72 | 0.26 | 0.48 | 0.73 | 0.20 | 0.49 | 0.69 |
| Fifth | 0.22 | 0.49 | 0.70 | 0.24 | 0.48 | 0.71 | 0.20 | 0.48 | 0.68 |
| Sixth | 0.20 | 0.49 | 0.69 | 0.22 | 0.48 | 0.69 | 0.20 | 0.48 | 0.68 |
| Seventh | 0.19 | 0.49 | 0.68 | 0.20 | 0.48 | 0.68 | 0.16 | 0.49 | 0.65 |
| Eighth | 0.17 | 0.49 | 0.66 | 0.18 | 0.48 | 0.66 | 0.18 | 0.47 | 0.65 |
| Ninth | 0.15 | 0.49 | 0.64 | 0.17 | 0.48 | 0.65 | 0.17 | 0.47 | 0.64 |
| Top | 0.13 | 0.49 | 0.62 | 0.14 | 0.48 | 0.62 | 0.15 | 0.47 | 0.62 |

NOTE: The table reports the within-decile average ratio of carbon tax burden to current expenditure.



**Distribution of Total Burden: Current Expenditure**

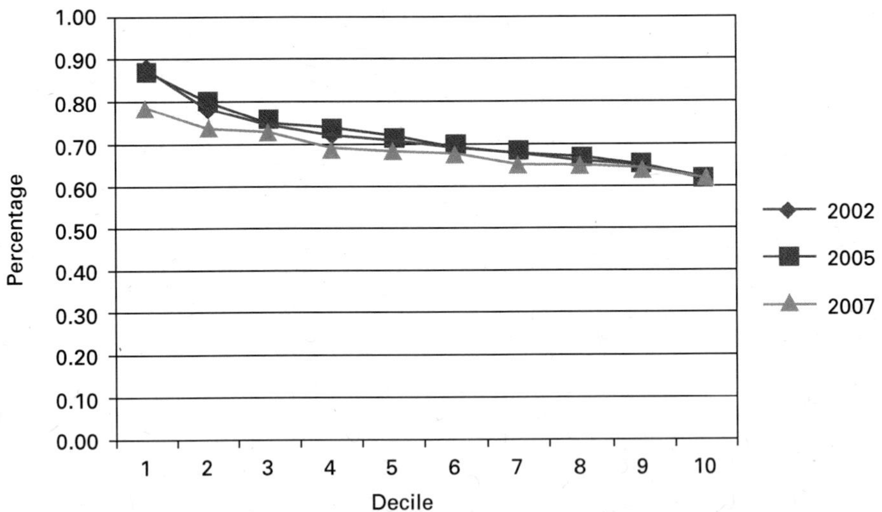


energy efficiency in the economy, which also offsets increasing household energy demand in such areas as automobiles, electricity use, and heating.

Figures 11.2 and 11.3 show the burden of the direct and indirect components of the tax in 2002, 2005, and 2007. The direct component of the tax is quite regressive: the average tax burden on the lowest decile is about three to four times the average tax burden on the highest decile. The indirect tax burden is less regressive than the direct burden: the burden on the lowest decile is only 1.43 to 1.56 times the burden on the top decile for all three years. The lesser regressivity for the indirect component is consistent with the observations of Herendeen, Ford, and Hannon (1981) and Hassett, Mathur, and Metcalf (2009).

Table 11.4 and figures 11.4, 11.5, and 11.6 show the distribution of the carbon tax in the three years when households are sorted by current consumption/expenditure instead of annual income. Similarly, the tax burden is calculated corresponding to current expenditure. Now the total carbon tax is less regressive: the ratio of average taxes paid by the bottom and the top varies from about 1.27 to 1.40 across

**FIGURE 11.5**

Distribution of Direct Burden: Current Expenditure

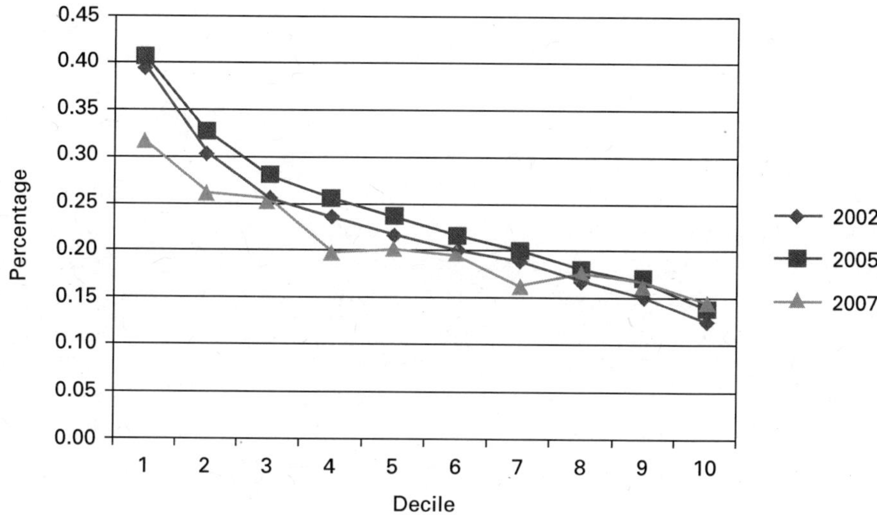


**FIGURE 11.6**

Distribution of Indirect Burden: Current Expenditure

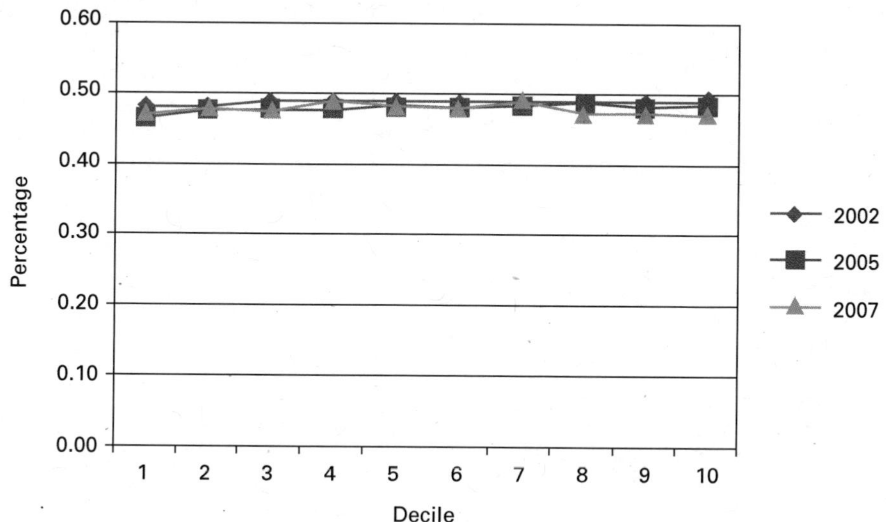

the three years, with the lowest difference in 2007. Nearly all the regressivity can be accounted for by the direct component of the tax, because the indirect component is roughly the same, around 0.46 to 0.49, across all deciles for all three years. This result is also similar to that for the United States in Hassett, Mathur, and Metcalf (2009), although their indirect component in 1987 is actually slightly progressive. The results in both the annual-income and consumption/expenditure cases show that the tax burden in 2007 is less regressive than it is in 2002 and 2005.

If the carbon tax rate is the same, but the revenue is used to reduce other preexisting distortionary taxes instead of being recycled to households in a lump sum, as suggested in equation (2), the tax becomes more regressive for all three years. This result is intuitive because rich people have more capital assets than poor people; thus, a reduction in corporate taxes is likely to subsidize rich people. This makes the carbon tax regime more regressive than transferring the benefits to households in a lump sum.

## Conclusion

The results presented in this chapter are similar to those of the studies of the United States by Metcalf (2007) and Hassett, Mathur, and Metcalf (2009). They suggest that a carbon tax in China is likely to be regressive, although the regressivity will decrease if it is assessed on a lifetime basis. Rich people own most of the property, such as land and housing, so capitalization effects tend to exacerbate the regressivity. Finally, most manufacturing sectors are concentrated in urban areas, so a carbon tax tends to bring more benefits to those areas, where more rich or middle-class people reside. From this perspective, the environmental benefits are likely to accrue to upper-income households, so even consideration of the benefits side will not outweigh the regressivity results.

Because a carbon tax policy will be regressive in China, an important question for future research is, what kind of public policies can be instituted with the carbon tax reform so that the overall policy reform can neutralize these adverse distributional effects? It is also important for future work to quantify all the economic and environmental costs and benefits, as well as capitalization effects and scarcity rents, to provide an unbiased measure of carbon tax incidence.

## References

Bento, Antonio, Lawrence Goulder, Mark Jacobsen, and Roger von Haefen. 2009. Distributional and efficiency impacts of increased US gasoline taxes. *American Economic Review* 99(3):667–699.

Blackman, Allen, Rebecca Osakwe, and Francisco Alpizar. 2011. Fuel tax incidence in Costa Rica: Gasoline versus diesel. In *Fuel Taxes and the Poor: The Distributional Effects of Gasoline Taxation and Their Implications for Climate Policy*, ed. Thomas Sterner, 106–118. Washington, DC: RFF Press and Routledge.

Bull, Nicholas, Kevin Hassett, and Gilbert Metcalf. 1994. Who pays broad-based energy taxes? Computing lifetime and regional incidence. *The Energy Journal* 15(3):145–164.

Cao, Jing, Mun Ho, Yu Lei, Chris Nielsen, Yuxuan Wang, and Yu Zhao. 2010. Reconciling control of carbon and air pollution with economic growth in China: Interim report on carbon tax. Interim Report. Beijing: Energy Foundation Research.

Datta, Ashokankur (2011), Are Fuel Taxes in India Regressive? In *Fuel Taxes and the Poor: The Distributional Effects of Gasoline Taxation and Their Implications for Climate Policy*, ed. Thomas Sterner, 141–170. Washington, DC: RFF Press and Routledge.

Friedman, Milton. 1957. *A theory of the consumption function*. Princeton, NJ: Princeton University Press.

Fullerton, Don, and Garth Heutel. 2010. Analytical general equilibrium effects of energy policy on output and factor prices. Presented at the Energy Policy Symposium "Distribution Aspects of Energy and Climate Policy" sponsored by Resource for the Future (RFF), the University of Chicago, and University of Illinois at Urbana-Champaign (UIUC), Washington, DC (January 20–21).

Hassett, Kevin, Aparna Mathur, and Gilbert Metcalf. 2009. The incidence of a U.S. carbon tax: A lifetime and regional analysis. *Energy Journal* 30(2):155–177.

Herendeen, Robert, Charlotte Ford, and Bruce Hannon. 1981. Energy cost of living, 1972–1973. *Energy* 6(12):1433–1450.

IEA. 2008. World Energy Outlook. 2008. http://www.iea.org/textbase/nppdf/free/2008/weo2008.pdf

Jorgenson, Dale, Daniel Slesnick, Peter Wilcoxen, Richard Goettle, and Mun Ho. 2010. The distributional impact of climate policy. Presented at the Energy Policy Symposium "Distribution Aspects of Energy and Climate Policy" sponsored by Resource for the Future (RFF), the University of Chicago, and University of Illinois at Urbana-Champaign (UIUC), Washington, DC (January 20–21).

Metcalf, Gilbert. 1994. The lifetime incidence of state and local taxes: Measuring changes during the 1980's. In *Tax progressivity and income inequality*, ed. Joel Slemrod, 59–88. New York: Cambridge University Press.

———. 1999. A distributional analysis of green tax reforms. *National Tax Journal* 52(4):655–682.

———. 2007. A proposal for a U.S. carbon tax swap: An equitable tax reform to address global climate change. *The Hamilton Project*. Washington, DC: Brookings Institution.

Pechman, Joseph. 1985. *Who bears the tax burden?* Washington, DC: Brookings Institution.

Poterba, Joseph. 1989. Lifetime incidence and the distributional burden of excise taxes. *American Economic Review* 79(2):325–330.

———. 1991. Is the gasoline tax regressive? In *Tax policy and the economy*, vol. 5, ed. David Bradford, 145–164. Cambridge, MA: The MIT Press.

Rausch, Sebastian, Gilbert Metcalf, John Reilly, and Sergey Paltsev. 2010. Distributional implications of US greenhouse gas control measures. Presented at the Energy Policy Symposium "Distribution Aspects of Energy and Climate Policy" sponsored by Resource for the Future (RFF), the University of Chicago, and University of Illinois at Urbana-Champaign (UIUC), Washington, DC (January 20–21).

Sterner Thomas, ed. 2011. *Fuel Taxes and the Poor: The Distributional Effects of Gasoline Taxation and Their Implications for Climate Policy*. Washington, DC: RFF Press and Routledge.

Sterner, Thomas, and Ana Lozada. 2012. The income distribution effects of fuel taxation. In *Fuel Taxes and the Poor: The Distributional Effects of Gasoline Taxation and Their Implications for Climate Policy*, ed. Thomas Sterner, 119–127. Washington, DC: RFF Press and Routledge.

West, Sarah, and Roberton Williams III. 2004. Estimates from a consumer demand system: Implications for the incidence of environmental taxes. *Journal of Environmental Economics and Management* 47:535–558.

# The Effectiveness of Pollution-Control Policies in China

YAO QI, SHUNSUKE MANAGI, AND TETSUYA TSURUMI

Since economic reform began in the 1970s, China has achieved rapid economic growth, but at the cost of severe environmental damage. Currently, China is suffering from severe surface-water pollution (Managi and Kaneko 2009b). The seven major rivers are polluted, and major lakes have prominent eutrophication problems. According to the State of Environmental (SOE) Report of 2008 published by the Ministry of Environmental Protection (MEP), among 409 monitored sections of 200 rivers, 20.8 percent had water quality worse than grade V, which means that water cannot be used for any purpose. Among the 28 major lakes, 39.3 percent had water quality worse than grade V (MEP 2008). In 2007 cyanobacteria erupted in Taihu Lake and caused a severe drinking-water crisis in Wuxi city (Xinhua 2007).

Because water pollution affects human health directly and is also associated with other environmental problems, such as biodiversity loss in water bodies, the Chinese government has always made it a priority in pollution control. During the past 30 years, a series of environmental laws and regulations have been established, various environmental protection organizations have been founded in all provinces, and billions of yuan have been invested in water abatement projects. During the 11th Five-Year National Development Plan (FYNDP) period, the State Environmental Protection Administration was upgraded to the Ministry of Environmental Protection (MEP) (Xinhua 2008). The whole nation is trying its best to achieve the challenging target of a 10 percent emissions reduction in chemical oxygen demand (COD) (Xinhua 2006), and over 10 billion yuan has been invested in special projects for technology to control water pollution (Lu, Chunxiang 2009). All these efforts demonstrate the great determination of the central government to solve this problem.

Research for this chapter was funded by the Grant-in-Aid for Scientific Research, the Ministry of Education, Culture, Sports, Science and Technology (MEXT), Japan, and the Ministry of Environment, Japan.

Comments from official Chinese publications have all been positive. For example, a message from Xinhua News says, "Under recovery strategy, China's water pollution control in major water bodies has achieved initial success, especially Huai River and Songhua River" (Xinhua 2009). The *China Economic Daily* published an article titled "Remarkable success on energy-saving, emission reduction and environmental protection" (Su and Wang 2009). On the other hand, however, foreign commentators paint a totally different picture. For example, Economy finds that "water pollution and water scarcity are burdening the economy, rising levels of air pollution are endangering the health of millions of Chinese, and much of the country's land is rapidly turning into desert" (Economy 2007). Lim writes that "an official from the environmental watchdog openly blamed the crisis on improper policies and poor government administration" (Lim 2005). Which view is correct? This chapter tries to answer the question: are China's environmental policies effective in reducing water pollution?

There are increasing concerns about China's environmental policies. The pollution levy has attracted the most attention. H. Wang and Wheeler (1996) and T. S. Jiang and McKibbin (2002) studied pollution supply and demand using province-level panel data. Both found that the pollution levy has a significant and negative impact on water pollution in China. Using firm-level cross-sectional data, previous studies also found evidence on the effectiveness of the pollution levy on industrial water pollution in China (Wang, H. 2000; Wang, H., and Jin 2002; Wang, H., and Wheeler 2000; 2005). Other factors, such as inspections, citizens' complaints, ownership, scale, and sector are also found to be significant in industrial water pollution. Studies also show that besides a firm's characteristics, social pressure, such as citizens' complaints, and pollution accidents mainly account for the implementation of the pollution levy (Wang, H., et al. 2002; Wang, H., and Wheeler 2005). However, the estimation techniques used in previous studies still need to be explored; the influence of other environmental policies besides the pollution levy has not been fully studied; and regional differences in the implementation of environmental policies have not been examined.

In order to compensate for deficiencies in previous studies, this chapter contributes in the following aspects. First, a generalized method of moments (GMM) is used in estimations to solve the endogeneity problem in policy variables, as well as other potential statistical issues. Second, the role of many environmental policies is analyzed. In addition to the pollution-levy system, the environmental impact assessment (EIA) system, the three-simultaneities system (TTS), the emissions permit system, pollution abatement for noncompliance by designated date (PAND), and shutting down, merging, and transferring (ST) are all included as explanatory variables in the model. Third, detailed policy-transmission processes are analyzed in a series of models, such as the influence of income on citizens' complaints, the influence of social pressure on policy implantation, the effect of policy implementation on abatement investment, and the influence of abatement investment on industrial water pollution. Finally, regional characteristics in policy implementation are taken into consideration by dividing the samples into three income groups: advanced regions, middle-income regions, and low-income regions.

The first main section of this chapter provides an introduction to China's environmental management system, as well as water-pollution-control policies. The second section reviews related theories on law enforcement, compliance, and pollution. The third section describes the model, and the fourth section shows the data. Econometric results are presented and discussed in the fifth section. The final section provides concluding remarks.

## China's Water Pollution Control Policies

### Legal System and Organizations

China's water environmental legal system consists of the constitution, the Environmental Protection Law, the Water Pollution Prevention and Control Law, the Water Law, a series of administrative regulations and rules, and local laws and decrees. The constitution has the highest status in the legal system and provides basic guidelines for other laws. Articles 9, 10, 22, and 26 explicitly stipulate: "The country protects proper use of natural resources, precious animals, and plants. The country protects living environment and ecology and prevents and controls environmental pollution." The Environmental Protection Law, enacted in 1989, is a comprehensive instructional law that establishes objectives, scope, guidelines, basic principles, policies, key measures, and organizing structures of environmental protection. The Water Pollution Prevention and Control Law and the Water Law are individual environmental laws that follow the guidelines of the constitution and the Environmental Protection Law and define concrete, meticulous regulations on management. The Water Pollution Prevention and Control Law places more emphasis on pollution control, while the Water Law places more emphasis on resource development (MEP 1999; 2005). Administrative regulations such as Implementation Details of Water Pollution Prevention and Control Law and Provisional Regulation on Water Pollution Prevention and Control of Huai River are promulgated to compensate for the inadequacies of the laws, as well as to specify enforcement procedures. Local laws and decrees are enacted to adapt to local conditions. The People's Congress is in charge of making laws, and environmental authorities are responsible for administrative regulations and rules (Chen, H., and Piao 1994).

The State Council of the People's Republic of China, namely, the central people's government, is the highest authority for environmental management. The most important work of the central government is to balance environmental protection and economic development by producing the national development plan. It is also responsible for setting guideline principles and policies, submitting proposals to the National People's Congress, and coordinating conflict among various departments. The MEP is the administrative department in charge of environmental protection under the State Council. Its work includes making environmental policies, setting emissions-reduction objectives, instructing environmental investment, releasing information, and promoting international cooperation. Local governments participate in environmental protection by making integrated development plans that consider environmental benefits. Local environmental protection bureaus (EPBs) are in charge of environmental protection in each region. They not only are supervised by upper-level environmental authorities, but also are responsible to local governments. EPBs at the provincial level are mainly in charge of making macrolevel guidelines, policies, and draft regulations. EPBs at county and township levels are mainly in charge of microlevel supervision, such as implementation of state policies, laws, and regulations; monitoring pollution sources; supervising reporting and registration of pollution discharges; and issuing pollution discharge permits. Municipal EPBs have both macro and micro functions. They can make environmental policies and rules, but they also have to directly enforce implementation of various laws and regulations (Managi and Kaneko 2009a).

## Administrative Measures for Implementation of Environmental Laws

Environmental laws and regulations play their role through strong implementation measures. Eight major legal/administrative measures are prescribed in the Water Pollution Prevention and Control Law: the EIA, the TTS, the pollution-levy system, the total emissions control system, the system of pollution discharge reporting, the emissions permit system, the PAND, and the ST. Among these measures, the EIA and the TTS are preventive measures that aim to control new pollution sources; the pollution levy, total emissions control, pollution discharge reporting, and emissions permits are regular restrictive measures for industrial enterprises; the PAND and the ST are ultimate punishment measures for serious pollution sources (Zhang, K., 1994; Zhang, K., Wen, and Peng 2007).

The EIA policy stipulates that it is necessary to forecast and evaluate the negative affect towards environment and take prevention measures before starting a construction project (Chen, H., and Piao 1994). The purpose of the EIA is to alleviate potential environmental hazards of new construction projects and promote sustainable development. EPBs make the final decisions on the basis of EIA reports submitted by industrial firms or local governments.

The TTS policy stipulates that for all the construction projects which have potential environmental hazard, the facilities for pollution control must be designed, constructed, and used at the same time with the main part (Chen, H., and Piao 1994). The target of the TTS is new construction projects with potential environmental risks. This system, together with the EIA system, carries out the concept that prevention should be the first priority. The EIA focuses on making pollution prevention plans, and the TTS focuses on the implementation of those plans (Chen, Q., and Liang 2006). EPBs are responsible for acceptance check of abatement facilities.

Under the pollution-levy system, environmental administrative authorities can charge enterprises for the part of pollutant emission which excess the emission standard and waste water which discharge into surface water system (Chen, H., and Piao 1994). There are two kinds of pollution levies. One punishes pollution emissions that exceed standards, such as levies on wastewater, waste gas, solid waste, noise, and radioactivity. The other is resource occupation fees, such as the wastewater discharge fee. This system acts as an economic incentive for enterprises to practice proper environmental management within their companies. The pollution levy is also a stable financial source for point-source pollution abatement. In this procedure, EPBs collect money according to emission reports and monitoring data. In 2003 the pollution-levy system was revised: the part of wastewater discharge under standard is increased into levy objects, and price rate rises in large scale to compensate environment damage (Yu and Cui 2004; Zhang, Y., and Li 2006).

The total emissions control system aims to control total pollution emissions within the scope of the environmental carrying capacity on the basis of environmental characteristics and the self-purification capacity of a particular area. Because a long period of concentration control had not stopped severe pollution, the Chinese government started total emissions control in 1996 (Xinhua 2005). The targeted pollutants have changed three times, and now only COD is being controlled. The MEP is responsible for setting national emissions-reduction targets and dividing them among provinces. In the 11th FYNDP, the Chinese government set an emissions-reduction target of 10 percent of COD (MEP 2008). Total emissions control is the most important component of this campaign.

Under the system of pollution discharge reporting, all enterprises that discharge pollutants directly or indirectly should report the type, quantity, and concentration of pollutants to local environmental administrative authority and provide materials of pollution abatement (Chen, H., and Piao 1994). The purpose of this system is to build a basic database on environmental pollution. With information from this system, environmental administrative authorities will be able to develop working plans to control pollution and prevent accidents. Furthermore, this system also acts as the precondition of the emissions permit system, the total emissions control system, and the pollution-levy system.

Under the emissions permit system, enterprises can only discharge pollutants less than the amount permitted by environmental administrative authority (Chen, H., and Piao 1994). EPBs are responsible for dividing emission amounts among enterprises and issuing licenses according to the total emissions-reduction target set by the MEP and pollution discharge reports submitted by enterprises (Chen, X., and Zhou 1999). The main purpose of this system is to protect major river basins and seriously polluted areas. This system and the system of pollution discharge reporting are important components of total emissions control.

The PAND applies to enterprises that seriously pollute the environment or enterprises located in special natural protection areas that exceed emission standards. These enterprises must reduce their pollution to a specified level by a designated date. Otherwise, they will be fined or shut down. This system was created by the Chinese government to improve regional environments. The PAND differs from other measures in that EPBs are not the only competent authorities; local governments have great influence over PAND decisions (Liu 2008). This system was used in "zero-point" actions in the Huaihe River basin and the Taihu River basin, in which industrial point-source pollution was well controlled and water quality improved immediately (Li, Wang, and Huang 2008).

Under the ST, enterprises that have low profit, high environmental pollution levels and have high impact on the daily life of nearby residents must stop producing and improve their pollution control level; enterprises that have low resource utilization and high environmental pollution level, especially small sized, county level firms of papermaking, chemical industry, dying, and printing, among others, must be enforced to pollution abatement by designated date or enforced to shut down, merged or transferred; enterprises that harm drinking water sources must be shut down (Chen, H., and Piao 1994). Enterprises that cannot accomplish environmental abatement by a designated date must be shut down. This system is the ultimate punishment for illegal pollution enterprises. Its purpose is to promote structure upgrade and improve resource allocation.

Previous studies have pointed out some common problems in the implementation of these measures. First, local governments often interfere in environmental pollution issues under the ideology of local protectionism. Second, some EPBs have corruption problems, such as embezzling pollution discharge fees. Third, many enterprises carry out pollution control passively, partly because of low environmental awareness. Fourth, enforcement of some measures may lack flexibility or long-term effectiveness. Finally, insufficient environmental supervision capacity limits the effectiveness of these measures (Chen, Q., and Liang 2006; Chen, X., and Zhou 1999; Liu 2008; Xia, Feng, and Cheng 2005; Xiang 2004; Yu and Cui 2004; Zhang, Y., and Li 2006).

## Conceptual Background

Environmental pollution is a by-product of economic activities, especially industrial production. Economic activities influence the environment in three ways: scale effects, structure effects, and technique effects. The scale effect refers to the increased amounts of pollution caused by increases in outputs. The structure effect refers to the upgrade of the economic structure from pollution-intensive industries to high-tech industries and services. The technique effect refers to environment-friendly production methods that improve efficiency in the use of raw materials in production processes and reduce pollutant emissions through end-of-pipe treatment.

Environmental policies, however, are underlying causes, which can have an effect only via the three proximate variables (Copeland and Taylor 2004; Managi, Hibiki, and Tsurumi 2009; Stern 2004). Usually, environmental policies are considered to influence the technique effect because they are designed to encourage technical improvement instead of hindering economic growth.

At the micro level, environmental pollution is the result of interactions among many players. Industrial firms produce pollution; citizens face pollution; and governments are referees who make judgments on "proper pollution level" (Esty and Winston 2006). Classical supply-and-demand theory describes the relationship between industrial firms and local citizens. Industrial firms are on the demand side; they demand more pollution to satisfy production needs. Citizens are on the supply side; they provide environmental goods to the extent that they are willing to sacrifice. The environmental demand function indicates optimal pollution intensity at a certain pollution price, which reflects cost-minimizing abatement by industries. The environmental supply function indicates pollution prices set under certain social pressures and partly reflects marginal damage (Jiang, T. S., and McKibbin 2002; Wang, H., and Wheeler 1996).

Governments play their role by adjusting pollution prices to maximize social welfare, and they achieve this goal by using policy instruments. In some studies, industrial firms are regarded as rational actors who always try to maximize their economic interest. Industrial firms calculate the potential benefit from illegal pollution and the expected cost of such behavior to make their decision on compliance. If the cost is considered to exceed the benefit, polluters will attempt to abate their pollution. Under this hypothesis, governments should ensure compliance by increasing the frequency of inspections or raising the severity of punishment (INECE 2005).

Other studies regard industrial firms as good-faith actors who always want to obey the law if they can. In this case, successful enforcement relies largely on the capacity and commitment of the firms. "Capacity" refers to knowledge of the rules and regulations, as well as the financial and technological ability to comply. "Commitment" refers to social norms of certain behaviors. It is determined by deterrence, remuneration, moral reasoning, and group identification (Cohen 1998; INECE 2005). Under this hypothesis, governments should ensure compliance by providing necessary support in funding and technology, as well as strengthening social norms by education and deterrence.

## Models

### The Environmental Kuznets Curve Model

The environmental Kuznets curve (EKC) is an inverted-U-shaped curve that depicts the relationship between environmental pollution and per capita income. It is derived from the empirical phenomenon that pollution increases with economic growth at the early stage and declines after the economy has reached a certain level (Grossman and Krueger 1995). This hypothesis is tested by using industrial COD emission intensity as the environmental indicator. To allow flexibility, the cubic term of income is included in model specifications, as shown in equation (1):

$$\log CODI_{it} = \alpha_0 + \beta_1 GDPC_{it} + \beta_2 GDPC_{it}^2 + \beta_3 GDPC_{it}^3 + \varepsilon_{it}, \tag{1}$$

where $CODI$ refers to industrial COD emissions per unit of output; $GDPC$, $GDPC^2$, and $GDPC^3$ refer to provincial income per capita, income squared, and income cubed; $\alpha_0$ is the intercept term; and $\varepsilon_{it}$ is the error term. In order to include province-specific effects and allow for feedback from pollution to income, a GMM technique is applied. However, the reduced form sometimes provides the illusion that pollution will decrease automatically with economic growth. Because of this limitation, the EKC model is used only as the first step in this research.

### Alternative Models

In order to explore the mechanisms behind the simple relationship of income and pollution, alternative models are employed. Economic growth acts on pollution in several stages. Initially, when people become rich, they tend to care more about the environment. They exert pressure on governments to control pollution by complaints. In order to protect human rights and solve the conflict, governments establish and implement laws and regulations. Implementation methods include commands and controls, incentives, information disclosure, financial support, and technological assistance. Finally, industrial firms choose to comply with laws by improving their technology level (either in end-of-pipe abatement or in production processes). This leads to less pollution and a better environment. The effectiveness of a law can be measured by how successful it is in solving the problem it was designed to address, and compliance is a good proxy for the final result. Because of data availability, the implementation rate of environmental policies is used to represent both the role of laws and regulations and their enforcement. The focus is on command-and-control measures. Citizens' complaints are used to represent social pressure on the environment, and industrial firms' investment in pollution abatement is used to represent law compliance. Figure 12.1 shows the revised models used in empirical analysis. The transmission model is detailed step by step.

**FIGURE 12.1**

Transmission Processes from Income to Pollution

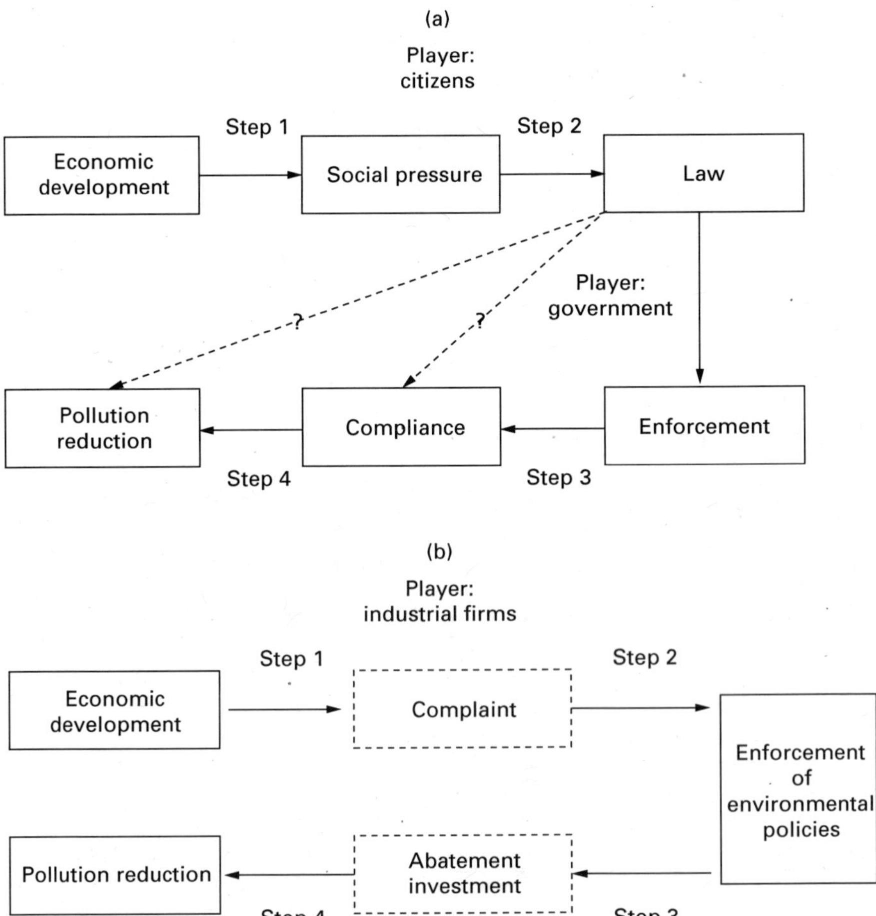

## Step 1: Income-Complaint Model

After people reach a certain level of material wealth, they may start to care about the environment, and they may express their demands by complaining to the government. Complaints are assumed to be positively related to income, education, population density, and pollution situation. In this step, factors that affect citizens' complaints are explored, as shown in equation (2):

$$compr_{it} = \alpha_0 + \beta_1 GDPC_{it} + \beta_2 edu_{it} + \beta_{3it} + \beta_4 ww_{it} + \varepsilon_{it}, \tag{2}$$

where *compr* refers to complaints about water pollution received by local government per 10,000 population; *edu* refers to the proportion of the population with at least nine years of education; *popd* refers to the population density of each province; and *ww* refers to the amount of industrial wastewater discharged. In order to exclude time-constant effects from the error term, a fixed-effect technique or a random-effect technique is used.

## Step 2: Complaint-Policy Model

In this step, the aim is to test whether the government responds positively to citizens' complaints and other pressures. Six enforcement measures are tested in the model, including the EIA, the TTS, the pollution-levy system, the emissions permit system, the PAND, and the ST. Because the PAND is defined as the number of completed projects in the current year, it is almost the same as the number of commands given one year earlier, so a one-year lead of the PAND is used in estimations. The explanatory variables are income per capita, the number of complaints, the economic loss from pollution accidents, and the rate of compliance with effluent standards. Income, complaints, and pollution accidents are assumed to have a positive effect on the enforcement of policies, while the compliance rate has a negative effect. The relevant equations are as follows:

$$eiar_{it} = \alpha_0 + \beta_1 GDPC_{it} + \beta_2 comp_{it} + \beta_3 wpae_{it} + \beta_4 stra_{it} + \varepsilon_{it}, \tag{3}$$

$$ttsr_{it} = \alpha_0 + \beta_1 GDPC_{it} + \beta_2 comp_{it} + \beta_3 wpae_{it} + \beta_4 stra_{it} + \varepsilon_{it}, \tag{4}$$

$$pltiu_{it} = \alpha_0 + \beta_1 GDPC_{it} + \beta_2 comp_{it} + \beta_3 wpae_{it} + \beta_4 stra_{it} + \varepsilon_{it}, \tag{5}$$

$$eptn_{it} = \alpha_0 + \beta_1 GDPC_{it} + \beta_2 comp_{it} + \beta_3 wpae_{it} + \beta_4 stra_{it} + \varepsilon_{it}, \tag{6}$$

$$pandn_{i,t+1} = \alpha_0 + \beta_1 GDPC_{it} + \beta_2 comp_{it} + \beta_3 wpae_{it} + \beta_4 stra_{it} + \varepsilon_{it}, \tag{7}$$

and

$$st_{it} = \alpha_0 + \beta_1 GDPC_{it} + \beta_2 comp_{it} + \beta_3 wpae_{it} + \beta_4 stra_{it} + \varepsilon_{it}, \tag{8}$$

where *eiar* refers to the implication rate of the EIA; *ttsr* refers to the successful implementation rate of the TTS; *pltiu* refers to the total income from the pollution levy divided by the total amount of wastewater discharged, a proxy for the unit price of wastewater; *eptn* refers to the total number of emission permits issued; *pandn* refers to completed projects of the PAND in the current year; *st* refers to the number of industrial firms shut down or transferred; *wpae* refers to the direct economic loss from water pollution accidents; *comp* refers to the total number of complaints about water pollution received by local government; and *stra* refers to the rate of compliance of industrial firms with effluent standards. Because policy enforcement is persistent and intensity of pollution emissions and per capita income are endogenous, a GMM approach is appropriate.

### Steps 3 and 4: Policy-Investment-Pollution Models

In these steps, the aim is to answer the following questions: Are China's policies to control environmental pollution effective in reducing industrial water pollution? Do they affect pollution directly or by inducing industrial firms' investment in abatement? The relevant equations are the following:

$$logCODI_{it} = \alpha_0 + \beta_1 GDPC_{it} + \beta_2 struc_{it} + \beta_3 eiar_{it} + \beta_4 ttsr_{it}$$
$$+ \beta_5 pltiu_{it} + \beta_6 eptn_{it} + \beta_7 pandn_{it} + \beta_8 st_{it} + \varepsilon_{it}, \tag{9}$$

$$inve_{it} = \alpha_0 + \beta_1 IFP_{it} + \beta_2 CODI_{it} + \beta_3 plti_{it} + \beta_4 eptn_{it} + \beta_5 pandn_{it} + \beta_6 st_{it} + \varepsilon_{it}, \tag{10}$$

and

$$CODI_{it} = \alpha_0 + \beta_1 GDPC_{it} + \beta_2 inve_{it} + \beta_3 inve_{it}^2 + \varepsilon_{it}, \tag{11}$$

where *inve* refers to investment in wastewater abatement made by industrial firms; *IFP* refers to total industry output; *plti* refers to the total pollution levy collected; and *struc* refers to industrial composition, which is defined as capital/labor. Equation (9) is used to test which policies contribute to industrial water-pollution reduction. Six enforcement measures are included: the EIA, the TTS, the pollution-levy system, the emissions permit system, the PAND, and the ST. Equation (10) tests whether these policies contribute to pollution reduction by inducing industrial firms to invest in abatement. Because the EIA and the TTS are preventive policies, they are not included. Equation (11) tests whether abatement investment contributes to pollution reduction. All policy variables are assumed to have a negative sign for pollution intensity and a positive sign for abatement investment, while investment is assumed to have a negative sign for pollution intensity. The GMM technique is used to control endogenity and dynamic issues.

## Methodology

When panel data are analyzed, the ordinary least squares (OLS) method often causes bias in estimators because of the existence of unobservable individual-specific terms that are correlated with explanatory variables. Although a fixed-effect approach eliminates time-invariant terms by using the within-transformation, it still cannot solve the potential problems caused by endogenity or autocorrelation. The GMM technique, which has become very popular in empirical analysis, solves these problems by introducing a lagged level of explanatory variables as instruments of first-differenced equations, or known as difference GMM (Arellano and Bond 1991). Alternatively, with further exploring moment conditions in level equations, system GMM is suitable for highly persistent models (Blundell and Bonds 1998). In addition, a two-step regression can be used to correct the potential problem caused by heteroscedasticity, together with finite sample adjustment on standard variance (Windmeijer 2005), and additional instrumental variables can help overcome the problem of weak instruments.

## Data

Province-level panel data from 1997 to 2007 are used. Data before 1997 are excluded because of the adjustment of administrative divisions in 1996.[1] Data on the emissions permit system are available only after 2002 because of a modification of variable definitions. The sample set includes 30 provinces; Tibet is excluded because of lack of data. Data on pollution and environmental policies are collected from the *China Environmental Statistical Yearbook*, while data on economics and social situations are collected from the *China Economic Yearbook*, the *China Statistical Yearbook for Regional Economy*, the *China Industrial Economy Statistical Yearbook*, and the *China Population and Employment Statistical Yearbook*. Table 12.1 provides definitions and explanations of variables, and table 12.2 provides description of variables.

Flow data on COD are used as a proxy for water quality. The emphasis is on industrial pollution, which is the biggest pollution source, because most policies are designed to control point-source pollution. Six enforcement measures (EIA, TTS, the pollution-levy system, the emissions permit system, the PAND, and the ST) are used to represent policies for two reasons. First, all provinces in China share the same environmental policies, which are established by the central government. Local governments adjust the implementation of policies to adapt to local characteristics by controlling key enforcement measures. Second, although other policy variables may exist, the lack of available data precludes their use. Luckily, these six variables include the most important policy instruments that are commonly used in China, so it is reasonable to expect that a full picture can be obtained from them.

Potential problems may arise because policy variables are aggregate, which means that their targets include not only water pollution, but also other kinds of pollution, such as gas pollution or solid waste pollution. For example, *st* refers to the number of industrial firms that are shut down or transferred because of heavy pollution of water, gas, or solid waste. Unfortunately, enforcement efforts solely for wastewater cannot be isolated from current data. One possible solution is to assume that wastewater-related implementation action accounts for a relatively large

---

[1] Chongqing became an independent municipality after 1997.

**TABLE 12.1**

Definitions of Variables

| Variable | Unit | Definition |
| --- | --- | --- |
| COD | Ton | Total amount of COD discharges in industrial wastewater |
| CODI | Ton/$10^9$ yuan | COD/industrial output, industrial COD emission intensity |
| CODA | Ton/$km^2$ | COD/area, industrial COD emission per square kilometer |
| IFP | $10^9$ yuan | Total industrial output |
| GDP | $10^9$ yuan | Gross regional product in each province |
| GDPC | $10^4$ yuan/person | Gross regional product per capita in each province |
| struc | $10^4$ yuan/person | Capital/labor, industrial composition |
| capital | $10^9$ yuan | Net value of fixed capital in industrial firms |
| labor | $10^4$ person | Annual average number of people engaged in industry |
| eiar | % | EIA implementation rate |
| ttsr | % | TTS successful implementation rate |
| plti | 10,000 yuan | Total income of pollution levy, including charges from wastewater, waste gas, solid waste, and others |
| pltiu | 1 yuan/ ton | Ratio of plti to industrial wastewater discharged, pollution levy per unit of industrial wastewater discharged |
| eptn | Unit | Number of pollution emission permits issued by government, including permits on wastewater, waste gas, and others |
| pandn | Unit | Number of completed PAND projects |
| st | Unit | Number of firms that are shut down or transferred |
| comp | Unit | Total number of citizens' complaints on water pollution, including letters and face-to-face complaints |
| compr | Unit/$10^4$ persons | Comp/population, complaint per $10^4$ persons |
| wpae | 10,000 yuan | Direct economic loss from water-pollution accidents |
| inve | 10,000 yuan | Investment in wastewater abatement by industrial firms |
| edu | % | Percentage of population with at least 9 years of education |
| popd | Persons/$km^2$ | Population density |

portion of enforcement efforts; this assumption is quite reasonable because water pollution has always been the highest priority of the Chinese government.

Some data processing must be done before regression can be performed. First, nominal prices are converted into real prices (2000 fixed prices) by using regional consumer price indexes. Second, the *China Environmental Yearbook* does not cover full samples of industrial firms, but collects data only on firms that report their pollution to local EPBs. The *China Economic Yearbook*, the *Regional Economic Statistical Yearbook*, and the *Industrial Economic Statistical Yearbook* are supposed to cover full samples of industrial firms. In order to achieve consistency among different data sources, data on COD emissions and abatement investment are adjusted by using the ratio of industrial output from the *China Environmental Yearbook* and the *Industrial Economic Statistical Yearbook*. However, data on environmental policies do not need any sample adjustment because they are collected from local EPBs and reflect the real status of policy enforcement. Third, because there are many undefined blanks in policy variables that will disturb regression, they are filled with either 0 or the average value of one year before and one year after, according to the characteristics of the variables.

**TABLE 12.2**

Descriptive Statistics

| Variable | Mean | Standard Deviation | Minimum | Maximum |
| --- | --- | --- | --- | --- |
| COD | 353,456.70 | 323,873.30 | 3,412.97 | 1,925,618.00 |
| *CODI* | 133.10 | 148.00 | 1.86 | 1,021.36 |
| CODA | 3.00 | 3.88 | 0.005 | 30.29 |
| *IFP* | 5,424.63 | 8,030.44 | 143.17 | 51,695.37 |
| GDP | 4,699.21 | 4,543.47 | 196.24 | 29,083.01 |
| *GDPC* | 1.19 | 1.02 | 0.21 | 6.62 |
| *struc* | 13.41 | 7.48 | 3.15 | 47.48 |
| *eiar* | 95.90 | 8.33 | 37.00 | 100.00 |
| *ttsr* | 92.55 | 9.57 | 26.90 | 100.00 |
| *pltiu* | 0.48 | 0.55 | 0.07 | 6.30 |
| *eptn* | 5,754.99 | 8,161.19 | 0 | 43,869.00 |
| *pandn* | 767.12 | 906.77 | 0 | 6,263.00 |
| *st* | 434.15 | 787.22 | 0 | 9,860.00 |
| *comp* | 1,857.54 | 2,306.93 | 12.00 | 15,003.00 |
| *compr* | 0.43 | 0.47 | 0.0029 | 3.31 |
| *wpae* | 238.67 | 1413.18 | 0 | 21,197.75 |
| *inve* | 6,8456.12 | 100,279.20 | 231.97 | 751,800.40 |
| *edu* | 54.39 | 11.35 | 27.22 | 83.27 |
| *popd* | 383.57 | 483.04 | 6.89 | 2,987.62 |

Researchers often question the reliability of statistical data in China. Data on the environment are collected through a self-reporting system. The Environmental Protection Law defines compulsory reporting responsibilities of industrial firms. Reported data are also monitored by local EPBs through either online monitoring (still limited coverage) or routine on-site monitoring and inspection. Because small-scale firms in small towns or villages may discharge their pollutants illegally, the data on COD emissions are adjusted as described earlier. Although China's statistical data are far from perfect, they reflect objective facts of the real world to some extent and thus can be used by researchers. Research using macrolevel data of China already exists (Managi and Kaneko 2009b; Wang, H., and Wheeler 1996).

## Results and Discussion

### Results of the EKC Model

The results of the EKC model are presented in table 12.3. There is a strong negative relationship between per capita income and industrial COD emission intensity. Although the quadratic and cubic terms are statistically significant, they are dominated by the linear term, as shown in figure 12.2. The results are consistent with research by De Groot, who found a monotonically declining relationship between industrial wastewater and per capita income on the basis of Chinese province-level data from 1982 to 1997 (De Groot, Withagen, and Zhou 2004). Other studies found similar results (Managi and Kaneko 2009b; Song, Zheng, and Tong 2008). Therefore,

**TABLE 12.3**

Estimations of the EKC Model

| Variables | log(CODI) | |
|---|---|---|
| | Quadratic | Cubic |
| GDPC | −1.71*** (−9.95) | −2.62*** (−8.14) |
| GDPC² | 0.14***(5.33) | 0.55*** (4.81) |
| GDPC³ | — | −0.04*** (−3.92) |
| AR(1) test (*p*-value) | 0.81 | 0.56 |
| AR(2) test (*p*-value) | 0.08 | 0.03 |
| Sargan test (*p*-value) | 0.00 | 0.00 |
| Hansen test (*p*-value) | 0.60 | 0.99 |

NOTE: Values in parentheses are *t*-values.

* Significant at the 10% level; ** significant at the 5% level; *** significant at the 1% level.

**FIGURE 12.2**

Relationship Between Log(*CODI*) and *GDPC*

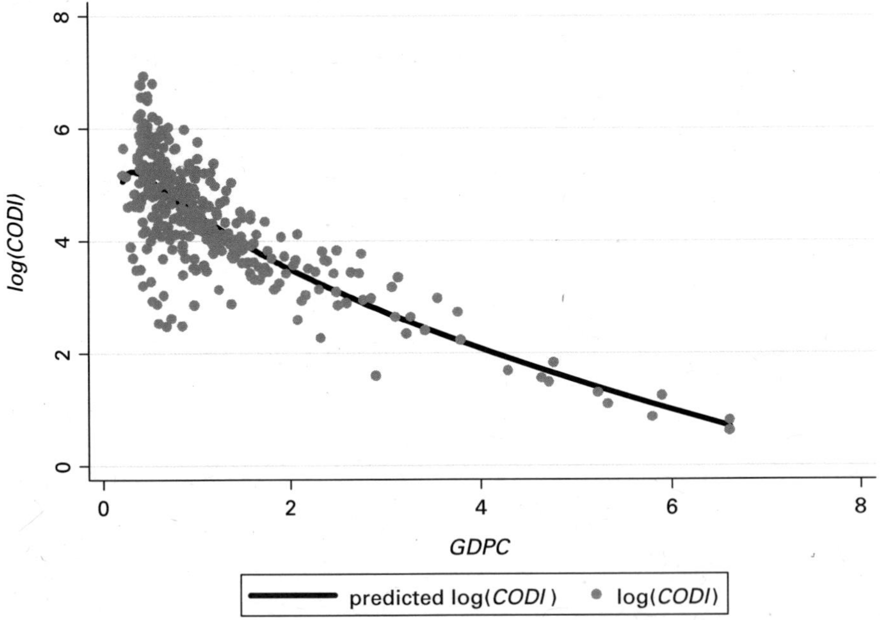


the data do not support the EKC assumption of an inverted-U-shaped relationship between pollution and income.

As incomes rise, industrial sources will exert increasing pressure on the environment. Because non-point-source pollution is currently difficult to control and residential pollution can be reduced only through infrastructure construction, it is industrial pollution that could be controlled through enforcement of environmental policies. Since 2001 COD has been designated as one of the most important emissions-reduction targets proposed by the Chinese central government in the last two FYNDPs. Policies, technological improvement in production processes, and industrial upgrades together explain the reduction of industrial COD emission intensity. The detailed mechanisms behind this reduction are discussed further in the following sections.

## Results of the Income-Complaint Model

Estimation results of the income-complaint model are presented in table 12.4. Both a fixed-effect approach and a random-effect approach are used in this analysis. Because the Hausman test rejects the null hypothesis that the unobserved time-invariant error term is not correlated with explanatory variables, the fixed-effect approach is appropriate. Thus, only fixed-effect results are reported. Because there are potential problems of multicollinearity between income and education and between income and population (Dasgupta and Wheeler 1997), three different specification forms are used in the regression. The results show that income, education, population density, and amount of wastewater discharge have a significant and positive impact on citizens' complaints.

With more education, people tend to be more aware of the hazards of environmental pollution, as well as the political right to protect their interests through complaints. With higher income, demands for better environmental quality will increase. Population density also has a positive and significant effect on citizens' complaints. Cities with high population may be more fragile, because environmental pollution will cause health damage to more people. Therefore, citizens in densely populated areas tend to complain more about environmental pollution.

The right to petition is a basic human right in China that is stipulated in the constitution. The environmental petition method was established in a regulation enacted by the Ministry of Environmental Protection in 1997 that aims to specify the procedures of citizens' complaints about environmental pollution. This method seems to work well in China and provides low-cost information to environmental authorities. The data set shows that high-income provinces, such as Jiangsu, Zhejing, and Guangzhou, have more complaints about water pollution. Empirical analysis

---

**TABLE 12.4**

Estimations of the Income-Complaint Model

| Variables | *compr* | |
|---|---|---|
| | Equation (3) | Equation (4) |
| *GDPC* | −0.06 (−1.30) | 0.49*** (4.62) |
| *GDPC²* | — | −0.10*** (−5.86) |
| *edu* | 0.02*** (4.14) | −0.001 (−0.22) |
| *popd* | 0.001* (1.88) | 0.004*** (4.30) |
| *CODA* | −0.02 (−1.10) | −0.02 (1.20) |
| Hausman test (*p*-value) | 0.00 | 0.00 |

NOTE: Values in parentheses are *t*-values.

* Significant at the 10% level; ** significant at the 5% level; *** significant at the 1% level.

Estimations of the Complaint-Policy Model

| | System GMM | | | | | |
|---|---|---|---|---|---|---|
| Variables | eiar | ttsr | pltiu | eptn | pandn | st |
| GDPC | 30.58*** | 30.26*** | 0.27*** | 588.65 | 263.56* | 130.02** |
| | (5.32) | (5.57) | (3.93) | (1.29) | (1.93) | (2.20) |
| CODI | 0.23*** | 0.22*** | 6.09e-4** | 5.44 | 1.63** | 0.83* |
| | (4.12) | (4.05) | (2.43) | (1.19) | (2.32) | (1.73) |
| comp | 0.006** | 0.005** | −1.03e-5 | 1.85*** | 0.08** | 0.04** |
| | (2.50) | (2.47) | (−0.72) | (5.17) | (2.02) | (2.03) |
| l.wpae | 0.001** | 0.001** | 1.61e-5 | 0.05 | 0.06* | 0.008 |
| | (2.24) | (2.18) | (1.23) | (0.37) | (1.75) | (1.35) |
| AR(1) test ($p$-value) | 0.68 | 0.35 | 0.13 | 0.05 | 0.00 | 0.007 |
| AR(2) test ($p$-value) | 0.88 | 0.87 | 0.19 | 0.53 | 0.18 | 0.087 |
| Sargan test ($p$-value) | 0.00 | 0.00 | 0.00 | 0.00 | 0.00 | 0.00 |
| Hansen test ($p$-value) | 0.99 | 0.99 | 0.99 | 0.96 | 0.98 | 1.00 |

NOTE: Values in parentheses are $t$-values.

* Significant at the 10% level; ** significant at the 5% level; *** significant at the 1% level.

indicates that income, education, and population density are proved to contribute positively to complaints. Thus, it is clear that the first step to combat environmental pollution when income rises is educating people to care about the environment.

## Results of the Complaint-Policy Model

The results of estimations of the complaint-policy model are presented in table 12.5, where *comp* has a positive and significant impact on enforcement of most policies (the EIA, emissions permits, the PAND, the ST). This finding is supported by similar previous studies that demonstrate that citizens' complaints have a positive effect on inspection and environmental law enforcement (Dasgupta, Huq, and Wheeler 1997; Dasgupta et al. 2000; Wang, H., et al. 2002; Wang, H., and Wheeler 2005). Thus, it is implied that governments are responsible on environmental issues in the sense that they respond to social pressure positively. However, other parts of assumptions are not supported by the results.

When governments receive complaints from citizens, they will probably adopt a series of reactions. First, they will inspect the pollution spot immediately to check the situation. If illegal pollution behavior is confirmed, polluting firms are supposed to be severly punished by either the PAND or the ST. Then the complaint will be converted to social environmental pressure signals, which will direct the allocation of monitoring resources. Most important, the signals will also affect decisions on the construction of new projects or factories, known as regional restrictions.[2] Regional restrictions are implemented through the EIA system.

---

[2] It is stipulated in The Decision on Strengthening Environmental Protection in 2005 of the State Council.

However, this model may have some problems because of omitted variables. Besides environmental pressure from citizens, pressure from the central government and personal willingness of top leaders of local governments also play important roles in the enforcement of environmental policies, but it is difficult to define these factors quantitatively.

## Results of the Policy-Investment-Pollution Models

Results of estimations of the policy-pollution model are presented in table 12.6. Column 1 reports results from OLS; column 2 reports results from fixed effect, which eliminates time-invariant unobserved terms by using within-transformation; column 3 reports results from two-step difference GMM, with lagged two to three periods of explanatory variables used as (IVs) in differenced equations; and column 4 reports results from system GMM.

The OLS results in column 1 are inconsistent because they fail to account for the time-invariant effect in the error term. Within results are also inconsistent because they fail to account for the correlation between endogenous policy variables and the error term. The GMM results are consistent as long as instrumental variables are valid and there is no serial correlation among external shocks. The former can be tested by the Sargan test (homoscedasticity) or the Hansen test (heteroscedasticity), while the latter can be checked by the AR(1) and AR(2) tests. In the estimations, both conditions are satisfied because both the Hansen test and the AR(2) test accept the null hypothesis. Comparison between differenced GMM and system GMM is ambiguous. Although the additional IVs introduced by system GMM may improve efficiency, the validity of system GMM requires specific initial assumption which cannot be confirmed, and too many IVs may also be a potential risk in estimation (Roodman 2009). As a result, the results from both difference GMM and system GMM are considered to be reliable.

Columns 3 and 4 of table 12.6 show that the data more or less support the prediction. Per capita income has a significant and negative impact on industrial COD emission intensity. Two policy variables out of six, *pandn* and *st*, have a negative sign and are significant.

In the estimation model, the scale effect is eliminated because relative data are used here. Among variables, *GDPC* is intended to capture the technique effect; *struc*, the capital-labor ratio, represents the structure effect because capital-intensive goods might be considered as pollution goods (Cole and Elliott 2003). Policy variables capture both the technique effect and the structure effect. The variables *eiar* and *st* focus more on structure upgrade, while others emphasize technology more. It is demonstrated that the technique effect and the structure effect both contribute to pollution reduction in China.

As in the EKC model, *GDPC* is highly significant and has a negative effect on industrial COD emission intensity. The coefficient can be interpreted as showing that an increase of 1,000 yuan in per capita income will lead to a decrease of about 3.9 percent to 5.1 percent in *CODI*. This variable captures the effects of other policies besides those included in the model, such as total emissions control, the environmental compensation tax, and higher emissions standards. More important,

Estimations of the Policy-Pollution Model

| | Dependent Variable: log(*CODI*) | | | |
| Independent variables | OLS | Within | Differenced GMM | Differenced GMM + IV |
| | 1 | 2 | 3 | 4 |
|---|---|---|---|---|
| *GDPC* | −0.66*** | −0.53*** | −0.50*** | −0.48*** |
| | (−15.29) | (−10.65) | (−5.21) | (−6.19) |
| *struc* | −0.007 | −0.01 | −0.01 | −0.01 |
| | (−1.03) | (−1.40) | (−0.66) | (−0.83) |
| *eiar* | −0.002 | −0.01 | 0.01 | 0.01 |
| | (−0.13) | (−1.11) | (0.74) | (0.84) |
| *ttsr* | −0.002 | 1.86e-4 | −0.001 | −8.01e-4 |
| | (−0.35) | (0.06) | (−0.33) | (−0.17) |
| *pltiu* | −0.32*** | −0.19*** | −0.24 | −0.25 |
| | (−4.13) | (−3.50) | (−1.36) | (−1.48) |
| *eptn* | 7.23e-06 | 3.20e-06 | −2.64e-5 | 2.5e-5 |
| | (1.21) | (0.43) | (−1.47) | (−1.43) |
| *pandn* | −7.33e-05 | −1.02e-4** | −1.38e-4*** | −1.40e-4*** |
| | (−1.21) | (−2.54) | (−4.22) | (−4.23) |
| *st* | 2.10e-4** | −1.11e-4* | −1.88e-4*** | −1.80e-4*** |
| | (2.40) | (−1.83) | (−2.82) | (−3.01) |
| Adjust $R^2$ | 0.63 | 0.64 | — | — |
| AR(1) test (p value) | — | — | 0.10 | 0.10 |
| AR(2) test (p value) | — | — | 0.73 | 0.70 |
| Sargan test (p value) | — | — | 0.31 | 0.37 |
| Hansen test (p value) | — | — | 1.00 | 1.00 |

NOTE: Values in parentheses are t-values.

*significant at the 10% level. **significant at the 5% level. ***significant at the 1% level.

income per capita also captures non-policy-induced technological improvement because innovations are more likely to occur in a rich society. However, further decomposition of this variable is beyond the scope of this research.

The results for *pandn* are also highly significant and show a negative impact on industrial COD emission intensity. The coefficient can be interpreted as showing that one additional complete PAND project will decrease *CODI* by 0.019 percent to 0.024 percent. The PAND is a type of compulsory administrative order for construction of pollution-abatement facilities. Firms with a good financial situation and enough technological capacity try to achieve pollution abatement by investing in new and better end-of-pipe technologies, improving management methods, while firms without enough capacity will probably continue polluting before the designated date and will be shut down after it. Of course, more completed projects under the PAND result in less pollution.

However, there are some criticisms of the PAND (Liu 2008). First, enforcement authority is unclear. In some areas, only local governments have the right to issue PAND orders; in other areas, environmental authorities also have this right.

Sometimes, conflicts can arise between local governments and local EPBs over PAND decisions. Second, restrictions on polluting firms' operations during the PAND period are ambiguous. Polluting firms can usually continue operating before the abatement deadline, and EPBs will not inspect them before the deadline. In this case, the designated abatement period (from one to three years) becomes a supervision interregnum. Finally, punishment of those firms that cannot achieve the abatement target during the period is weak. Local governments, which place more emphasis on economic growth, are reluctant to execute a shutdown. Often a small fine will be imposed.

To resolve these problems, PAND regulations were revised in the new version of the Water Pollution Prevention and Control Law enacted in 2008. In the new law, EPBs are designated as the enforcement bodies of the PAND. During the specified abatement period (which must be less than one year), EPBs may require polluting firms to limit or to stop production. Finally, shutdown is the only possible punishment when the required target is not achieved, but local governments are still the enforcement bodies of this punishment. If the revised PAND system is understood and well implemented by EPBs and local governments, it will play a more important role in industrial water-pollution reduction in the future.

The variable $st$ has a negative impact on industrial COD emission intensity. It is significant in difference GMM but not in system GMM. This result provides some evidence about the effectiveness of the ST. The coefficient in differenced GMM can be interpreted as the shutting down of one more pollution-intensive enterprise, which will reduce *CODI* by 0.04 percent. The ST as both industrial policy and environmental policy reduces industrial water-pollution intensity passively. It helps adjust the structure of the economy by forcibly crowding out dirty industries. Small-scale township and village enterprises in 15 heavily polluting industries, such as chemicals, papermaking, printing and dyeing, thermoelectricity generation, and cement manufacturing, that use outdated technology and equipment are the main shutdown targets. In addition, as the ultimate punishment measure, the ST also has a deterrent effect on other polluters because it is supposed to raise the expected cost of environmental pollution.

However, the ST may bring conflict between environmental protection and economic growth, and it is often criticized for its provisionality. If it is overused, it can sometimes cause social problems, as in the case of shutting down ceramic firms in Foshan city. Also, while governments are shutting down heavily polluting firms, new firms that pollute at the same level are being built up. The targets of this policy are mostly small-scale township and village enterprises. Although they are more pollution intensive, they are the most active players in China's industrialization and are believed to contribute greatly to absorbing rural excess labor and accelerating urbanization (Dacosta and Carroll 2001; Fu and Balasubramanyam 2003; Lin, Cai, and Li 2002). Their existence shows China's comparative advantage in energy-intensive and labor-intensive industries at the stage of primitive capital accumulation (Lin, Cai, and Li 2002). Otherwise, it is impossible to jump directly from agriculture to high-tech industry. Also, these firms usually do not have the necessary capacity for proper pollution abatement. Even if some of them have the willingness to comply with environmental laws and regulations, current conditions restrict them from doing so. The ST should be used with great caution, and the government should give more financial and technical support to small-scale township and village enterprises.

The variable *eiar* is not significant, and its sign is opposite to the assumption. According to previous studies, there are unknown stories behind statistical data. In some places, local governments interfere with EIA decisions made by environmental authorities; in other places, the order between EIA and construction is even reversed (Zhao 2005). Data on the implementation rate cannot reflect the degree of strictness in decision making on each project; this partly explains why this variable is insignificant.

Although the sign of *ttsr* is consistent with the assumption, this variable is not significant. Although the TTS ensures the construction of pollution-abatement facilities of new firms, as well as the appropriateness of the technology used for pollution abatement, it cannot ensure the operation of those facilities. Many abatement facilities are set aside just after the acceptance check of new projects in industrial firms. Without an effective daily monitoring system, the role of the TTS is limited.

The variable *pltiu* is negative but insignificant, contrary to the assumption and results of previous studies. The pollution levy has always been the focus of policy research in China. Previous studies published several analyses of China's water pollution-levy system (Jiang, T. S., and McKibbin 2002; Lu, B., Lu, and Wang 1999; Wang, H. 2000; Wang, H., and Jin 2002; Wang, H., and Wheeler 1996; 2000; 2005). All of them reported a highly significant effect of the levy on water-pollution reduction. The study in this chapter differs from others in the following ways: First, most of them use firm-level cross-sectional data with the OLS estimation method, while in this chapter, province-level panel data and the GMM technique are used. Second, all of them employ the water levy or the levy on wastewater above the emissions standard, while in this study aggregate data on the pollution levy are used. Finally, the other studies include only the water levy to represent environmental policies, while this study also includes other policy variables. Of course, data problems may be one cause of different results. Another reason might be that the effect is dominated by other policies instead of the pollution levy.

The variable *eptn* is insignificant. A data problem also exists here because this variable cannot represent restriction of total emissions systems. *GDPC*, which catches the influence of total emissions, shows a strong impact on pollution reduction. A more plausible explanation is that the emissions permit system currently does not have much impact on emissions reduction. This policy still covers less than 50 percent of industrial sources. In daily operation, the permitted pollution amount is not well referenced, and the validity of pollution emissions allocation still needs investigation. Furthermore, monitoring capacity is too weak to enforce this policy (Sun 2003; Xia, Feng, and Cheng 2005). According to the experience in developed countries, it is better to set up an emissions-trading system in the future to lower costs and improve efficiency.

The sign of *struc* is negative, contrary to the results of previous studies (Cole and Elliott 2003; Managi, Hibiki, and Tsurumi 2009). Although it is believed that an economy grows primarily via capital accumulation in the early stages of development and by human capital acquisition in later stages (Copeland and Taylor 2004), there may also be an intermediate stage in which the economy upgrades from resource-intensive industries to capital-intensive high-tech industries. In this stage, although economic growth is capital oriented, its impact on the environment is less than in the initial stage. China's case is similar to this because China's economy is upgrading from manufacturing to the information industry and other high-tech industries. However, because *struc* is not statistically significant, this assumption remains ambiguous.

In summary, concentrated efforts in pollution-reduction campaigns (the PAND, the ST) dominate other regular water-pollution-control policies (the pollution-levy system, the emission permit system) and preventive policies (the EIA, the TTS) and have more impact on reduction of industrial water pollution. This result supports the commonly heard remark about China's water-pollution control that policies have only a temporary and partial effect on water environmental protection. Although China's water-pollution-control policies as a whole are effective in reducing pollution, the system is unhealthy.

Table 12.7 shows the estimation results of the policy-investment model. Among various factors, *pltiu* and *pandn* are significant and have a positive effect on investment. The result for the pollution levy is consistent with previous studies (Wang, H. 2002; Wang, H., and Chen 1999). According to rational theories, industrial firms will put efforts into pollution abatement if the actual pollution levy is higher than the abatement cost. The significant result for *pandn* supports the explanation of the PAND's role in pollution reduction in the previous model, that it reduces pollution by encouraging technical improvement.

The variable *eptn* is insignificant. As in the results of the previous model, the emissions permit system does not show a significant effect on either abatement or pollution reduction. Therefore, its effectiveness as a pollution-control policy is

**TABLE 12.7**

Estimations of the Policy-Investment Model

| Variables | Differenced GMM<br>*inve* |
|---|---|
| *IFP* | 7.18*** (4.34) |
| *CODI* | −51.12 (−0.81) |
| *pltiu* | 24,885.08** (2.15) |
| *eptn* | 0.06 (0.06) |
| *pandn* | 10.15* (1.74) |
| *st* | −1.40 (−0.09) |
| AR(1) test (*p*-value) | 0.06 |
| AR(2) test (*p*-value) | 0.22 |
| Sargan test (*p*-value) | 0.00 |
| Hansen test (*p*-value) | 1.00 |

NOTE: Values in parentheses are *t*-values.

*Significant at the 10% level; **significant at the 5% level; *** significant at the 1% level.

**TABLE 12.8**

Estimations of the Investment-Pollution Model

|  | Differenced GMM |
| --- | --- |
| Variables | *CODI* |
| *GDPC* | −43.13** (−2.14) |
| *inve* | −4.76e-4** (−2.04) |
| *inve*$^2$ | 4.49e-10** (2.65) |
| AR(1) test (*p*-value) | 0.68 |
| AR(2) test (*p*-value) | 0.30 |
| Sargan test (*p*-value) | 0.00 |
| Hansen test (*p*-value) | 0.96 |

NOTE: Values in parentheses are *t*-values.

*Significant at the 10% level; **significant at the 5% level; *** significant at the 1% level.

doubtful. The variable *st* is also insignificant, which is reasonable. Firms that have been shut down will not have a chance to invest in pollution abatement. This variable is included to check whether there is a deterrent effect on other firms. Unfortunately, it fails to have this effect.

Table 12.8 presents estimation results of the investment-pollution model. As expected, more compliance leads to less pollution, so investment has a significant and negative impact on COD intensity. However, the scale of the impact may decrease with increased investment. This result is consistent with that of the previous study by Managi and Kaneko (2009a), which also obtains a negative relationship between abatement effort and water pollution. The negative relationship between investment and pollution is the indispensable last step of this analysis. It once again confirms the policies' technique effects: they encourage industrial firms to invest in pollution-abatement technology, and the new technologies reduce pollution effectively.

Stories behind the income-pollution relationship can be explored using alternative models. From estimation results, it is demonstrated that education and income stimulate social pressure on environmental pollution; governments respond to this social pressure by better implementation of environmental policies. Among existing policies, the PAND and the ST have a significant negative impact on water pollution. The PAND contributes to pollution reduction by inducing industrial firms to invest in pollution abatement, but the ST does not. The role of the pollution levy is ambiguous. It encourages abatement investment, but it does not show a significant direct effect on pollution reduction. The PAND shows perfect results in each step.

## Comparisons among Different Regions

China is a big country with considerable regional gaps in economic development and environmental pollution. Therefore, there may necessarily be differences in the implementation of environmental policies among different provinces. In this section, differing foci of different income groups on environmental policies are investigated.

Thirty Chinese provinces are classified into three groups according to average per capita income ranking from 1997 to 2007 (table 12.9). Water pollution is ranked

**TABLE 12.9**

Regional Ordering Based on Economic Development

| High Income | Middle Income | Low Income |
| --- | --- | --- |
| Shanghai (H) | Hebei (H) | Qinghai (L) |
| Beijing (M) | Inner Mongolia (L) | Ningxia (M) |
| Tianjin (H) | Xinjiang (L) | Shannxi (L) |
| Zhejiang (H) | Jilin (M) | Jiangxi (L) |
| Guangdong (H) | Hubei (M) | Anhui (M) |
| Jiangsu (H) | Hainan (L) | Sichuan (M) |
| Fujian (M) | Shanxi (M) | Guangxi (H) |
| Liaoning (H) | Chongqing (M) | Yunnan (L) |
| Shandong (H) | Henan (H) | Gansu (L) |
| Heilongjiang (L) | Hunan (M) | Guizhou (L) |

NOTE: H refers to heavy pollution; M refers to moderate pollution; L refers to light pollution.

according to average industrial COD emissions per area over 1997–2007. Interestingly, the classification of water pollution is similar to that of income. Most of the advanced regions have serious water pollution, and most of the backward regions have light or moderate pollution.

Table 12.10 shows the estimation results of the policy-pollution model for each income group. In order for the results to be consistent with those in 5.4 of table 12.7, the same variables and the same method (system GMM) are used for analysis, except that two-step regressions cannot be used here because of the singularity problem. However, because the sample size is so small, the number of IVs exceeds the number of individual groups, which will reduce efficiency to some extent. As a result, the IVs in the middle- and low-income groups cannot pass the Sargan test. In these cases, the evidence provided by these results is not very reliable, and they should be interpreted with caution.

From the results, it is clear that environmental policies play different roles in water-pollution control in different income groups. In high-income regions, *pandn* and *pltiu* are significant and have a negative impact on *CODI*; in middle-income regions, *st* and *pltiu* are negative and significant; and in low-income regions, *ttsr* and *pltiu* are negative and significant. These results imply that environmental policies are relatively healthy in high-income regions, because both regular measures and intensive abatement campaigns are effective in controlling water pollution, and both of them stimulate compliance behaviors and thus reduce pollution through technical improvements. In middle-income regions, the ST plays a more important role than the PAND; this is less desirable because the ST controls environmental pollution by sacrificing economic growth and does not stimulate technical improvements. In low-income regions, the preventive measure TTS plays a more important role than intensive abatement campaigns. This seems sound because environmental protection relies on regular measures, but local governments may be reluctant to give PAND or ST orders because of economic interests.

Although the pollution levy does not have a significant effect on water pollution in national samples, it has a highly significant negative effect on water pollution in

**TABLE 12.10**

Estimations of the Regional Policy-Pollution Model

| | Differenced GMM Dependent Variable: log(*CODI*) | | |
|---|---|---|---|
| Independent Variables | High Income | Middle Income | Low Income |
| *GDPC* | −0.39*** (−4.94) | −1.01*** (−5.05) | −2.66*** (−3.67) |
| *struc* | 7.31e-4 (0.05) | −0.007 (−0.55) | 0.13* (2.04) |
| *eiar* | −0.03 (−1.72) | −0.02 (−1.68) | 0.02 (0.50) |
| *ttsr* | 0.002 (0.13) | 0.005 (0.98) | −0.003 (−0.71) |
| *pltiu* | −0.80** (−2.22) | 0.02 (0.49) | −0.67*** (−3.45) |
| *eptn* | −5.15e-6 (−0.53) | −2.82e-6 (−0.18) | −1.41e-5 (−1.00) |
| *pandn* | −1.31e-4*** (−3.88) | −6.60e-5 (−0.95) | −5.08e-5 (−0.72) |
| *st* | −1.56e-4** (−2.41) | −8.13e-5** (−2.26) | −7.51e-5 (−0.90) |
| AR(1) test (*p*-value) | 0.06 | 0.07 | 0.21 |
| AR(2) test (*p*-value) | 0.63 | 0.12 | 0.09 |
| Sargan test (*p*-value) | 0.09 | 0.00 | 0.01 |
| Hansen test (*p*-value) | 1.00 | 1.00 | 1.00 |

NOTE: Values in parentheses are *t*-values.

* Significant at the 10% level; ** significant at the 5% level; *** significant at the 1% level.

regional samples, and the magnitude of the response elasticity is also significant. This implies that the pollution levy, as an economic incentive policy, is implemented well and plays an important role in industrial water-pollution control in different income group. This result may explain the conflict with previous studies, because most of them collect data in advanced provinces, like Zhejiang or Jiangsu. A plausible explanation may be that each income group adjusts the levy price by different implementation to adapt to the economic situation in that region. The implementation gap between high-income regions and low-income regions may be too large to obtain significant estimations.

## Is the Pollution Levy Effective?

The preceding analysis does not give a clear evaluation of the effectiveness of the pollution-levy system. It is not statistically significant with regard to industrial COD intensity in the policy-pollution model and the national sample, but it becomes significant in the regional samples. Also, *pltiu* is significant for industrial firms' abatement efforts in policy transmission loops.

These results can be used to compare the costs of wastewater treatment and the pollution levy. According to the Administrative Regulations on Pollution Discharge Levy (2003), the pollution levy is charged on the first three pollutants with most pollution equivalent for the amount that meet effluent standard, with additional twice price for the amount that fail to meet effluent. The unit price for one pollution equivalent of COD is 0.7 yuan. If the COD concentration of typical industrial water is 800 mg/L, then the pollution levy for one ton of untreated industrial wastewater is about 1.7 yuan. According to collected data on operation costs of wastewater treatment plants, as well as information from books and the Inter-

Comparison of Three Kinds of Cost

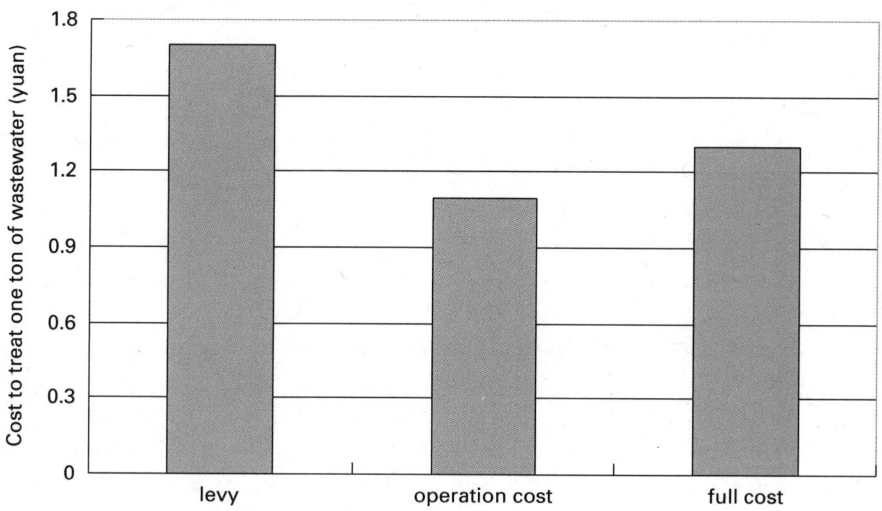


net, the operation cost for one ton of wastewater is about 1 yuan (Wang, F., and Li 1992). If 80 percent of COD can be eliminated by treatment plants, then the cost of treating one ton of wastewater at a treatment facility is around 1.1 yuan. However, the construction cost of wastewater treatment plants, which is around 1,000 yuan for one ton of wastewater, should also be included. If the lifespan is 15 years with an additional overhaul cost of 10 percent, the full cost of treating one ton of wastewater is 1.3 yuan. A comparison of the three kinds of costs is shown in figure 12.3.

From the figure, it is clear that the pollution levy is higher than the abatement cost. Thus, it will stimulate enterprises' efforts to abate pollution if it is well implemented. However, the real levy may be lower than the price stipulated in regulations, and the levy is collected on the basis of PDR without enough inspections. Also, industrial firms may be shortsighted, and the initial construction cost is often beyond their capacity. As a result, the real expected abatement cost may be higher than the pollution levy, and enterprises may choose to pay the levy instead of doing abatement. Therefore, key points for the pollution levy are raising the real levy through better enforcement and providing technical and financial support to enterprises.

## Why Are Economic Incentives Not as Effective as Expected?

The results of the preceding analysis imply that the PAND and the ST are effective in water-pollution control, the pollution levy is effective to some extent, and emissions permits are less effective. The PAND and the ST are typical command-and-control policies, while the pollution levy and emissions permits are considered economic incentives. From the literature, it is known that many of China's economic incentives cannot graduate from trial implementation (Jiang, H., et al. 2009). It can be concluded that command-and-control policies dominate in water-pollution control, while economic incentives are less effective. This is consistent with viewpoints of China's domestic publications, which regard economic incentives and voluntary plans as supplements of commend-and-control policies (Wang, J., Jiang, and Ge 2008).

These results are not surprising because China has not yet completed its reform of the market economy, which is the necessary condition for economic incentives to play their role. According to U.S. documents, the criteria for the market economy are currency convertibility, wages determined by free bargaining between labor and management, joint ventures and other investments, the extent of government ownership or control of the means of production, and the extent of government control over the allocation of resources and over the price and output decisions of enterprises (Stewart et al. 2005). There are still many distortions in the Chinese market. For example, in 2008 state-owned enterprises still accounted for one-third of gross domestic product and one-fourth of the total labor force and dominated vital industries, such as financial services, power, and telecommunications; the government still has strong control over allocation of resources, such as loans and land; and China's currency is still not convertible. Although self-evaluation of China's marketization was 77.8 percent in 2006, China has not been admitted as a market economy by the European Union. Evaluation of China's economy as a market economy is complex and is beyond the scope of this chapter. The argument here is that China's market condition limits the effectiveness of environmental economic measures. However, because China has been making great efforts to reform its market economy, especially since it became a member of the World Trade Organization in 2001, economic measures will become increasingly important in the future.

## Conclusion

The results presented in this chapter cannot refute the commonly heard criticism of China's water-pollution control that its policies have only a temporary and partial effect on improvement of water quality. China needs to place more emphasis on preventive and regular pollution-control measures, strengthen monitoring capacity to support implementation of these policies, and give more assistance to small-scale township and village enterprises for pollution abatement.

## References

Arellano, Manuel, and Stephen Bond. 1991. Some tests of specification for panel data: Monte-Carlo evidence and an application to employment equations. *Review of Economic Studies* 58(2):277–297.

Blundell, Richard, and Stephen Bonds. 1998. Initial conditions and moment restrictions in dynamic panel data models. *Journal of Econometrics* 87(1):115–143.

Chen, H., and G. Piao. 1994. *Foundation of environmental law.* Beijing: China Environmental Science Press.

Chen, Q., and P. Liang. 2006. Comment on EIA system and "three simultaneity" system. *Environmental Protection* 12A(23):42–45.

Chen, X., and Z. Zhou. 1999. Application of emission permit system on business management. *China Environmental Management* 6:29–30.

China Water Network. 2010. Raising effluent standard in Taihu River Basin. http://www.gong kong.com/Common/Details.aspx?c=1&m=7&l=5&Type=mknews&CompanyID=8-B9F2 -1F2B4D8D438E&Id=2010060214095700006

Cohen, Mark A. 1998. Monitoring and enforcement of environmental policy. In *International yearbook of environmental and resource economics*, ed. Tom Tietenberg and Henk Folmer, 44–106. New York: Edward Elgar.

Cole, Matthew A., and Robert J. R. Elliott. 2003. Determining the trade-environment composition effect: The role of capital, labor and environmental regulations. *Journal of Environmental Economics and Management* 46(3):363–383.

Copeland, Brian R., and M. Scott Taylor. 2004. Trade, growth, and the environment. *Journal of Economic Literature* 42(1):7–71.

Dacosta, Maria, and Wayne Carroll. 2001. Township and village enterprises, openness and regional economic growth in China. *Post-Communist Economies* 13(2):229–241.

Dasgupta, Susmita, Mainul Huq, and David Wheeler. 1997. Bending the rules: Discretionary pollution control in China. Policy Research Working Paper Series, No. 1761. Washington, DC: World Bank.

Dasgupta, Susmita, Benoit Laplante, Nlandu Mamingi, and Hua Wang. 2000. Industrial environmental performance in China: The impact of inspections. Policy Research Working Paper Series. Washington, DC: World Bank.

Dasgupta, Susmita, and David Wheeler. 1997. Citizen complaints as environmental indicators: Evidence from China. Policy Research Working Paper Series. World Bank.

De Groot, Henri L. F., Cees A. Withagen, and Min-Liang Zhou. 2004. Dynamics of China's regional development and pollution: An investigation into the environmental Kuznets curve. *Environment and Development Economics* 9:507–537.

Development Research Center of the State Council. *China Economic Yearbook*. Beijing: National Bureau of Statistics.

Economy, Elizabeth C. 2007. The great leap backward? The costs of China's environmental crisis. *Foreign Affairs* 86(5):38–59.

Esty, Daniel C., and Andrew S. Winston. 2006. *Green to gold*. New Haven, CT: Yale University Press.

Fu, Xiao-Lan, and Vudayagi N. Balasubramanyam. 2003. Township and village enterprises in China. *Journal of Development Studies* 39(4):27–46.

Grossman, Gene M., and Alan B. Krueger. 1995. Economic growth and the environment. *Quarterly Journal of Economics* 110(2):353–377.

Industry and Transportation Department and the National Bureau of Statistics. *China Industrial Economy Statistical Yearbook*. Beijing: China Statistics Press.

International Network for Environmental Compliance and Enforcement (INECE). 2005. *Making law work: Environmental compliance and sustainable development*. London: Cameron May.

Jiang, H., J. Wang, C. Ge, and D. Cao. 2009. Evaluation and prospect of China's environmental pollution control policies. *Environmental Policy in China* 5:193–232.

Jiang, T. S., and Warwick J. McKibbin. 2002. Assessment of China's pollution levy system: An equilibrium pollution approach. *Environment and Development Economics* 7:75–105.

Li, Z., Q. Wang, and X. Huang. 2008. Zero-point action of Huai River. *Environmental Economy* (9):55–58.

Lim, Louisa. 2005. China warns of water pollution. *BBC News*. http://news.bbc.co.uk/2/hi/asia -pacific/4374383.stm

Lin, J. Y., F. Cai, and Z. Li. 2002. *The China miracle: Development strategy and economic reform*. Shanghai: Shanghai People's Press.

Liu, Chao. 2008. Exist or revocation: Performance investigation of deadline governance system. *Journal of Yunnan University: Law Edition* 21(2):78–82.

Lu, B., G. Lu, and Q. Wang. 1999. Quantitative research on effects of existing measures of environmental management on pollutant discharge of enterprise. *China Environmental Science* 19(4):369–372.

Lu, Chunxiang. 2009. Special projects for water pollution control technology in the eleventh FYNDP. http://www.cuwa.org.cn/zwdt/swyw/68114.shtml

Managi, Shunsuke, Akira Hibiki, and Tetsuya Tsurumi. 2009. Does trade openness improve environmental quality? *Journal of Environmental Economics and Management* 58(3):346–363.

Managi, Shunsuke, and Shinji Kaneko. 2009a. *Chinese economic development and the environment.* Cheltenham, UK: Edward Elgar.

———. 2009b. Environmental performance and returns to pollution abatement in China. *Ecological Economics* 68(6):1643–1651.

Ministry of Environmental Protection. 1995. http://www.mep.gov.cn/xcjy/zwhb/200806/t20080604_123452.htm

———. 2005. *China Environmental Statistical Yearbook.* Beijing: China Statistics Press.

———. 2008. Report on the state of the environment in China. http://english.mep.gov.cn/standards_reports/soe/ soe2008/201002/t20100224_186070.htm

National Bureau of Statistics. *China Population and Employment Statistical Yearbook.* Beijing: China Statistics Press.

———. *China Statistical Yearbook for Regional Economy.* Beijing: China Statistics Press.

Roodman, David. 2009. A note on the theme of too many instruments. *Oxford Bulletin of Economics and Statistics* 71(1):135–158.

Song, T., T. G. Zheng, and L. J. Tong. 2008. An empirical test of the environmental Kuznets curve in China: A panel cointegration approach. *China Economic Review* 19(3):381–392.

Stern, David I. 2004. The rise and fall of the environmental Kuznets curve. *World Development* 32(8):1419–1439.

Stewart, Terence P., et al. 2005. Statutory criteria for changing China's non-market economy status. U.S. China Economic and Security Review Commission. http://www.uscc.gov/researchpapers/2005/05_08_18_trade_group_law_postion_paper.php

Su, Min, and Wang Ling. 2009. Remarkable success on energy-saving, emission reduction and environmental protection. *China Economic Daily.* (August 3). http://www.ce.cn/cysc/hb/gdxw/200908/ 03/t20090803_19526019.shtml

Sun, L. 2003. Function and standing of total control of pollutants for discharge permit system. *Jiangsu Environmental Technology* 16(3):38–40.

Wang, F., and X. Li. 1992. *Technical economy handbook for industrial waste water.* Beijing: Tsinghua University Press.

Wang, Hua. 2000. Pollution charges, community pressure, and abatement cost of industrial pollution in China. Policy Research Working Paper Series. Washington, DC: World Bank.

———. 2002. Pollution regulation and abatement efforts: Evidence from China. *Ecological Economics* 41(1):85–94.

Wang, Hua, and Ming Chen. 1999. How the Chinese system of charges and subsidies affects pollution control efforts by China's top industrial polluters. Policy Research Working Paper Series. Washington, DC: World Bank.

Wang, Hua, and Yanhong Jin. 2002. Ownership and industrial pollution control: Evidence from China. Paper presented at Annual Conference of the American Agricultural Economics Association, Long Beach, CA (July).

Wang, Hua, Nlandu Mamingi, Benoit Laplante, and Susmita Dasgupta. 2002. Incomplete enforcement of pollution regulation: Bargaining power of Chinese factories. Policy Research Working Paper Series. Washington, DC: World Bank.

Wang, Hua, and David Wheeler. 1996. Pricing industrial pollution in China: An econometric analysis of the levy system. Policy Research Working Paper Series. Washington, DC: World Bank.

———. 2000. Endogenous enforcement and effectiveness of China's pollution levy system. Policy Research Working Paper Series. Washington, DC: World Bank.

———. 2005. Financial incentives and endogenous enforcement in China's pollution levy system. *Journal of Environmental Economics and Management* 49(1):174–196.

Wang, J., H. Jiang, and C. Ge. 2008. Innovation of environmental economic policies under new era in China. *Environmental Economy* 12(2):45–35.

Windmeijer, Frank. 2005. A finite sample correction for the variance of linear efficient two-step GMM estimators. *Journal of Econometrics* 126(1):25–51.

Xia, G., D. Feng, and L. Cheng. 2005. Report about situation of the permit system of pollutant discharge operation in six provinces and cities. *Environmental Protection* 6:57–62.

Xiang, Z. 2004. Exploration of EIA system. *Administrative Tribune* 66:76–77.

Xinhua. 2005. Why should China establish total emission control system. http://news.xinhua net.com/environment/2005-12/20/content_3946332.htm

———. 2006. The eleventh Five-Year National Development Plan. http://news.xinhuanet.com /misc/2006-03/16/content_4309517.htm

———. 2007. Tracking of algae blooming in Taihu Lake. http://news.xinhuanet.com/video/2007 -06/08/content_6215092.htmXinhua

———. 2008. Law of China in the past 30 years: 4 level jumps of environmental protection agency. http://news.xinhuanet.com/legal/2008-11/23/content _10399594_1.htm

———. 2009. China's water pollution control in major water bodies has achieved initial success. http://news.xinhuanet.com/politics/2009-08/08/content_ 11846929.htm

Yu, H., and J. Cui. 2004. Assessment and analysis on pollution levy system in China. *Yunnan Environmental Science* 23(3):28–31.

Zhang, K. 1994. The environmental policies in China. *World Environment* 1:3–6.

Zhang, K., Z. Wen, and L. Peng. 2007. Environmental policy of modern China: Formation, characteristics and evaluation. *Population, Resource and Environment in China* 17(2):1–7.

Zhang, Y., and B. Li. 2006. Pollution levy system in China. China Environmental Science Conference, 1694–1698, Beijing, China (July).

Zhao, L. 2005. Study on environment impact assessment in China. Master's thesis, Northeast Forestry University.

# Contributors

**Editor**

JOYCE YANYUN MAN
Director
Lincoln Institute of Land Policy
Cambridge, Massachusetts
Peking University–Lincoln Institute
    Center for Urban Development and
    Land Policy
Beijing, China

Professor of Economics
College of Urban and Environmental
    Sciences
Peking University
Beijing, China

**Authors**

JING CAO
Associate Professor
School of Economics and
    Management
Tsinghua University
Beijing, China

GREGORY C. CHOW
Professor of Economics
Princeton University
Princeton, New Jersey

DABO GUAN
Senior Lecturer
School of Earth and
    Environment
University of Leeds
Leeds, United Kingdom

CANFEI HE
Professor
College of Urban and Environmental
    Sciences
Peking University
Beijing, China

Co-Director
Peking University–Lincoln Institute
    Center for Urban Development and
    Land Policy
Beijing, China

JUAN JING
Research Fellow
Peking University–Lincoln Institute
    Center for Urban Development and
    Land Policy
Beijing, China

Postdoctoral Fellow
College of Urban and Environmental
    Sciences
Peking University
Beijing, China

MATTHEW E. KAHN
Professor of Economics, Political Science,
    and Public Policy, Emeritus
Institute of Environment, Department
    of Economics, Department of Public
    Policy
University of California, Los Angeles

National Bureau of Economic Research
Los Angeles, California

SHUNSUKE MANAGI
Associate Professor
Graduate School of Environmental
   Studies
Tohoku University
Sendai, Miyagi, Japan

FENGHUA PAN
Assistant Professor
Department of Geography
Beijing Normal University
Beijing, China

YAO QI
M.A. Candidate
Graduate School of Frontier Sciences
University of Tokyo
Kashiwa, Ibaraki, Japan

YUN QIAN
Assistant Professor
Beijing Forestry University
Beijing, China

MINJUN SHI
Professor
Research Center on Fictitious Economy
   and Data Science
Graduate University of Chinese Academy
   of Sciences
Beijing, China

TETSUYA TSURUMI
Assistant Professor
Graduate School of Frontier Sciences
University of Tokyo
Kashiwa, Ibaraki, Japan

RUI WANG
Assistant Professor
Luskin School of Public Affairs
University of California, Los Angeles

YAN WANG
Lecturer
School of Science
Communication University of China
Beijing, China

ZHONGXIANG ZHANG
Distinguished Professor
School of Economics
Fudan University
Shanghai, China

YINGER ZHENG
Ph.D. Candidate
College of Urban and Environmental
   Sciences
Peking University
Beijing, China

# Index

abatement investment, for pollution, 21, 22

accidents, environmental, 25–26

administrative regulations, 17

agencies, for environmental protection, 16

air pollution: ambient, 96–97, *97, 98*; in
Chinese cities, 96–101; urban, 100–101

Air Pollution Prevention and Control Law of
1987, 4

air quality, 28

alternative energy, 7–8

alternative greenness systems, 80–88

ambient air pollution, 96–97, *97, 98*

ambient sulfur dioxide levels, *97*

automobile consumption tax, 152

base-case simulation, 161

Beijing, 30, 32, 55, 100; Forbidden City in,
110, *110*; Old Town in, 110, *110*

bioenergy, 9

blacklisted cities, 28, 28*n*1, 29

bulletin system, 30, 30*n*2

burden: of carbon tax incidence, *168,*
168–172, *169, 170, 171*; financial, of local
governments, 34

buses greenhouse gas emissions, *77*

capital stock, in computable general
equilibrium model, 160

carbon capture, 10

carbon dioxide ($CO_2$) emissions, 3, 4, 6, 44,
129; consumption-induced, 63–67, *65,*
68–70, *69, 70*; data sources about, 62;
estimating methods for, 60–62; factor
decomposition of, 67; findings and policy
implications of, 70–71; of Guangyuan, 140,
*140, 141*; across income groups, 64–66;
increase of, 59, 68, 107, *108*; input-output
analysis of, 60; in Nantong, *125*; in reform
era, 114; regulations of, 11–12; scenario
simulation for, *61,* 61–62; structure
decomposition analysis of, 60–61;
structure of, 119–120, *120*; in United States,

119, *120*; with urbanization, *67. See also* per
capita carbon dioxide emissions

carbon footprint: in least developed regions,
129–141, *130, 131*; scenarios of, 133–135.
*See also* Guangyuan's carbon footprint

carbon intensity, of Guangyuan, 135

carbon tax incidence: assumptions of, 164–167;
burden of, *168,* 168–172, *169, 170, 171*;
distributional effects of, 157–159; estimates
of, 167–172, *168*; literature about, 158, 159;
measurement of, 163–167; microlevel
household surveys of, 163–167; as regressive,
160, 164, 167, 168, 169, 170, 171, 172; studies
of, 157–158, 159, 163–167. *See also*
computable general equilibrium model

carbon tax policy, 160–163, *163*

changing consumption patterns, 134, 138

chemical oxygen demand (COD): control of,
179; data on, 185, 186–188; in model, 181,
191, 196, 197; reduction in, 175

China Academy of Social Science, 108

*China Economic Yearbook,* 185, 186

*China Energy Statistical Yearbook,* 62

*China Environmental Statistical Yearbook,*
185, 186

China Guodian Corporation, 30

*China Industrial Economy Statistical
Yearbook,* 185, 186

*China Population and Employment Statistical
Yearbook,* 185

*China Statistical Yearbook,* 62, 97, 103

*China Statistical Yearbook for Regional
Economy,* 185, 186

Chinese cities: air pollution in, 96–101;
blacklisted, 28, 28*n*1, 29; carbon
dioxide emissions in, 119–120, *120*;
decentralization in, 54–56; greenhouse gas
emissions in, 76, *76,* 96; greenness of,
95–104; household carbon dioxide
emissions in, 101–103; large, 95–96;
modernization of, 111, 112; ongoing
population and income growth of, 96;

# About the Lincoln Institute of Land Policy

The Lincoln Institute of Land Policy is a private operating foundation whose mission is to improve the quality of public debate and decisions in the areas of land policy and land-related taxation in the United States and around the world. The Institute's goals are to integrate theory and practice to better shape land policy and to provide a nonpartisan forum for discussion of the multidisciplinary forces that influence public policy. This focus on land derives from the Institute's founding objective—to address the links between land policy and social and economic progress—that was identified and analyzed by political economist and author Henry George.

The work of the Institute is organized in three departments: Valuation and Taxation, Planning and Urban Form, and International Studies, which includes programs on Latin America and China. We seek to inform decision making through education, research, demonstration projects, and the dissemination of information through publications, our Web site, and other media. Our programs bring together scholars, practitioners, public officials, policy advisers, and involved citizens in a collegial learning environment. The Institute does not take a particular point of view, but rather serves as a catalyst to facilitate analysis and discussion of land use and taxation issues—to make a difference today and to help policy makers plan for tomorrow. The Lincoln Institute of Land Policy is an equal opportunity institution.

113 Brattle Street
Cambridge, MA 02138-3400 USA

Phone: 1-617-661-3016 x127 or 1-800-526-3873
Fax: 1-617-661-7235 or 1-800-526-3944
E-mail: help@lincolninst.edu
Web: www.lincolninst.edu